STUDIES ON ETHNIC GROUPS IN CHINA

Stevan Harrell, Editor

Empire and Identity in Guizhou

Local Resistance to Qing Expansion

※

JODI L. WEINSTEIN

UNIVERSITY OF WASHINGTON PRESS / SEATTLE AND LONDON

Publication of this book was supported by a generous grant from
the Association for Asian Studies First Book Subvention Program.

University of Washington Press
PO Box 50096, Seattle, WA 98145, USA
www.washington.edu/uwpress

Library of Congress Cataloging-in-Publication Data
Weinstein, Jodi L.
Empire and Identity in Guizhou : local resistance to Qing expansion /
Jodi L. Weinstein. — 1st edition
    p.   cm. — (Studies on Ethnic Groups in China)
Includes bibliographical references and index.
ISBN 978-0-295-99326-3 (hardback : alk. paper);
978-0-295-99327-0 (paperback : alk. paper)
1. Bouyei (Chinese people)—China—Guizhou Sheng—History—18th century.
2. Guizhou Sheng (China)—Ethnic relations—History—18th century.
I. Title.   II. Title: Local resistance to Qing expansion.
DS793.K8W444   2014
951'.3400495919—dc23   2013020635

CONTENTS

FOREWORD

An old Chinese saying goes, "Those on top have policies; those below have counterstrategies" (*Shang you zhengce, xia you duice*). This adage sums up several millennia of relationships between East Asian imperial regimes, which ruled from the productive and powerful center in China, and their poorer, less powerful subjects living in the borderlands. It is still true in the twenty-first century: the People's Republic tries to consolidate its control over its border regions and solidify the loyalty of border peoples to the regime, while border peoples (now called *shaoshu minzu*, or "minority nationalities") deal with the state's efforts in various ways. They do not always resist or always accommodate, but they act strategically, joining in when it appears advantageous or when they have no choice, but resisting when it appears intolerable not to. Since the regime they deal with assumes itself to be morally as well as economically and materially stronger, peoples on the periphery face the prospect not just of being ruled, but of being absorbed into the more "civilized" culture and polity of the center.

This kind of relationship is not new. The last empire with an actual emperor, the Qing (1644–1911), was not even ruled by ethnic Chinese, but rather by Manchus, originally a peripheral people from the northeast. But in its southwestern domains, the Qing, like its predecessors, assumed the moral superiority of the center and attempted to balance the advantages of letting peripheral peoples be, against the costs of trying to consolidate their control and assure the peripheral people's loyalties.

One of the peripheral peoples the Qing regime had considerable trouble controlling were the Zhongjia, a Tai-speaking group of Guizhou, now incorporated into the Buyi or Bouyei *minzu*, or "nationality." Well before the Qing, the Zhongjia were formulating counterstrategies as both Chinese immigration and imperial policy impinged on their livelihoods and social structures. By the time Jodi Weinstein's narrative begins, in the mid-Qing, the Zhongjia were practicing the familiar mix of going along and joining the civilization with resisting and defending their local autonomy and their own livelihoods.

Weinstein tells the story of the counterstrategies of the Zhongjia in the eighteenth century. She begins with the history of Qing attempts to consolidate their rule, switching from indirect rule through native leaders to direct rule by appointed magistrates. She then gives us a rich account of how some Zhongjia resisted, indirectly through schemes of trickery and evasion and more directly through rebellion, in the Nanlong area in 1797. Importantly, though, not all Zhongjia resisted, and not all resistance was direct confrontation, let alone military confrontation.

This story points out to us, in clear and lively fashion, how little has changed even as so much has changed. The People's Republic is orders of magnitude more powerful than the Qing state; it can deploy not only force but also persuasion much more pervasively than could its Qing predecessor. But it still faces the same problems, and peoples of the borderlands buy in when they see it as advantageous or resist when they see it as necessary.

This story is also important for another reason. The state narrative of the People's Republic stresses that the Qing was a Chinese regime, an earlier version of themselves. That the rulers were Manchus is of little import in this telling of history; Manchus were then and are now one of the many groups that makes up the Chinese nation. This state narrative has been strongly challenged by advocates of the "New Qing History," who are much more inclined to see the Qing as a multinational empire than they are to see it as a Chinese nation that happened to be ruled by a monarch in sumptuous robes instead of by a committee of bureaucrats in dark, pinstriped suits and red neckties. But Weinstein's book tells a more complex story: the Qing emperor and the twenty-first-century bureaucrats were facing the same problems: ethnic and cultural difference combined with unequal power leading to the disinclination of ruled people to submit uncritically, but leaving open to them various strategies of accommodation and resistance.

Finally, the book is noteworthy because it introduces another historical narrative alongside those coming from the center and from outside critics: the narrative of the Zhongjia themselves. As Weinstein examines the different stories of the rebellion coming from the official Qing history and the oral history collected from the rebels' descendants, we see clearly that not only are policies from above opposed by counterstrategies from below, but also historical narratives from above are countered by different stories from below. Weinstein's sensitive and multifaceted account of one small corner of Guizhou in the eighteenth century helps us, in the words of Prasenjit Duara, rescue history from the nation.

STEVAN HARRELL

June 2013

ACKNOWLEDGMENTS

In the many years since I started this project, I have benefited from the advice, wisdom, and encouragement of many people, and it is now my pleasure to acknowledge them. First, I must thank Beatrice S. Bartlett for drawing me into the world of eighteenth-century China and inspiring me to explore the uncharted landscapes of Guizhou. Thanks are also due to Jonathan Spence, James C. Scott, John Faragher, Annping Chin, and Jonathan Lipman, whose work inspired many of the theories examined here, and to the late Hugh Stimson for his instruction in literary Chinese.

This book would not have been possible without support and encouragement from my students and colleagues in the Department of History at the College of New Jersey. I wish to express my gratitude to the department chair, Professor Celia Chazelle, for creating such a welcoming place to teach. I also wish to thank the current and former students who have contributed to this book in more ways than they can image. I hope they will enjoy reading it as much as I have enjoyed crafting it. I am especially grateful to Professor Daniel Crofts for his comments on successive drafts of the manuscript, and for our many fruitful conversations about Guizhou history. Professor Cynthia Paces also offered much encouragement during the final weeks of revision and pointed me toward a fine cartographer in Bill Nelson. Special thanks must also go to Megan Tavares for her assistance with the technical aspects of manuscript and CD preparation, and to the staff at the TCNJ Library for accommodating my numerous interlibrary loan requests.

My research received generous funding from a variety of sources. The Yale Council on International Studies provided a grant to support research in Yunnan and Guizhou. Grants from the Yale Council on East Asian Studies and an Enders Grant from the Yale Graduate School of Arts and Sciences financed my research in Taiwan's Palace Museum. A Fulbright Grant administered through the Institute of International Education supported eleven months of research in Beijing and Guizhou. In subsequent years, I received support from the Chiang Ching-kuo Foundation and from an East Asian Studies Prize Fellowship provided by the Yale Council on East Asian Studies. I wish to thank all those who reviewed my work and awarded these grants. Special thanks must also go to James Millward and Robert Jenks for commenting on my East Asian Studies Prize Fellowship proposal, and to Abbey Newman for administering the grant. In addition, I wish to record my gratitude to the Association for Asian Studies for providing a subvention to support the publication of this book.

I am also indebted to a number of people in China and Taiwan for their assistance. In Kunming, I received a warm welcome and much support from Professor Lin Chaomin of the Yunnan University History Department and his students. My research at the Taipei Palace Museum was greatly facilitated by museum director, Ch'in Hsiao-i, the library director Wang Ching-hung, Chuang Chi-fa, and the entire library staff. In Beijing, I received guidance from Professor Cheng Chongde of the Institute of Qing Studies at People's University. Also in Beijing, Zhu Shuyuan, Li Jing, and other members of the staff at the Number One Historical Archives offered advice and assistance. Professor Zhou Guoyan of the Central Minorities University in Beijing provided many hard-to-find books and journals on the Buyi ethnic group. I am also grateful to Dan St. Rossy, formerly of the Education Section at the U.S. Embassy in Beijing, for his logistical support and hospitality. In Guiyang, Professor Weng Jialie of the Guizhou Minority Nationalities Research Institute supplied background information on the history of that province and opened his home to me. Invaluable help and support also came from Professor Yang Shaoxin of the History Department at Guizhou Normal University, from his student Li Yuanpeng, who served as my tireless guide on the long trip from Guiyang to Xingyi and back, and from the staff of the rare books collection at the Guizhou Provincial Library.

Over the years, Yong Xue, Shou-chih Yan, Jacob Whittaker, Charles McKhann, James Z. Lee, John Herman, David Bello, C. Patterson Giersch, David Atwill, Jean Michaud, Sarah Turner, Christine Bonnin, John Kelley, Candice Cornet, and Kenneth Pomeranz have all offered suggestions on the work in progress. Yu Luo's many insights on Buyi history, culture, and religion proved invaluable throughout the revision process, as did Beatrice Kwok's comments on early drafts of Chapters 2 and 5. I am also grateful to Alice Davenport for her careful copyediting and her many helpful suggestions, and to Roberta Engleman for her expert work in compiling the index. Finally, I thank Lorri Hagman, Stevan Harrell, Marilyn Trueblood, Jacqueline Volin, Beth Fuget, Rachael Levay, and Tim Zimmermann of the University of Washington Press for their confidence in my work and for their detailed feedback and patient guidance throughout the review, revision, and production process.

This work would not have been possible without my family and friends. My husband, Rob Barrish, has traveled this long journey alongside me with patience, good humor, and kindness, cheering me on when I needed it most. My parents, Stephen and Felice Weinstein, have also offered unflagging support, and I am thankful to them for instilling in me a lifelong desire to read, learn, and explore the world. Warm encouragement also came from my in-laws, Gil and Lois Barrish, from my brothers and sisters-in-law, from Dr. Eliana Perrin and her family, and from my training partners on the Jersey Area and Princeton Area Masters swim teams. My cats, Cougar and Ketzel, bemusedly observed the entire endeavor. To all, I am grateful.

MAP 1. Guizhou's location in China and eighteenth-century administrative divisions within Guizhou

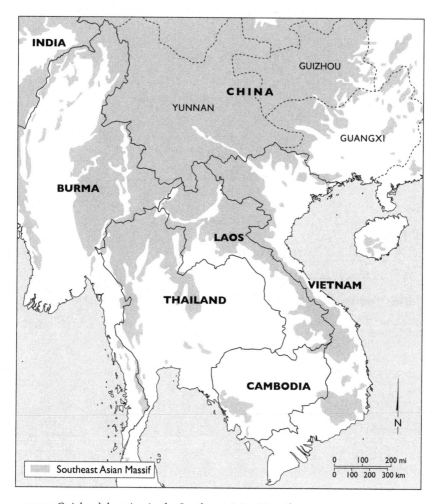

Southeast Asian Massif

MAP 2. Guizhou's location in the Southeast Asian Massif

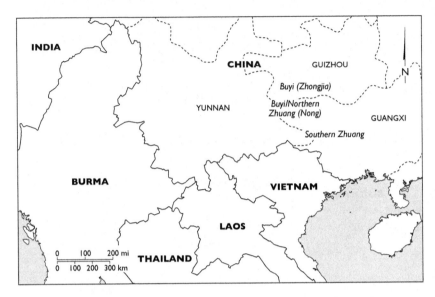

MAP 3. Distribution of the Zhongjia (Buyi) and Nong (Northern Zhuang)

Empire and Identity in Guizhou

Chapter 1

GUIZHOU AND THE LIVELIHOODS
APPROACH TO ZHONGJIA HISTORY

※

China's imperial officials seldom had anything positive to say about Guizhou province. In his account from the mid-eighteenth century, Guizhou governor Aibida offered this blunt analysis of the region's harsh terrain, limited economic prospects, and unruly non-Chinese inhabitants:

> The [Guizhou] countryside is gloomy and impenetrable. Heavy rains are frequent. The fields must be terraced [because] the soil is stony. Slash and burn agriculture prevails. The paddies and marshes yield no abundance, and the mulberry trees and hemp do not yield much profit. The annual tax revenue does not equal that of a large county in China Proper (*neidi*). . . . Miao, Zhong, Ge, Luo, Yao, and Zhuang tribes swarm like bees and ants. Many of them still believe in ghosts and spirits. They are addicted to violence, whether it be major retaliatory attacks or smaller acts of banditry and plunder. They are easy to incite and difficult to pacify. As a result, it is not easy for the imperial court to find steadfast and competent local officials. Those who are appointed place little importance on their positions. They disdain and neglect Yi barbarians and Han alike. They are dissolute and let matters drift; nothing is of consequence to them. In this way, poison brews and becomes thick. Once released, it cannot be stopped. . . . Thus it is that no benefit can be derived from Guizhou.[1]

Aibida's pessimistic assessment obscured a fundamental reality. The imperial ambitions of China's last dynasty, the Qing (1644–1911) extended to Guizhou and beyond. However much government officials disdained this remote corner of southwestern China, they had to create some semblance of order there. During the eighteenth century, the Qing drive for expansion, centralization, and social stability encountered a tenacious effort by Guizhou's local residents to defend their autonomy and livelihoods. This book investigates the resulting tensions in three contiguous prefectures (*fu*), Guiyang, Nanlong, and Anshun, during the period from 1725 to 1797.

Although this study strives to create a panoramic view of all three prefectures, its focus is most often limited to Zhongjia ethnic communities in Nanlong and Guiyang. A Tai-speaking people concentrated in central and southern Guizhou, the Zhongjia are now called the Buyi (also spelled Bouyei in the People's Republic of China) [布依]).[2] Today, the Buyi are one of the lesser-known ethnic minorities (*shaoshu minzu*) in Guizhou, at least relative to such groups as the Yi, the Miao, or the Dong, but this quiet existence in contemporary China belies an eventful past. Throughout the eighteenth century, Zhongjia communities and individuals challenged the imperial enterprise in Guizhou with striking regularity and creativity. Indeed, two major Zhongjia clashes with Qing authority provide both the starting point and the endpoint for the narrative in this book, as well as many of the intervening episodes. At one end of the time frame are the reforms implemented in southwestern China during the reign of the third Qing emperor, Yongzheng (r. 1723–35). In an effort to exert greater control over non-Han communities in Guizhou, Yunnan, Guangxi, Hunan, and Sichuan, the central government implemented a program known as "reforming the native and returning to the regular" (*gaitu guiliu*).[3] Under this policy, Qing officials used a combination of moral suasion and military force to depose hereditary native rulers (*tusi*) and incorporate their domains into regular administrative units. The ultimate goal was to bring hitherto autonomous communities under direct imperial rule and transform non-Han peoples into law-abiding Qing subjects.

Long considered the most intractable of Guizhou's non-Han populations, the Zhongjia became the first targets of this campaign. In 1725, Zhongjia communities in the Guiyang region served as the proving ground for the earliest prototypes of the Yongzheng-era initiatives.

Reforms in the Nanlong region followed two years later. Many Zhongjia acquiesced to the new order and settled into quiet lives centering on agriculture, textile production, and small-scale commerce.[4] More enterprising individuals developed illicit business ventures that mixed local religious beliefs with anti-dynastic slogans and millenarian rhetoric. These schemes sent a clear signal that the state's presence was not altogether welcome in the Zhongjia heartland, and that Qing priorities were seldom compatible with the needs and values of local residents. In 1797, a half-century of sporadic unrest culminated in full-scale rebellion when Zhongjia insurgents from Nanlong laid siege to every major town in central and southwestern Guizhou. This book provides the first Western-language account of this rebellion, which Chinese historians usually call the Nanlong Uprising.

The purpose of this study, then, is twofold. One goal is to introduce the Zhongjia to a wider readership and illuminate their role in the history of late imperial China. A related goal is to show how members of this ethnic group created viable livelihoods and maintained their identity while negotiating the imperial state's plans for standardization and centralization. My understanding of livelihoods draws inspiration from Jean Michaud and his colleagues in anthropology and human geography. It encompasses not only the activities that people use to make a living, but also the social, ethnic, and religious resources at their disposal, and the decisions they make in view of local conditions and external forces.[5] An exploration of livelihoods can reveal "the unexpected ways in which people on the margins do not just get onboard and accept . . . modernization but, rather, use their agency to maintain direction over their lives and livelihoods despite current and far-reaching changes to economic conditions and political authority."[6]

Thus far, the livelihoods approach has mostly been applied to twenty-first-century communities in the Southeast Asian Massif, an area defined as "the highlands of all the countries sharing a large chunk of the southeast Asian portion of the Asian land mass. These lie roughly east of the lower Brahmaptura River, in India and Bangladesh, and south of the Yangzi River in China, all the way to the Isthmus of Kra at its southernmost extension."[7] This is the same region that James Scott defines as "Zomia," a refuge for stateless people and populations seeking refuge from surrounding "civilizations."[8] Michaud and other scholars engaged in livelihoods research seek to expand on Scott's analysis with a "more refined reflection from the ground up and a more dynamic understanding of the relationships between (marginal) local subjects, (global) market forces, and (national) states."[9]

Christine Bonnin and Sarah Turner have shown, for example, how Hmong and Yao farmers in northern Vietnam resist or selectively implement Hanoi's attempts to project modernity into their communities. In recent years, the Vietnamese government has sought to increase grain production by introducing hybrid rice and maize varieties to upland areas. Although the new strains yield larger crops, Hmong and Yao villagers often reject them in favor of indigenous varieties that produce superior rice, both as a food product and as material for distilling alcohol. Villagers acknowledge that the new seeds might be more profitable, but local tastes and cultural preferences clearly outweigh economic considerations. Moreover, families with land to spare use it not to plant hybrid rice and sell the surplus, but instead to continue planting the indigenous varieties. Less well-off farmers purchase or barter small quantities of the traditional rice, especially for ritual purposes. In this way, a lively informal trade in indigenous rice flourishes beyond the confines of the state-directed market economy.[10]

In this book, I suggest that the livelihoods approach can be applied to historical settings as well as modern ones. It offers a particularly fruitful way to examine Zhongjia interactions with the Qing state. The Zhongjia heartland is, after all, located on the northeastern edge of the Southeast Asian Massif. Its eighteenth-century inhabitants confronted many of the same ecological and economic challenges now facing modern-day inhabitants of China, Vietnam, and Laos, and they responded to these challenges in similar ways. Like the Hmong, the Yao, and many other communities living in the Massif today, the Zhongjia did not submit uncritically to state demands. They weighed all of their options and made livelihood choices that best suited their immediate needs and accorded with their understanding of the world.[11]

In order to provide a full understanding of Zhongjia livelihood choices, I seek to give equal voice to imperial and indigenous perspectives on the events described in this book. The Qing state's perspective is easy to locate and analyze, thanks to the abundance of archival sources and other official and semi-official writings. It is more difficult to find indigenous voices. Unlike other non-Han groups in southwestern China such as the Nasu Yi and the Tai, the Zhongjia did not maintain written records of their encounters with China's rulers.[12] They did, however, cultivate a rich oral tradition to preserve and transmit memories of important events. This study utilizes Chinese translations of Zhongjia poems and folk songs, treating them less as accurate historical records than as selective historical memories, or a way communities have chosen to perceive and remember their past.[13] Although the Zhongjia did not commit historical events to writing, they did use modified Chinese characters to produce religious texts such as creation stories, prayers for the souls of the dead, entreaties to various spirits, and incantations to dispel evil and bring good fortune.[14] Many of these scriptures are available in Chinese translation, and a few have been published in English.[15] Throughout this book, I use some of these texts as a window on the beliefs and rituals that shaped Zhongjia worldviews and informed their livelihood choices. When indigenous sources are unavailable, I follow the advice of James Scott and Peter Perdue and read against the grain to glean local voices from official Qing documents.[16]

The sources reveal a complex dynamic between state entities and local residents. Despite its sophisticated bureaucracy and technologically advanced armies, the Qing could never claim a total monopoly on political or cultural space in the Zhongjia heartland. Even after the *gaitu guiliu* reforms of the Yongzheng reign, regular administrative rule was largely confined to prefectural seats and a few smaller administrative centers. Much of the countryside remained under the control of indigenous landlords who, though nominally subordinate to the provincial bureaucracy, nevertheless enjoyed considerable autonomy in day-to-day affairs. Equally important, indigenous beliefs, customs, and priorities did not melt away with the arrival of Qing officialdom. Imperial rule did not deprive the Zhongjia of the capacity to think and act for themselves—that is, to choose the livelihoods they considered optimal. Local residents accepted, adapted, circumvented, or rejected state directives as they saw fit.[17] Individuals could make risk-benefit analyses to determine when it made sense to follow Qing legal and cultural norms, and when it made more sense to bend or defy them. The decision to follow these norms had the advantage of keeping the state at a safe distance, as Qing officials rarely intervened in the affairs of law-abiding Zhongjia, but it could also mean passing up opportunities for social and economic mobility. Conversely, the decision to pursue illicit activities might bring greater prosperity and an enhanced sense of autonomy, but only if plans were executed well enough to elude detection by local authorities. If plans failed, the masterminds and many of their followers were likely to face imprisonment or even execution. Local residents were fully cognizant of all choices and their possible consequences.[18] They exercised the sort of agency that Sherry Ortner describes as "the forms of power people have at their disposal, their ability to act on their own behalf, influence other people and events, and maintain some kind of control in their own lives."[19]

The livelihoods approach to Zhongjia history adds a new dimension to the terrain charted by C. Patterson Giersch, John Herman, and Jacob Whittaker. Giersch's work on southern Yunnan demonstrates how eighteenth-century Qing officials and Tai indigenous leaders established a relationship based on mutual respect and common strategic concerns. The Qing used the Tai polities as a buffer against potentially aggressive Southeast Asian kingdoms, while the Tai maintained some autonomy by playing regional powers against one another. Herman's work on the Mu'ege kingdom of the Nasu Yi people in northwestern Guizhou illustrates how indigenous rulers took advantage of the Ming dynasty's (1368–1644) political and economic institutions to enhance their own power. Whittaker examines another Nasu Yi state, the Lu-ho polity in Yunnan, to show how indigenous elites appropriated elements of Confucian culture for their own purposes while preserving rituals and institutions that distinguished them from the Chinese.[20]

The idea of indigenous agency is clearly at the heart of these stories, but it resides primarily—though by no means exclusively—with indigenous elites. The livelihoods approach in this book focuses on the agency of commoners such as farmers, vagabonds, disgruntled intellectuals, and self-styled magicians. These people all employed the resources at their disposal to engage the state in a meaningful way and assert their own sense of identity.

This book is organized chronologically, pursuing the twin trajectories of Qing expansion into Guizhou and the ways in which Zhongjia livelihoods adapted to changing political and economic circumstances. The discussion begins with an overview of Guizhou's natural environment, followed by an introduction to Zhongjia history, culture, and socioeconomic organization (chapter 2). The next chapter describes the Qing state's gradual penetration into central and southwestern Guizhou during the late seventeenth and early eighteenth centuries. The Qing conquest and reforms of the Kangxi period (1662–1722) mainly affected native elites and did not have an immediate impact on local communities. The social and political landscape of the region was forever altered with the ascension of the Yongzheng emperor in 1723. The new emperor took deep offense at what he perceived as endemic lawlessness in Guizhou and elsewhere in southwestern China. Together with a coterie of trusted officials, he engineered a plan to make the region tractable by eliminating native rulers and bringing local populations under direct Qing control. Among his first targets were Zhongjia communities in the central Guizhou region of Dingfan-Guangshun (Guiyang prefecture) and the Guizhou-Guangxi borderlands (Nanlong prefecture). Chapter 3 suggests that Qing reforms in these regions constituted an exercise in what James Scott calls "seeing like a state"—an attempt to transform peripheral territories into more governable spaces.[21]

Gaitu guiliu in southwestern Guizhou highlighted the imperial state's ability to create new administrative spaces and staff them with functionaries, but it did not guarantee greater control over the human activities within those spaces. During the mid-eighteenth century, Qing officials found themselves confronting a series of criminal cases that underscored the fundamental discrepancies between imperial visions for the region and realities on the ground. These cases involved moneymaking schemes masterminded by individuals whose livelihood choices made perfect sense in the context of their own lives, but little sense from the perspective of imperial authorities anxious to maintain the hard-won order in southwestern China. Although these cases never involved armed violence, they did feature symbolic attacks on Qing authority that hinted at the potential for more serious unrest (chapter 4). These latent tensions erupted in late 1796, when government troops stationed in southwestern Guizhou were called away to quell rebellions in other provinces. Within weeks, a local religious leader from Nanlong took advantage of the sudden power vacuum and organized a rebellion against the Qing. Spurred on by their charismatic leaders and by supernatural beliefs, the rebels soon controlled all of central and southwestern Guizhou. Qing troops eventually regained control of the region, but sporadic unrest and illegal activities continued into the nineteenth century, an indication that local residents persisted in making livelihood choices that conflicted with state ideals (chapter 5).

The final chapter (chapter 6) situates Guizhou's indigenes in the Qing vision of multicultural empire. James Millward has proposed a model called "Five Nations Under Heaven" in which the empire's five major ethnic groups—Han, Manchu, Tibetan, Mongol, and Muslim—occupy parallel positions in relation to the Qing imperial house.[22] Conspicuously absent from this model are the indigenes of southwestern China and Taiwan. Emma Teng suggests that this omission signals that the native Taiwanese were superfluous to the Qing conception of "great unity."[23] Chapter 6 will discuss whether or not this held true for the Zhongjia as well; and will also examine the legacy of Qing ethnic policy in contemporary China, with particular reference to the livelihood choices available to the Buyi.

Chapter 2

NATURAL, HUMAN, AND

HISTORICAL LANDSCAPES

No three days are clear, no three feet of land are level,
and no one has three ounces of silver.

Tian wu san ri qing, di wu san chi ping, ren wu san fen yin.
天無三日晴,地無三尺平,人無三分銀

— *Guizhou saying*

In 1638, during the waning days of the Ming Dynasty and the twilight of
his own career, the famed explorer Xu Xiake (1587–1641) embarked on a
journey through the mountains, caverns, and forests of Guizhou. His
travels took him through many of the regions explored in this book. He
entered the province from its southeastern border with Guangxi, made
his way northwestward to the provincial seat of Guiyang, and then negoti-
ated a series of meandering paths into the little-known reaches of Guizhou's far southwest. After three weeks of arduous travel, he reached his
destination at the confluence of the North Pan (Beipan) and South Pan
Rivers (Nanpan) near Guizhou's southwestern border with Guangxi.[1]

Xu considered the writing of travel diaries his most important responsibility as an explorer, and each night he penned succinct yet vivid
accounts of that day's experiences.[2] These journal entries represent much
more than a traveler's jottings. Xu's adventures—and occasional misad-

ventures—encapsulate the human and geographic features that made Guizhou such a challenge for both its inhabitants and the imperial states that sought to govern it. Although some of Xu's entries from Guizhou reflect genuine delight with the natural landscape, many more evince his frustration with the region's stony mountain paths, foul weather, and hostile "Miao" natives.[3]

Frequent rains, heavy fog, and hilly terrain often led Xu to believe that nature was conspiring against him. On several occasions, heavy downpours forced him to cancel or postpone planned expeditions. When he hiked to high elevations to capture a panoramic view of the valley below, he found the scenery enveloped in clouds and mist, but when he traveled at low elevations, numerous hills and mountains blocked his view.[4]

Xu's interactions with local residents did not improve his opinion of the region. The prospect of violence threatened his journey as he traveled into increasingly remote areas. On one occasion, he heeded the advice of a friendly Buddhist monk and took a long detour to avoid "Miao" bandits known to lie in wait for unsuspecting travelers.[5] The indirect route provided safe passage, but Xu encountered new problems when he reached his destination, a small "Miao" settlement. The villagers refused to accept him as an overnight guest and sent him to another nearby hamlet, where the residents hid in their houses and refused to open their doors when he knocked. Xu proceeded to the next settlement, where he "forced himself into [the villagers'] midst." After much haggling, a farmer agreed to put him up for the night, but the accommodations were rustic in the extreme. Xu found himself bedding down for the night on a pile of filthy straw amid the family's livestock. The experience left him grumbling over the crudeness of the "Miao."[6]

The following morning brought further difficulties when Xu tried to hire a porter to accompany him on the next leg of his journey. No one wanted the job, even though Xu promised to pay well. After a full day of bargaining, a "Miao" man finally agreed to make the journey for what Xu considered an exorbitant fee. Night had already fallen by this time, so they decided to set out the following morning. Xu awoke at daybreak to discover that the porter had absconded with a large sum of money—the promised wages for the journey and then some. He tried in vain to find the miscreant and then spent the next day hunting for another porter. He resumed his journey several days behind schedule and with fewer coins in his pocket, thanks to the thieving "Miao."[7]

These episodes illustrate the relationship between the natural setting and human behaviors in Guizhou. The rough terrain and dank weather that occasionally foiled Xu's plans had a much more profound impact on the daily lives of Guizhou's inhabitants. The chilly reception he received in "Miao" hamlets stemmed from the residents' poverty and their instinct for self-preservation. The villagers probably viewed Xu as an extra mouth to feed, a burden they could not bear. Perhaps they even feared that he might pilfer from their meager grain supply or seize their livestock. Such suspicions were not unwarranted in a land where banditry was a way of life, and people were alternately victims and perpetrators of property theft. It is not surprising that Xu himself fell prey to petty crime. Whereas Xu viewed the event as one of the many insults he endured in Guizhou, the porter probably saw an opportunity to take advantage of an unwary stranger. Perhaps the money he stole amounted to more than he might have otherwise earned in a year, or perhaps even a lifetime—enough to feed and clothe his family, repay any debts, and cover other expenditures. Such behavior made little sense to Xu Xiake, but it might have provided the best solution for satisfying the porter's immediate and future needs.

The porter's actions represent one small example of the livelihood choices examined in this study. The remainder of this chapter examines the ecological conditions that shaped these choices, looks at the people who made the livelihood decisions, and analyzes the political arrangements that helped sustain them. The first section provides a detailed investigation of Guizhou's climate and topography, explaining how the scarcity of fertile land forced people to find other ways to supplement their livelihoods. The discussion then turns to the various peoples who shared this fragile ecological space, namely the Zhongjia, Lolo, Miao, and Han.[8] The chapter concludes with an overview of Guizhou's political history to 1659. In view of the region's challenging terrain and ethnic diversity, the imperial governments of the Yuan (1279–1368) and Ming dynasties eschewed direct governance in favor of indirect rule through hereditary native officials. This arrangement allowed the imperial court to exercise a modicum of control over Guizhou at minimal expense. It also meant that state intervention at the local level was relatively infrequent, leaving people more or less free to pursue a wide range of livelihood choices.

NATURAL LANDSCAPES: CLIMATE, TOPOGRAPHY, AND AGRICULTURE

The mists and rains that annoyed Xu Xiake have always been a fact of life in Guizhou. Annual rainfall does range from 850–1600 mm (33–63 inches), but other provinces (Fujian, Guangdong, Guangxi, and Hunan) all report significantly more.[9] However, although Guizhou is not China's wettest province, it is one of the cloudiest. In 2004, the provincial capital of Guiyang, situated in central Guizhou, reported just 989 hours of sunshine, making it the third-most-overcast city in China behind the Sichuan cities of Wenjiang (984 hours of sunshine) and Chongqing (974.9 hours).[10] Guiyang and nearby Anshun are mild year-round, with winter temperatures that seldom drop below 5 degrees Celsius (41 degrees Fahrenheit) and summer temperatures that rarely exceed 27 degrees Celsius (81 degrees Fahrenheit). Nanlong, situated in southwestern Guizhou, has a similar range, with slightly warmer winter averages and extreme humidity year-round.[11]

Although these temperatures look moderate, Guizhou's unrelenting humidity makes the colder months unpleasantly damp and the warmer months uncomfortably sticky. It also produces the recurrent mists and fog described in Xu Xiake's diary. Xu considered these mists a mere inconvenience, but many other Chinese intellectuals of the imperial era viewed them as a serious health risk. It was widely believed that Guizhou's atmosphere produced miasmas (*zhangqi*), or noxious vapors thought to cause disease. The miasmas of Nanlong were considered particularly insalubrious. In the words of one eighteenth-century official, "Hot weather is common and cold days are rare. When spring changes to summer, there are sudden, violent rainstorms, and the hills are shrouded in a miasma of suffocating vapors. People suffer from headaches, pressure in the chest, diarrhea, and other illnesses. Epidemics of malaria are not infrequent."[12]

Guizhou's terrain created problems far more serious than the real or imagined health risks posed by the weather. Modern estimates indicate that 87 percent of the land in Guizhou is mountainous, and only 3 to 5 percent is flat.[13] The region occupies the eastern edge of the Yunnan-Guizhou Plateau, a southeastern extension of the Tibetan Plateau, which slopes southeastward from the Yunnan highlands through Guizhou and into Guangxi. This plateau is composed primarily of Devonian limestone, which, through a weathering process known as carbonation, has produced the landscapes of fancifully shaped karst mountains seen throughout southwestern China and northern Vietnam.[14]

Guizhou's combination of relative warmth, high humidity, and heavy rainfall provides the ideal conditions for karst formation. The carbon dioxide that occurs in both the soil and the atmosphere is highly soluble in water. When carbon dioxide mixes with rainwater and groundwater, it forms carbonic acid, which then forms hydrogen ions and bicarbonate ions. The hydrogen ions wear away at the calcium carbonate of the limestone. Over the millennia, as large quantities of solid rock are eaten away, caves and sinkholes form underground, and then, as the land surface collapses, the characteristic karst topography takes shape.

This landscape places severe constraints on Guizhou's agriculture. Farming is mostly confined to the small, isolated valleys produced by the karst topography. Hillside cultivation is also carried out wherever possible, with terraces built all the way to the tops of the highest peaks. Infertile soils further limit agricultural productivity. Much of the soil in western Guizhou is either red podzolic earth, which is too eroded and leached to support good farming, or yellow podzolic earth, which is too acidic. To make matters worse, karst topography has poor drainage and absorbs water rapidly; thus, instead of draining away, the excess water from heavy rains can build up and cause devastating floods.[15]

The peasants of Guizhou coaxed what foodstuffs they could from this unforgiving terrain. The best land in the valleys of Guiyang, Anshun, and Nanlong was reserved for paddy rice. Even with terracing, however, the amount of land level enough for rice cultivation was very limited. Winter wheat was also common in the valleys and on terraced hillsides. Upland areas were given over to maize, often intercropped with sweet potato, soybeans, or squash. Buckwheat, the hardiest of grains, also grew well in the harsh, mountainous areas of Guizhou's far northwest.[16] Other crops included green and yellow beans, sorghum, millet, barley, potatoes, gourds, sesame, mushrooms, and various fruits. Important commercial crops included cotton, tea, indigo, sugar cane, tobacco, medicinal plants, lacquer, and tung oil. Because the soil lacked nutrients, fertilizers (usually in the form of night soil, animal manure, ashes from burned vegetation, or plant oils) were required to produce adequate harvests.[17]

Population and Land Use

The increasing population pressed hard on Guizhou's available land.[18] It is clear that the province experienced a demographic explosion between the sixteenth and nineteenth centuries, although precise population figures remain a matter of debate. Qing government enumerations suggest that the registered population was approximately 528,000 in the mid-sixteenth century; and that the population increased to 2.4 million by 1741, to 3 million by 1746, to 3.3 million by 1756, to 3.4 million by 1765, and then jumped to more than 5 million in 1778.[19] However, as Ho Ping-ti explained in his pioneering 1957 study, Qing population registers reflected not the actual population, but rather, the fiscal population (the number of tax-payers).[20] James Lee's careful demographic studies have shown that fiscal population figures grossly underestimate the actual population. In the case of Guizhou, according to Lee, non-Han populations were usually not included in census figures, nor were the large numbers of immigrants who settled in Guizhou. After accounting for the people omitted from official registers, Lee offers much higher population figures for the province–that is, a population of approximately 1.5 million in the mid-sixteenth century, a doubling to 3 million by 1733 and a doubling again to 6 million by 1775.[21] Yang Bin's more recent study offers slightly more conservative estimates, suggesting that the population was around 2.06 million in 1661, and that it increased to 4,574,900 in 1753, and to 5,410,035 in 1840.[22]

Calculating the amount of cultivated land in seventeenth- and eighteenth-century Guizhou is equally problematic because land-use figures were also underreported throughout the late imperial period.[23] One recent study estimates that the amount of registered land under cultivation was around 654,120 hectares (1.6 million acres) in 1685, 991,420 (2.5 million acres) hectares in 1724, and 1.4 million hectares (3.5 million acres) in 1784.[24] Despite the steady increase in cultivated area, land use in Guizhou remained significantly lower than in other provinces. Neighboring

Guangxi, for example, had approximately 2.6 million hectares under cultivation in 1784 (6.4 million acres), while Jiangsu had 5.3 million (13.1 million acres) of cultivated land.[25] Guizhou's hilly terrain and poor soils were undoubtedly factors in this province's low numbers—but so was the persistent problem of underreporting. In any case, the scarcity of cultivable and cultivated land gives credence to Aibida's complaint, quoted on the first page of this book, that the entire province could not produce as much tax revenue as a single county in China Proper.

HUMAN LANDSCAPES: GUIZHOU'S ETHNIC MOSAIC

A variety of peoples vied for the resources of Guizhou's ecologically precarious space.[26] Throughout history, the province has been an ethnic mosaic. In northwestern Guizhou, the Lolo, known today as the Yi predominated, interspersed with small settlements of Han immigrants and Miao. The southwest had a high concentration of Zhongjia (Buyi), but also had small Miao settlements in the mountains and ever-increasing numbers of Han immigrants. As the ethnic crossroads of the province, the areas around Guiyang and Anshun were home to all four groups.

Over the centuries, Chinese imperial officials attempted to classify the peoples of Guizhou into clearly delineated groups. Every local gazetteer from the sixteenth century onward included several chapters devoted to the dress, customs, and languages of non-Han populations. The eighteenth century saw the emergence of a genre of illustrated manuscripts known as Miao albums (*Miao tu*), a collection of drawings and texts that delineate and categorize the different groups in China's southern provinces. As Laura Hostetler explains, the genre originated as an administrative document created by and for officials responsible for governing the people represented therein. The albums generally classified ethnic groups according to their geographic location, the color or appearance of their clothing, physical attributes, distinctive features of their dwellings, and other characteristics remarkable to their observers. The albums also commented on the ethnic groups' behavioral tendencies, and the extent to which the groups had adopted Han cultural norms.[27]

Today, Guizhou's non-Han populations count among the fifty-five ethnic minorities (*shaoshu minzu*) officially recognized in the People's Republic of China. Scholars in the fields of ethnology (*minzu xue*) and ethnohistory (*minzu shi*) have written extensively on the history and political economy of these groups. This body of work is structured around a political agenda that portrays the history of China's non-Han groups as just one small chapter in the nation's larger history. Pivotal events such as rebellions are not examined in light of their significance to a given ethnic group, but only as steps in that group's inexorable progress toward "liberation" by the Chinese Communist Party. This rhetoric constrains this type of scholarship but does not necessarily compromise it. Despite its ideological overtones, research in *minzuxue* and *minzushi* does yield up some valuable historical and ethnographic data; and recent work from younger Chinese scholars also suggests a gradual movement away from the nationalistic paradigm. The following sections synthesize information from these *minzu* studies with the findings of Western anthropologists and historians in order to introduce the four main ethnic groups of central and southwestern Guizhou.

The Zhongjia (Modern Name: Buyi, Bouyei)

The historical record from the eighteenth century finds this ethnic group at the center of every major event in the region. The alleged misdeeds of Zhongjia chieftains provided the pretext for Yongzheng-era officials to implement the *gaitu guiliu* reforms of the 1720s. Over the next few decades, when instances of social unrest occurred, Zhongjia villagers were often the instigators. At the peak of the unrest, in 1797, the masterminds behind the Nanlong Uprising and the majority of their followers were all Zhongjia. Members of the region's other ethnic groups, namely the Han, Miao, and Yi, played much smaller roles in these events—sometimes as victims, sometimes as antagonists, sometimes as bystanders. Who were the Zhongjia, and why did they play such a pivotal role in the upheavals of the eighteenth century? The following section seeks to answer these questions, at least in part, by providing an introduction to Zhongjia language, history, and socioeconomic institutions.[28] Although the discussion focuses primarily on the imperial era, it also touches upon ethnic policy in the People's Republic of China.

Who Are the Zhongjia?

To begin answering the question "Who are the Zhongjia?" it will be useful to first examine some modern demographic and ethnographic data. As noted earlier, the Zhongjia have been called the Buyi since 1953. Numbering around 2.9 million, the Buyi today constitute the eleventh-largest minority nationality in the People's Republic of China. Approximately 2.5 million Buyi live in Guizhou, mainly in the two Buyi–Miao Autonomous Prefectures of Qianxinan (Southwestern Guizhou) and Qiannan (Southern Guizhou), and in the regions of Anshun, Guiyang, and Liupanshui, while the rest are scattered throughout southeastern Yunnan and southeastern Sichuan. Small numbers of Buyi also live in northeastern Vietnam, where they constitute two officially recognized ethnic groups, the Bo Y and the Giay.[29]

The Buyi represent one of many Tai groups in southern China and Southeast Asia. More precisely, their language is classified as a Northern Tai language within the Kam-Tai branch of the Kadai (sometimes called Tai-Kadai) language family. Their closest kin in both ethnolinguistic and geographic terms are the Northern Zhuang, a subgroup within the much larger Zhuang nationality that is found mostly in Guangxi. The present-day Northern Zhuang correspond to an ethnic group called Nong in Qing sources.[30] The Buyi and Northern Zhuang share so many cultural and linguistic similarities that it is impossible to study one group without reference to the other; indeed, for the purposes of this book, scholarship on the history, political life, religious traditions, and oral literature of the Northern Zhuang often proved as useful as similar research on the Buyi. More distant relatives of the Buyi include the Southern Zhuang of Guangxi and the Nung and Tay of Vietnam.[31] The Buyi also share some cultural and linguistic features with the Dai of southern Yunnan as well as the Thai, Lao, and Shan populations of mainland Southeast Asia. Their extended ethnic family also includes the Dong (Kam), Shui, and Maonan ethnic groups dispersed throughout Guizhou, Guangxi, and Hunan, and the Li of Hainan.[32]

Archeological findings, linguistic data, and DNA evidence suggest that these Tai-speaking populations all descended from the Hundred Yue (Baiyue) peoples who occupied a vast area of eastern, central, and southern China as early as 2000 B.C.E. Two Baiyue civilizations in particular have been linked to the Buyi of Guizhou and their Zhuang neighbors. The Buyi and Northern Zhuang seem to share ancestral ties to the Xi'ou people who inhabited the West River basin along Guangxi's present-day border with Guangdong. The Southern Zhuang, along with the closely related Nung and Tay, may have descended from the Luoyue people who lived in the area extending from Guangxi's current provincial capital of Nanning to the Red River basin of northern Vietnam. Like their contemporaries in other Yue societies, the inhabitants of Xi'ou and Luoyue relied primarily on rice farming and other agricultural activities for their livelihood.[33]

Contact between the Xi'ou peoples and the Han probably began during the Qin Dynasty (221–206 B.C.E.), when China's imperial government began sending expeditionary forces into the southern realms.[34] Interaction, intermarriage, and mutual acculturation between indigenous communities and various immigrant groups continued until the eighteenth or nineteenth century C.E. as successive waves of Han soldiers and civilians settled in the southwest.[35] Thus, today's Buyi population developed from more than two millennia of cultural exchanges in the Guizhou-Guangxi borderlands.[36]

These exchanges were multi-directional. Some Han colonists were absorbed into local populations and effectively became Zhongjia.[37] At the same time, many Zhongjia internalized Chinese cultural norms and tried to "pass" as Han. As the Zhongjia gained familiarity with Chinese culture, they perceived that the Han enjoyed one particular advantage that they did not, namely the opportunity to participate in the imperial examinations. In order to enjoy the same privilege, many Zhongjia began identifying themselves as immigrants from Shandong, from Huguang (a province during the Yuan and Ming, comprising present-day Hubei and Hunan) or from Jiangnan; and they produced fictive genealogies to legitimize these claims.[38] To this day, many Buyi still maintain both the genealogies and the claims to ancestral homes in eastern or central China.[39] The Zhuang often assert similar claims to Han ancestry, a phenomenon that ethnologist David Holm traces to prejudices against the indigenous peoples of southern China that only began to fade after the Zhuang received official recognition as an ethnic group. "Before . . . the 1950s, discrimination against 'southern barbarians' was such that many villagers tried to assimilate and . . . fitted themselves up with Chinese-style genealogies that purported to prove that their remote ancestors came from northern Chinese provinces . . . and had been sent to Guangxi in order to garrison the frontiers against the southern barbarians."[40]

It is worth noting, however, that some Buyi may in fact descend from so-called southern barbarians—namely the Zhuang of Guangxi who tried so hard to hide their own "barbarian" origins. A number of historical writings from the Ming and Qing periods suggest that the Zhongjia were the progeny of garrison troops sent from Guangxi to Guizhou during the Five Dynasties and Ten Kingdoms Period (906–960 C.E.). The *Official History of the Ming Dynasty* (*Ming shi*) described the Zhongjia as soldiers who had immigrated to Guizhou from Guangxi, an idea that Tian Wen expounded in his 1690 *A Book of Guizhou* (Qian shu): "From whence did the Zhongjia come? During the Five Dynasties Period, the Chu king Ma Yin sent them from Yongguan [in present-day Guangxi] to garrison [Guizhou]."[41] The idea of Guangxi origins was reiterated in the 1751 *Qing Imperial Illustration of Tributaries,* and again in an early twentieth-century account by the British missionary Samuel Clarke.[42] Zhou Guoyan finds an element of truth in such assertions, but cautions that the entire Buyi population cannot possibly claim descent from this small contingent of Guangxi soldiers. Although the troops' ethnic origins have not been firmly established, Zhou finds it reasonable to assume that they were Zhuang. "According to textual research, Yongguan was in the central part of Guangxi where its capital city—Nanning—is situated. It is one of the areas inhabited mainly by Zhuang people today, and it was also a Zhuang area during the Five Dynasties, according to historical studies."[43]

Changing Names: From 'Buzhuang' to 'Zhongjia' to 'Buyi'

If some modern-day Buyi are indeed the descendants of Zhuang immigrants to Guizhou, these ancestral ties represent just one example of the enduring historical, cultural, and linguistic linkages between the two ethnic groups. These Guangxi origins may also help explain the provenance of the old ethnonym *Zhongjia*. Both *Zhong* (as in Zhongjia) and *Zhuang* are short forms of the word *Bouxcuengh* (in Chinese: *Buzhuang*), a self-appellation used by the ancient Tai-speaking inhabitants of northern Guangxi and still heard in Zhuang-speaking communities today.[44] *Boux* (*Bu*) means "people," and *cuengh* (*zhuang*) means "narrow, flat-bottomed river valleys in the mountains." Thus, *Bouxcuengh* signifies "people of the river valleys," an apt appellation for people who relied on agriculture for their livelihood.[45]

According to Zhou Guoyan, the tenth-century settlers from Guangxi probably imported the term *Zhuang* (variously written 撞, 獞 or 僮 in Chinese sources) to Guizhou.[46] There, it acquired the variant pronunciation "Zhong," eventually giving rise to the terms *Zhongjia* (狆/仲家) and *Zhongmiao* (狆/仲苗) found in Chinese documents from the Yuan dynasty onward.[47] These ethnonyms became common currency, broadly applied by Han residents and government officials alike, and were generally accepted by the communities so named. For most Zhongjia, however, the term was more of an exonym than an autonym—that is, it was a name introduced by outsiders rather than one that people used to refer to themselves. The term *Zhuang/Zhong* apparently fell into disuse among local residents after that initial influx of Guangxi immigrants.[48] A more common autonym was *Bouyeix*, meaning "native people," a term that local residents used to distinguish themselves from the various Han groups in the area, such as "recent immigrants" (*bouxhek*), "people of the army" (*bouxgun*) or "officials" (*bouxhak*).[49] The Bouyeix further classified themselves according to the quality and elevation of the land they farmed.[50] Lowland dwellers were often called "people of the rice paddies" (*bouxnaz*), a name that differentiated them from "people beyond the rice paddies" (*bouxnongz*) and "people of the hills" (*bouxloeh*).[51] These autonyms were relational terms that reflected the ways people thought of themselves in contradistinction to other nearby groups. As such, the names probably provided what David Holm calls "badges of self-identity," but they did not imply any real sense of primordial or monolithic ethnic solidarity.[52]

The name *Zhongjia* remained in use until the Nationalities Identification Project was implemented during the early years of Communist rule in China. Working at the behest of central and local government authorities, researchers in Guizhou determined that the most common autonym among the so-called Zhongjia was *Buyi* or some variant thereof.[53] Thus, the group was officially renamed *Buyi* in August 1953.[54] The dialects spoken in northern Guangxi also bore closer resemblance to Buyi dialects in Guizhou than to the local languages of southern Guangxi. Nonetheless, local and central authorities determined in the early 1950s that the Tai-speaking populations of northern and southern Guangxi would all be classified as Zhuang (now written 壮) despite their linkages to the Buyi and apparent lack of internal cohesion.[55] These classifications supposedly reflected popular sentiment on both sides of the Guizhou-Guangxi border. The Guizhou Buyi did not want to be classified under the same ethnonym as their Zhuang neighbors in Guangxi.[56] The Zhuang, for their part, had resisted the Buyi label because the term was a local pejorative "applied by the more prosperous valley dwellers to the poor people who live[d] in the hills, and never used by any group of themselves."[57]

The purported opposition from both sides of the Guizhou/Buyi-Guangxi/Zhuang dispute fit neatly into the agenda of local and central authorities. Their goal all along, it seems, had been to establish two ethnic groups conveniently divided by a provincial boundary. As Katherine Kaup explains, "The division of nationalities, not surprisingly, often was determined more by where they lived than by any 'objective' Stalinist criteria. The division between the Zhuang and the Buyi nationality . . . was largely determined by provincial boundaries." Kaup also notes that many of the people labeled "Buyi" in Guizhou had blood relatives among the "Zhuang" across the border in Guangxi. In some cases, immediate family members were identified as two separate nationalities if they straddled the border.[58] This division was not altogether agreeable to members of Guizhou Nationalities Affairs Commission. Some of them reportedly told their colleagues in Yunnan that they would have preferred to see Guangxi reclassify its Zhuang population as Buyi "so that there might be a standardized understanding of ethnicity throughout the southwest. However, because the classification took place in strict accordance with provincial jurisdictions . . . this daydream never came true."[59]

This was not the first time central government authorities attempted to divide and control the inhabitants of the Guangxi-Guizhou borderlands. Eighteenth-century officials pursued a similar goal, but for different reasons and with very different results. As will be explained in chapter 3, the Yongzheng emperor's representatives in southwest China tried to subdue the Zhongjia by deposing a native official and redrawing the border between Guizhou and Guangxi. For the remainder of the Qing period, this boundary only existed on paper and in the minds of imperial authorities. It had little if any bearing on the lives of Zhongjia villagers, many of whom had family in both Guizhou and Guangxi. Cultural and clan ties remained strong within the communities straddling the two provinces, as local residents frequently crossed back and forth to visit friends and relatives, conduct business, study religion and magic, and, on occasion, participate in illegal activities or rebellions.

The decisions following the Nationalities Identification Project of the 1950s might be viewed as an attempt to replace this porous geographic frontier with an impermeable ethnic boundary, much as Qing officials of the eighteenth-century sought to impose order in the same region by creating a hard provincial boundary. The reforms of the Yongzheng period established the Hongshui River that runs along Guangxi's northwestern frontier with Guizhou as the boundary between the two provinces. Since the 1950s, this river has also marked the theoretical divide between the Buyi and the Zhuang. David Holm suggests a different regional cartography based on dialect distribution and river systems. He identifies the You River in south-central Guangxi as the dividing line between the Northern Zhuang/Buyi and Southern Zhuang dialects.[60] Given that the Northern Zhuang—that is, those living between the Hongshui and Youjiang Rivers— share more traits with the Buyi than with the Southern Zhuang, it might have made more sense to use the Youjiang as both a provincial and an ethnic boundary. In other words, the territory north of the river might have been annexed to Guizhou and its inhabitants classified as Northern Zhuang or Buyi (or as something else altogether), while the territory south of the river might have remained part of Guangxi and its inhabitants classified as Southern Zhuang or Zhuang (or again, as something else altogether).[61]

Of course, the matter is purely academic, for it is highly unlikely that authorities in China will consider redrawing any ethnic or provincial boundaries in the foreseeable future.[62] More to the point, the ethnonyms "Buyi" and "Zhuang" have become thoroughly reified in the six decades since the Nationalities Identification Project.[63] Although Buyi and Zhuang intellectuals alike readily point to similarities in their languages and cultures, they are equally quick to stress that their ethnic groups are separate and distinct.[64]

'The greatest evil in all Guizhou': Portraits from Chinese and Western Sources

Having examined the ethnic and historical origins of the Zhongjia, it now remains for us to explore the reasons behind their role in Guizhou's tumultuous eighteenth century history. To begin, it will be useful to examine some ethnographic descriptions from the late imperial period. In many cases, these portraits are less than flattering and may even strike the twenty-first-century reader as downright racist, but it is precisely this negative viewpoint that makes these descriptions so useful. The accounts provide a sampling of official and literati views on the Zhongjia—and, even more importantly, shed light on the ways in which the Zhongjia responded to their environment and to real or perceived threats from their neighbors or from government authorities.

Ethnographic accounts from the late imperial era usually characterized the Zhongjia as "the fiercest of all the Miao," if not "the greatest evil in all Guizhou."[65] The Zhongjia earned this reputation as a consequence of their alleged propensity for violence and deceit, vividly described in the 1673 *Gazetteer of Guizhou province:*"[The Zhongjia are] dangerous and wily . . . and fond of killing. When they go out they must carry a strong crossbow and a sharp knife. If an enemy [so much as stares at them], they must take revenge."[66] In addition to their reputed penchant for brutality, the Zhongjia followed a lifestyle that Confucian scholar-officials found contemptible, as suggested in this excerpt from the 1673 *Gazetteer of Xilong district:* "[The Zhongjia] are completely lacking in courtesies. . . . After marriage, women return to their natal homes for a number of years. When ill, [the Zhongjia] do not consult with doctors but instead seek the advice of shamans. [They] use chicken bones for divination. . . . They lack metal tools, and salt is not part of their diet."[67] In these accounts and many others like them, the character for *Zhong* was usually written 狆, using the "dog" character component (*quan* 犭). This unsubtle pejorative reflected Confucian scholar-officials' attitudes about peoples they considered less than civilized—or even less than human. *Zhong* could be written 仲, using the "human" character component (*ren* 人), but this variant appeared with far less frequency in government communiqués, local gazetteers, and travel chronicles.[68]

Attitudes toward the Zhongjia were not static, however. During the eighteenth century, some imperial officials noted fractional advances toward the Confucian ideal of civilization. For example, a 1750 handbook reports: "The Zhongjia are the most clever and cunning of all the Miao.[69] In the past, they carried swords at their waist and crossbows under their arms. They would hide deep in the thickets or climb high into the hills [to launch surprise attacks and raids]; these were their finest tricks. Recently, they have advanced toward culture (*xianghua*) and developed awe and respect for the law. Their old customs have been eradicated. . . . Most men have adopted Han clothing, and many can understand the Chinese language."[70]

These comments seem to embody the values of the Confucian civilizing project undertaken during the Yongzheng and early Qianlong reigns, when local officials sought to bring non-Han peoples "toward culture"(*xianghua*) through education and moral suasion. To be sure, some Zhongjia villagers who lived near Han settlements did gain proficiency in Mandarin and adopted Chinese attire. After the Yongzheng-era reforms, many Zhongjia men also began to wear the queue, the distinctive braided hairstyle that signaled loyalty to the Qing.[71] But these outward manifestations of acculturation did not necessarily signal a change of ethnic identification or political allegiance, let alone the "awe and respect for the law" noted in the excerpt above.[72]

Accounts from the late Qing period portrayed the Zhongjia as both Sinicized *and* intractable. This dichotomy is particularly apparent in the 1911 account by British missionary Samuel Clarke. He observed a high degree of acculturation among the Zhongjia and, in some cases, even total assimilation. "Some of them engage in trade and settle in the Chinese cities and towns, and if they remain there, as many of them do, they bind the feet of their girls and are reckoned as Chinese."[73] His comments on Zhongjia bilingualism suggest a similar level of Sinicization: "Most of the men . . . and many of the women can speak Chinese. . . . We have heard them say, and we think the statement is true, that out of every three words they utter when speaking their own language, one is Chinese."[74] This portrait of acculturation receives further credence from Clarke's description of Zhongjia clothing and education: "The Chung-chia [Zhongjia] men can hardly be distinguished from the Chinese. . . . As most of them are agriculturists, the men dress exactly the same as Chinese farmers and village folk. . . . Many of them compete at the civil and military examinations and some of them have risen to high rank in the imperial service."[75] Despite these outward displays of Sinicization, Clarke noted that the Han still considered the Zhongjia an inferior race, a view that he evidently shared:

The Chung-chia [Zhongjia] appear to have all the defects of the Chinese and none of their better qualities. Among the Chinese are good, bad, and indifferent; among the Chung-chia some are bad and some perhaps not so bad. The Chinese generally describe the Miao as turbulent, simple, and without proper notions of propriety; while they describe the Chung-chia as crafty, lying, and dishonest. . . . The Chinese say that every Chung-chia is a thief, and from what we know of them, we should not feel justified in denying the charge. . . . The dishonest among the Chung-chia are sneak thieves who prowl around at night, and pilfer from their friends and neighbors.[76]

Clearly, the Zhongjia ran afoul of Confucian (and Western evangelical) sensibilities in myriad ways. With a century or two of historical hindsight and a greater understanding of the environmental conditions facing the Zhongjia, it is possible to interpret their real or imagined transgressions in a different light. Many of the behaviors depicted here—the supposed proclivity for violence, cunning, and thievery, and even the varying degrees of acculturation—exemplified different activities on a broad spectrum of livelihood choices. Thievery and pilfering were time-honored redistributive techniques employed by those who needed (or simply wanted) something their neighbors possessed. Acculturation, whether partial or complete, real or feigned, reflected a great flexibility and pragmatism in the Zhongjia approach to Chinese culture. Local residents adopted and adapted whatever served their immediate needs and rejected the rest. The Chinese language—or some local variant of it—was useful because it served as the lingua franca for commercial exchanges and the occasional encounter with imperial authorities. Chinese attire enabled Zhongjia villagers to blend in with other local residents, though apparently not enough if observers recognized them as non-Hans wearing Han clothing! The imperial education system enabled some Zhongjia to gain a modicum of literacy and at least a passing familiarity with the Confucian classics. The Zhongjia tolerated and even respected Qing laws, but never to the extent that these legal niceties impinged upon traditional livelihoods. At times, the Zhongjia manipulated Chinese culture in ways that enabled them to launch indirect attacks on Qing authority. On other occasions, most notably during the Nanlong Uprising, they rejected the

Confucian culture complex and mounted a direct assault on imperial institutions.

Zhongjia Political and Economic Institutions

During the imperial era, Zhongjia society was organized around an institution known as the *tingmu* system. The term *tingmu* referred to hereditary landowners who governed small fiefdoms along the Guizhou-Guangxi border. The residents of *tingmu* domains were divided into units known as *jia* (shields). The *jia* were subdivided into smaller units called *ting* (encampments). Each *jia* was composed of ten *ting*.[77] The people living in chieftain-controlled areas were divided into eight categories. The four highest classes all participated in government and administration. The chieftains occupied the highest rank. All the land and people belonged to them, and their name was law within the areas they governed. Next in rank were the local headmen (*tumu* or *toumu*), who were both the chieftains' assistants and enfeoffed officials. The village heads (*bashi*) were responsible for keeping the peace among local residents. Next in rank were the horse platoons (*mapai*), the soldiers who served in the chieftains' personal armies. Equal in rank to these soldiers were ritual specialists (*mogong*), who maintained the local shrines and organized various ceremonies.[78] Below these leaders and functionaries were the ordinary people, who were further subdivided into eight groups. The rice farmers, known as "grain-farming hundred names" (*liangzhuang baixing*) were the highest-ranking commoners. Below the rice farmers were servants and laborers (*fuyi*), who were usually immigrants from other areas. At first, these workers did not possess any land, but after a set period of service, they could obtain some fields of their own. Next in rank were the "privately-owned hundred names" (*sizhuang baixing*), immigrants and refugees who were effectively the chieftains' private property. These settlers were allowed to till the chieftains' poorest fields, but it was not a secure life, for they could be bought and sold along with the land. Their only protection was that the chieftains could not sell these cultivators separately from the land they tilled. The members of this *sizhuang baixing* class had no hope of upward social mobility; they could not become rice farmers or even servants. However, even lower in rank were maidservants (*nüpai*), who performed domestic tasks in the chieftains' households and who could be sold or married off like slaves.[79]

Lands under the chieftains' control were divided into public fields (*gongtian*), and private fields (*sitian*). Rice farmers rented parcels of the public land from the chieftains. Annual rents varied from place to place but usually ranged from 50 to 80 percent of the year's harvest. Private lands were the personal estates of the chieftains, local headmen, and village heads. Rice farmers were required to work the private lands as well as their allotment of public land.[80] Most landlords also required their tenants to provide set periods of labor, and to contribute food, money, or manpower for religious holidays and other celebrations. The tenants' quality of life ranged from miserable to tolerable, depending on the quality of the land they farmed, the size of the harvests in any given year, and the disposition of their landlords.[81] Some families supplemented their livelihoods by raising additional income from cash crops such as tobacco and indigo, or from the production and sale of textiles.[82]

The Lolo (Nasu Yi)

The Lolo, or Yi as they are known today, are Tibeto-Burman speakers who traditionally occupied a wide area including northwestern Guizhou, southwestern Sichuan, and northeastern Yunnan. Those living in northwestern Guizhou call themselves the Nasu (also known as the Nasu Yi).[83] Although the Nasu Yi play a relatively minor role in this book, it will be useful to take a general look at their political history and economic institutions.

The Nasu Yi were the most powerful non-Han group in Guizhou— perhaps in all of southwestern China—until the early years of the Qing dynasty. The Mu'ege kingdom of the Nasu Yi gained control over much of present-day Guizhou between about 300 and 1200 C.E. The kingdom's strength and its long-term survival stemmed from its geographic position between China proper and the expansionist kingdoms along the southwestern periphery. The Tang (618–907) and Song (960–1279) imperial governments both treated the Mu'ege realm as a buffer against rival states— against Nanzhao in the Tang, and against Dali in the Song.[84]

In 1280, the patriarch of the ruling An clan received a hereditary title from the government of the new Yuan dynasty [85] By the 1570s, the An family controlled a vast area that extended from the northwestern tip of Guizhou all the way to the Guiyang region, an area called Shuixi in Ming sources. This territorial expansion radically altered the kingdom's social and economic structure. When the An realm had been limited to the barren northwestern corner of Guizhou, the clan economy had centered on slash-and-burn agriculture. After the An rulers annexed more fertile territory to the south and east, they realized that paddy farming would yield far more revenue than slash-and-burn and they adopted Han agricultural techniques. This dramatic change to the region's economy required a skilled labor force, and in the minds of the kingdom's officials, there was no better source than the recent Han in-migrants to northwest Guizhou, northeast Yunnan, and southern Sichuan. These in-migrants had, to a great extent, been responsible for the introduction of Han agricultural methods to the southwestern periphery of the Ming empire. Thus, the An leaders considered it entirely logical to raid vulnerable Han settlements for captives to farm reclaimed lands. By the beginning of the seventeenth century, then, an extensive trade network stretched from northwest Guangxi to central Sichuan to supply Shuixi's expanding economy with slaves.[86] The slaves were a multi-ethnic group consisting of Lolo commoners, Chinese, Miao, and even Zhongjia. The An clan assigned certain tasks to specific ethnic groups. The Zhongjia, for example, were considered good farmers and were thus allocated the best land, while the Miao and Han were often assigned less fertile lands.[87]

The Ming and Qing states steadily eroded Nasu Yi political autonomy. The An family was deposed in the 1670s, but was restored to power after twenty years. During the 1720s, the Yongzheng court terminated the An family's hereditary title and incorporated the domain into regular administrative units.[88]

The Miao

Although their origins and ancient history remain obscure, the current scholarly consensus is that the earliest Miao moved southwestward from central China, under pressure from Han expansion.[89] They were usually characterized as a mountain-dwelling people, although it is not certain when or how willingly they became denizens of the uplands. The likeliest scenario is that, in the face of increasing pressure from Han immigrants, the Miao retreated into remote mountain regions of southwestern China, Laos, Thailand, and Vietnam.[90]

Over the centuries, the name *Miao* has acquired two related meanings. In its broadest sense, it is a generic term for the various non-Han groups in Guizhou and neighboring provinces. As we have seen throughout this chapter, Chinese literati and imperial officials sometimes used the term "Miao" when they were actually referring to the Zhongjia. In the narrowest sense, "Miao" denotes a broader ethnic group (*minzu*) that includes several subgroups in southwest China, as well as the Hmong of Vietnam, Laos, and Thailand.[91] Ming and Qing sources use the term *Miao* in the broader sense to refer more generally to the non-Han peoples of southern China. The sources often distinguished between Miao who were unassimilated barbarians ("strangers," or *sheng*) and those who had adapted to Chinese civilization ("acquaintances," or *shu*). The Miao who were "acquaintances" lived close to centers of Han culture and were either under direct state control or under the control of a state-appointed native official. These Miao adopted Han clothing, became conversant in Mandarin, and learned to read and write. The Miao who remained "strangers" were those who resisted assimilation, pacification, and state control.[92] Ming and Qing sources also classified Miao populations according to the color or appearance of their clothing, their physical attributes, distinctive features of their dwellings, or other characteristics remarkable to their observers. This practice gave rise to such names as the Flowery Miao, Red Miao, Short-skirted Miao, Dog's Ear Miao, and Pig-filth Miao.[93]

During the Ming and Qing periods, most Miao lived in hamlets (*zhai*) of one hundred or so families. These settlements were usually located high in the mountains and were often enclosed with heavy wooden fences to discourage outsiders from entering. Defensibility was the main consideration in choosing a place to settle. Even if a hamlet itself was not readily defendable, the surrounding mountains provided sanctuary for villagers in the event of an attack. The Miao depended primarily on agriculture for their livelihood. As mountain-dwellers, they relied on the slash-and-burn farming of hardy dryland crops such as buckwheat, oats, corn, and potatoes, often supplemented by hunting and gathering in the forest. Like the Zhongjia, they participated in local market systems, often exchanging forest products and handicrafts for sugar, salt, and metal tools. Those living in northwestern Guizhou also raised sheep and goats for sale at local markets.[94]

The Miao lacked the centralized political organization of the Zhongjia or the Nasu Yi and often occupied the lowest rungs of Guizhou's socioeconomic ladder.[95] As noted earlier, some Miao in southwestern Guizhou became the slaves of Zhongjia chieftains. The Miao living in northwestern Guizhou were often the tenants of Nasu Yi aristocrats, or, less frequently, of Han and Muslim (Hui) settlers.[96] Their rental obligations included crop payments, as well as labor service in forestry, agriculture, and transport. As chapter 4 will explain, the Miao often found themselves caught up in the schemes of their more resourceful neighbors, either as accomplices or as victims.

The Han

Han settlers began arriving in Guizhou during the last years of the Spring and Autumn Period (770–476 B.C.E.). From the Tang through the Ming and Qing periods, wave after wave of Han immigrants entered Guizhou from Shanxi, Jiangxi, Sichuan, Hunan, Anhui, and Jiangsu. The Ming government had a policy of sending soldiers and their dependents to Guizhou to establish military colonies (tuntian). After each Ming military campaign in the southwest, the state settled more Han in Guizhou. A number of people also immigrated to Guizhou of their own volition. Each new wave of immigrants placed increasing pressure on the area's non-Han inhabitants.[97] The Han settlers usually claimed the most fertile lands and applied their advanced farming techniques to their fields, thus giving a welcome boost to a province's tax base. In many areas, the Han gradually became the dominant ethnic group, and displaced native peoples were either forced into less desirable, hilly regions, or were driven to remote border areas. Those natives who remained in their home regions suffered a significant reduction in their social and economic standing. Many Han regarded their non-Han neighbors with the contempt we saw reflected in Xu Xiake's diary.

THE HISTORICAL LANDSCAPE: GUIZHOU DURING THE MING AND EARLY QING

During the Yuan dynasty, the lands constituting present-day Guizhou were divided among the neighboring provinces of Huguang (present-day

Hunan and Hubei), Yunnan, and Sichuan. Under the administration of these provinces were six "routes" (*lu*) in the Guizhou region.[98] Beneath the route-level administration, prefectures, counties, and departments were established wherever there were sufficient tax-paying populations. Where direct administration was not possible, the Yuan appointed hereditary native rulers (*tusi*) to administer local populations on behalf of the court.

The early Ming state oversaw a gradual administrative consolidation in the Guizhou region, culminating with the creation of Guizhou province in 1413. The process had begun in 1382, when the government established the Guizhou regional military commissioner (*duzhihui shi*), the first official devoted exclusively to the region. The commissioner was responsible only for military matters; provincial officials in Yunnan, Sichuan, and the Ming province of Huguang remained in charge of civil administration.

In 1413, two powerful native rulers in eastern Guizhou went to war over a disputed piece of land. When the fighting threatened to engulf a wider area, the Ming court sent troops to quell the violence. Eventually, the two feuding rulers killed each other. The central government claimed their lands and established regular administrative units—eight prefectures and four districts in all. The court then established a provincial administration commissioner (*buzheng shi*) to coordinate the administration of these new units.[99] This was the first Chinese government organization devoted entirely to the civil administration of the Guizhou region. In order to generate enough tax revenue for this new administrative apparatus, the Ming government soon encouraged immigrants from other provinces to settle in Guizhou.[100]

Native Officials in Ming Guizhou

Although the Ming established a provincial administrative apparatus in Guizhou, it continued the Yuan practice of establishing sub-provincial administrative units only where Chinese farming and taxpaying communities were large enough to support them.[101] In areas where non-Chinese populations predominated, the Ming state appointed native rulers to govern their own people according to local custom. When the court conferred native chieftain status upon a tribal leader, it classified him (or her, in rare instances) as either a civilian native official (*tuguan*) or a military native official (*tusi*). The civilian officials were under the direct supervision of the central government's Board of Appointments (*libu*), while their military counterparts came under the aegis of the Board of War (*bingbu*). Generally speaking, the civilian officials controlled areas within defined provincial boundaries, often where small numbers of Han had settled among indigenous populations. These officials held titles analogous to those in the Chinese administration system, with titles prefixed by the word *tu*: native prefects (*tufu*), native department magistrates (*tuzhou*), and native county magistrates (*tuxian*). Their staffs often included Chinese officials who served as secretary-archivists, translators, or sheriffs, and who helped mediate relations between the chieftains and the imperial state. The military officials, on the other hand, enjoyed a greater degree of institutional and territorial autonomy from China.

Regularly appointed imperial officials were seldom posted to areas controlled by these native rulers. These domains were usually located along or just beyond China's political borders, typically in areas without significant Han populations. Military officials were expected to command sizable armies to assist in the empire's defense.[102] Indigenous populations living under native rule were not subject to the standard forms of Ming and Qing taxation imposed on individuals and households. Native offices were subject to levies of goods and labor, and of soldiers when military emergencies arose. The Ming government took the collection of these levies very seriously, for, apart from their economic value, they signified the continued compliance and subservience of the native peoples.[103]

James Lee estimates that native officials controlled at least one-half of Guizhou during the Ming.[104] The institution did not always function effectively, however, as native officials often proved corrupt and unruly. Some native rulers failed to maintain peace and stability in the regions under their control, others threatened to rebel against the dynasty. Thus, after establishing many native offices early in the dynasty, the Ming government concluded that it needed a new governing method and opted to implement the policy known as "changing native officials to regularly appointed officials" (*gaitu guiliu*). The process created at least as many problems as the Ming hoped it would solve, as native populations did not always accept centrally appointed officials and were not always readily integrated into mainstream Chinese society.

By the seventeenth century, the administrative map of Guizhou resembled a patchwork quilt. Areas controlled by native officials overlapped with regular administrative units: in effect, everyone was in charge, and no one was in charge. As John Herman notes, even after Guizhou was organized as a province, Ming officials would continue to view it not so much as a contiguous part of "China Proper" (*neidi*), but as an internal frontier or semi-periphery defined roughly by provincial boundaries.[105]

The Qing Conquest of Guizhou

Although Qing armies captured Beijing in 1644, they did not gain control over southwestern China for another fifteen years. In the interim, Guizhou became a refuge for Ming loyalists. Following the suicide of the last Ming emperor, ministers in the secondary capital at Nanjing scrambled to piece together a resistance government. Several surviving members of the Ming royal family were thus maneuvered into leading a movement to overthrow the Qing. The restorationist government became known as the Southern Ming.

The most effective Southern Ming leader was Zhu Youlang, the Prince of Gui. In late 1646, he mounted a resistance campaign from the coastal province of Guangdong. At this time, he crowned himself emperor and assumed the reign title Yongli. Advancing Qing armies soon forced him westward into Guangxi, where he maintained a capital at the provincial seat of Guilin intermittently for three years. Qing incursions occasionally forced Yongli to flee northward to Hunan or Jiangxi, or southward, toward the border with Vietnam. With the help of skilled military leaders, he eventually succeeded in expanding the Southern Ming territories to include most of Guangxi, Guizhou, and Yunnan. The Qing court in Beijing kept a wary eye on Yongli and launched several military campaigns against him in the late 1640s and early 1650s. Qing advances forced the Southern Ming deeper and deeper into southwest China. For a time, Yongli governed his domain from Anlong, a remote town near Guizhou's border with Guangxi. In 1656, he fled to Yunnan, where he clung to power for another eighteen months before Qing armies deposed him.[106]

Guizhou served as an important staging ground for Qing campaigns against Yongli and his supporters. Qing armies invaded the province in early 1658, and met in Guiyang six months later to plan a strategy for consolidating power over Yunnan. In order to traverse Guizhou, Qing commanders had to secure the cooperation of the native officials who controlled the most strategic regions.[107] Jobtei, the general in charge of southwestern Guizhou, received military assistance from the native official whose domain included key routes into Guangxi and Yunnan.[108] Another Qing general, the infamous Wu Sangui, cooperated with the An rulers of northwestern Guizhou. Their alliance was so strong that the native official even led Wu's troops into battle. Wu also used An territory as a base for campaigns in nearby Sichuan.[109]

Once Guizhou was secured for the Qing, Wu Sangui led his troops into Yunnan in pursuit of the Yongli emperor. Yongli escaped into Burma and received asylum from the royal court at Ava. After lengthy negotiations between the Qing and Burmese courts, Wu Sangui received permission to cross into Burma. They arrested Yongli in Ava and escorted him back to Yunnan, where he was executed in May, 1662.[110] As a reward for the successful capture of the last Ming pretender, Wu Sangui was granted lifetime control over Yunnan and Guizhou, although the governors-general of both provinces remained in place.[111] Wu's new position gave him extraordinary powers. An imperial edict of December 1659 had already authorized him to appoint and dismiss officials and to handle all military, financial, and civil affairs without the intervention of the Board of Appointments or the Board of War.[112]

As Wu and other Qing generals moved across Guizhou, they accepted the submission of numerous native officials and usually renewed the officials' Ming titles and the terms of alliance. Almost immediately, however, the Qing court diverged from Ming policy on the *tusi*. Even as commanders on the ground were extending official recognition to native officials, policy makers in Beijing were planning a radical overhaul of the Qing state's relations with native communities. This restructuring and its effects on Guizhou's social and economic life will be the subject of chapter 3.

Chapter 3

THE CONSOLIDATION OF QING RULE

※

When Qing armies completed the military conquest of southwestern China in 1659, Guizhou was an unruly internal frontier. Although the Ming government had organized the region as a province in 1413, Guizhou still bore only the faintest imprints of imperial control. The province was an ethnic patchwork, populated by a variety of indigenous non-Han groups, each with its own languages and customs. Some of these groups showed varying degrees of assimilation with mainstream Chinese culture, but many others remained fiercely independent. Sub-provincial administrative units existed only where Han tax-paying populations were large enough to support them. Hereditary native officials (*tusi*) controlled most of the land within Guizhou and along its borders with other provinces. Although these native officials received their titles and legitimacy from the throne, most of them functioned beyond the reach of imperial law. The central government had little sway over such matters as criminal justice, or even over the rules governing inheritance of the titles it conferred upon the native officials.

It was not until the reign of the third Qing emperor, Yongzheng, that the imperial state took decisive steps to consolidate military, political, and cultural control over frontier communities throughout southwestern China. After consulting with officials in the region, Yongzheng endorsed a plan to "reform the native and return to the regular" (*gaitu guiliu*).

Under this policy, native rulers were deposed and their domains were incorporated into regular administrative units. Indigenous populations that had traditionally enjoyed relative autonomy were thus brought under direct rule for the first time.[1] Central and local authorities hoped that imperial law and Confucian ethics would eventually displace local customs, transforming Guizhou's indigenous peoples into civilized Qing subjects.

Both the process and the short-term effects of the Yongzheng-era campaigns in central and southwestern Guizhou are worth examination. Relatively tolerant attitudes of the first two Qing emperors, Shunzhi (1644–1661) and Kangxi (1662–1722), gave way to more confrontational tactics during the Yongzheng period. These tactics unfolded in the Dingfan-Guangshun region of central Guizhou, and Nanlong, in the province's far southwest. Both areas were home to large communities of the Zhongjia ethnic group whose penchant for banditry, raiding, and feuding had long been a source of consternation for imperial authorities. In 1724, officials in Dingfan-Guangshun started a campaign to bring order and civility to the region. The enterprise met with fierce resistance from villagers who deeply resented the state's intrusion. After two years of battling local vigilantes, provincial officials finally managed to lay the groundwork for a much larger military and administrative presence. Shortly after the campaign in Dingfan-Guangshun concluded, Qing authorities turned their attention to Guizhou's ill-defined boundary with Guangxi. For centuries, this region had been a no-man's-land rife with unresolved territorial disputes and blood feuds. In an effort to create a new administrative and social order, provincial officials deposed the inept native ruler whose family had controlled the region since the last decades of the Yuan period. After establishing a permanent boundary between Guizhou and Guangxi, the provincial officials cobbled together the recently annexed lands into a new prefecture, Nanlong.

This narrative covers both new and familiar terrain in the history of the Qing southwest, offering a reinterpretation of the events in Dingfan-Guangshun and providing the first English-language account of the campaign in Nanlong.[2] The reforms in southwestern China are most often associated with the Yunnan-Guizhou governor-general (*zongdu*) Ortai. Only after Ortai assumed his post in 1725 did Qing troops begin to gain any traction against the local bandits who plagued the area. In a matter of months, Ortai secured the region and began taking steps to integrate it into the Chinese world.[3] Ortai's efficient handling of the Dingfan-Guangshun crisis convinced the emperor that the success here could be replicated in other parts of Yunnan and Guizhou.[4] This proved a grave miscalculation, for subsequent campaigns proved far more complex and far bloodier than the engagement at Dingfan-Guangshun. Qing incursions into the Miao regions of southeastern Guizhou, the Lolo (Yi) heartland of northeastern Yunnan, and the Tai polities of southern Yunnan provoked violent opposition from local populations.[5]

Qing expansion in these regions was both an imperial and colonial phenomenon. The Yongzheng-era policies brought parts of southwestern China under direct imperial rule for the first time, and Han settlers soon displaced native populations. Some officials who advocated the overthrow of the native rulers voiced "overtly colonial" arguments, stating that "natural resources could be more efficiently tapped if the areas in question were brought under the direct control of the central government."[6] The colonial and imperial nature of the Qing enterprise in Dingfan-Guangshun and Nanlong is most apparent in the state's efforts to impose direct rule. "Overtly colonial" arguments were far less important in these regions than in other parts of the Qing southwest, particularly the copper-rich lands of northeastern Yunnan.[7] Dingfan-Guangshun had few natural products to offer. Nanlong was more richly endowed, with reserves of silver and other metals and an abundance of forest products, but economic exploitation does not appear to have been a major impetus in determining policy for this region.[8] Han settlement is a thornier issue. In theory at least, the policy of eliminating indigenous rulers was intended to protect Han Chinese living in or near native areas—not necessarily to attract new settlement.[9] Subsequent Han settlement of Dingfan-Guangshun and Nanlong appears to have been more of a by-product—albeit one welcomed by imperial authorities—rather than an express aim of the Yongzheng-era program.[10]

The correspondence between the emperor and his officials in the field suggests that policy in Dingfan-Guangshun and Nanlong was motivated above all by the desire to create order where none had existed before—or at least no order existed that the Qing considered recognizable or usable. In view of this, Yongzheng's plans for Dingfan-Guangshun and Nanlong appear to represent an exercise in what James Scott calls "seeing like a state." Here and elsewhere in southwestern China, the state took steps to rationalize and standardize "a social hieroglyph into a legible and administratively more convenient format. The social simplifications introduced not only permitted a more finely tuned system of taxation and conscription but also greatly enhanced state capacity."[11] Before the Yongzheng-era reforms, large areas of Guizhou resembled social hieroglyphs, indecipherable to Qing authorities. Many indigenous communities lived beyond the reach of direct administration, isolated by geography as well as their own languages and customs. Officials of the Yongzheng era hoped to transform these hieroglyphs into a legible form, enabling the state to better understand and control the region's population, land, and resources.

It may be useful to examine the matter in terms of *state space* and *non-state space*.[12] State spaces describe lowland areas where the ecology was conducive to stable human settlements and surplus grain production, two prerequisites for administrative oversight and revenue extraction. Non-state spaces, by contrast, were upland areas where the ecology did not support these preconditions, where inhabitants practiced slash-and-burn or shifting agriculture, or engaged in other economic activities that produced little surplus. In the absence of stable populations or steady sources of revenue, such areas remained largely impervious to state control and taxation. The central government generally regarded these non-state spaces as a source of violence and barbarism, and as places of sanctuary for bandits, rebels, and other dangerous characters who posed an immediate or potential threat to the state.[13]

With some refinement, these concepts carried deep resonance for Guizhou on the eve of the Yongzheng-era reforms. State spaces, such as they were, existed wherever the imperial government had managed to establish regular administrative units. Non-state spaces characterized areas without regular administrative units, native officials, or even centralized indigenous polities. Such regions were most commonly found in the Miao heartlands of southeastern Guizhou.[14] Between the state and the non-state spaces lay the Zhongjia regions of central and southwestern Guizhou—areas perhaps best labeled "semi-state spaces." These areas had both native officials and a smattering of regular administrative units, but neither functioned well enough to meet the government's increasing demand for standardization and centralization.[15] Yongzheng and his officials recognized that their capacity to "see like a state" would be severely constrained unless they reorganized space into a format that could accommodate their vision. One goal of *gaitu guiliu*, therefore, was to transform the semi-state spaces of central and southwestern Guizhou into full-fledged state spaces.

QING POLICY IN SOUTHWEST CHINA UNDER SHUNZHI AND KANGXI

During the Shunzhi and Kangxi reigns, the central government tried to operate within the existing framework of the native official (*tusi*) system. As noted in chapter 1, the military conquest of Guizhou in 1658 owed much to the cooperation of native rulers. When Qing troops marched across native domains, the local chieftains usually pledged loyalty to the new dynasty, exchanged their Ming seals for Qing ones, and then offered military assistance to the imperial armies. In this way, Beijing secured control over the region while leaving the institution of native rule largely intact.[16]

Although the native officials remained in power, the central government soon took steps to curb their traditional autonomy, beginning with new regulations on the inheritance of official titles. In 1659, the Shunzhi emperor moved to assert greater control over the succession process by stipulating that only direct, patrilineal descendants could inherit the Qing title. This marked a sharp departure from Ming precedents, which allowed native officials to designate heirs according to local custom or personal whim.[17] Under the new Qing rules, the court refused to consider a deceased leader's brothers, sons by concubines, or daughters for the post. In order to confirm the lines of descent, applicants for the titles were required to submit their genealogies to local officials. In addition, potential successors to the title were encouraged, but not required, to attend the nearest state-sponsored public school. These reforms affected the culture of native elites in two crucial ways. First, by assuming a direct supervisory role over the inheritance process, the Qing state greatly curtailed the political independence of indigenous frontier societies. Second, the opportunity to receive a Confucian education encouraged the native rulers to begin identifying more closely with Chinese culture.[18]

These reforms continued to evolve during the Kangxi reign as the court extended more educational opportunities to native populations. In 1682, the Guizhou public schools were opened to all male relatives of the native officials. Four years later, the schools were opened to all male children in the native domains. In 1703, the regular examination system was opened to students from native chieftain families, although their exams were graded separately from those written by Han Chinese candidates. Two years later, Beijing recommended that "charity schools" (*yixue*) be established throughout Guizhou for the designated heirs—that is, sons, and brothers—of the native officials. The court also stipulated that it would assign official titles only to candidates who could prove they had attended these state-sponsored schools.[19]

The purpose of these reforms was to tie the native rulers' political fortunes even more firmly to the Qing court. Kangxi preferred this approach to the more aggressive policies advocated by civil and military officials who pressed for the abolition of native rule. The emperor's attitude stemmed not from any particular affection for the *tusi*, but from profound mistrust of the provincial officials in southwest China, a product of his bitter experience with the traitor Wu Sangui.[20] As explained in chapter 2, Wu won hereditary control over Yunnan and Guizhou for his role in the Qing conquest of these provinces and the capture of the last Ming pretender. Beijing had intended for him to govern on the court's behalf, but he soon came to view the region as his personal empire. He amassed a small fortune by increasing taxes and establishing monopolies on salt wells, gold and copper mines, and trade in ginseng and rhubarb.[21] Wu supplemented the ill-gotten gains from his local enterprises with generous subsidies from Beijing, ostensibly provided to quell local uprisings. His modus operandi was to antagonize native officials until they took up arms, and then petition the court for funds and munitions to put down the uprisings that he himself had fomented.[22]

By the 1670s, the Kangxi emperor was convinced that Wu Sangui posed a grave threat to the dynasty's political and financial stability, but he was not sure how to deal with the powerful general.[23] An opportunity for action arose in 1673, when Wu Sangui asked Beijing for permission to retire to Manchuria. Wu's intentions were anything but sincere. He was simply trying to gauge the court's reaction to his petition and fully expected Beijing to reaffirm his authority over southwestern China. Instead, the court turned the tables on Wu and ordered his immediate transfer to Manchuria. Outraged, Wu decided to rebel against the dynasty, sparking an eight-year war.[24] In its aftermath, Kangxi remained wary of the provincial officials in Yunnan and Guizhou, finding echoes of Wu Sangui's treachery in every request for military action against the *tusi*.[25] Faced with the real or imagined threat of another war in the southwest, Kangxi preferred to forgive the native rulers' occasional transgressions.

THE YONGZHENG REIGN: ABOLISHING NATIVE RULE AND 'SEEING LIKE A STATE'

The Yongzheng reign saw a decisive shift in both central government attitude and policy toward southwest China. Whereas the Kangxi emperor had steered away from aggressive change in southwest China, his son was determined to transform the region's political, administrative, and cultural landscapes. Yongzheng's campaign in southwestern China represented an integral part of his mission to extend the imperial writ to the farthest-flung reaches of the Qing realm.[26] Although some historians have portrayed Yongzheng as an autocrat or a despot, he was above all committed to the pursuit of effective government.[27] He restructured state institutions and practices in ways that both increased his personal power and also promoted more honest, efficient administration at every level.[28]

Yongzheng's Mission in Southwest China: Local Security and Broader Strategies

Soon after ascending the throne, Yongzheng turned his reformist zeal to the chronic unrest and maladministration in southwestern China. His initial attempts at reform were fairly conservative, demanding nothing more than a stricter application of the existing laws on native rulers. In a 1724 edict, Yongzheng leveled a series of accusations at the native officials, charging that they possessed "only scant knowledge of the laws of the Empire" and governed their domains with cruelty and avarice. According to the emperor, native officials thought nothing of stealing their subjects' livestock, kidnapping women and children, and even murdering at will. Even worse, they colluded with fugitives from other provinces, the so-called "treacherous Han" (Han *jian*), to oppress and swindle the native commoners. After enumerating the native officials' many crimes, the emperor ordered provincial authorities to keep a closer watch on the *tusi* under their jurisdiction and strictly punish those who broke the law. Native officials who failed to mend their ways even after a reprimand were subject to impeachment, dismissal, and punishment.[29]

After this tentative start, the emperor moved toward a more aggressive policy. He began staffing key provincial posts in Guizhou and Yunnan with "new men," relatively young officials who shared his commitment to reform.[30] As disorders persisted throughout the region, these activists became increasingly convinced that the native official system had ceased to function as a viable means of governing non-Han areas. The chieftains continued to flout imperial law in numerous ways. Some were personally involved in banditry, while others provided sanctuary to criminals, Han and non-Han alike. The activists worried that if such infractions went unpunished, then even the more law-abiding native rulers might be emboldened to engage in illegal activities.[31] Even worse, as Ortai cautioned in a 1725 memorial, the continued presence of the *tusi* could undermine any chance for long-term stability in the region. "If we do not replace all the native rulers with regularly appointed officials . . . then even if the land tax, military affairs, and legal matters are managed with the utmost thoroughness, it will amount to nothing in the end. We dare not approach this matter with anything less than the greatest care and vigilance. . . . In my humble estimation, this is the first order of business in Yunnan and Guizhou."[32] Warnings like these persuaded the Yongzheng emperor of the need to overthrow native rulers and incorporate their domains into regular administrative units (*gaitu guiliu*).

It should be noted that broader strategic concerns also informed the decision to take action against the native officials. Southwestern China was vital to Qing interests in Inner Asia, and Yunnan occupied a key position as the gateway to Tibet, where the Qing had recently gained a foothold they could ill afford to lose. Tibet had become more and more important to the imperial state. During the late Kangxi period, imperial troops had engaged in fierce battles with the Western Mongols for dominance in Inner Asia. Qing authorities gradually came to realize that in order to contain this formidable adversary, it was essential to control the Mongols' religious leaders (who were loyal to the Yellow Hat school of Buddhism in Tibet). In addition to its role as a gateway to Tibet, Yunnan was also important in its own right, as the empire's chief source of copper, the primary ingredient in Qing coins. Qing policy in Guizhou was in some respects a by-product of Yunnan's importance. Imperial authorities hoped that pacifying Guizhou would ensure easier access to its neighbor to the west.[33]

Imposing Order in Dingfan-Guangshun

Dingfan-Guangshun, often abbreviated Ding-Guang in Qing documents, served as the laboratory for Yongzheng's activist policies in southwestern China. The transformation of this region occurred in four stages. The first stage involved the long and frustrating struggle to subdue Zhongjia bandits in the heart of Ding-Guang. The second stage entailed the abolition of a native chieftain whose family had controlled the lands just west of Ding-Guang. His surrender allowed provincial officials to consolidate and expand their control in central Guizhou. During the third stage, Qing authorities took armed action against local residents who obstructed the erection of military compounds in Ding-Guang. In the fourth and final stage, provincial officials enrolled residents of the newly annexed lands on tax rolls and issued last names to those who had none.

The name Dingfan-Guangshun refers to two small administrative centers in central Guizhou. The Ming government established Dingfan and Guangshun as departments (*zhou*) in 1587 and 1602, respectively. Both were subordinate to Guiyang prefecture, located 64 kilometers (40 miles) to the north.[34] Until the reforms of the Yongzheng period, Dingfan and Guangshun stood as tiny outposts of imperial rule in the heart of native territory. The surrounding countryside remained in the hands of native chieftains. In Ming and Qing sources, these chieftains were referred to by their surnames followed by the suffix *fan*, or "barbarian."[35] Indeed, "Ding-fan" means "pacified barbarians," a name that reflected imperial ambitions rather than realities on the ground. Like much of Guizhou, the region was an ethnic mosaic. The Zhongjia were the predominant non-Han group, but Miao and other indigenous populations lived in the area. Small numbers of Han Chinese also began to settle in the region during the Ming period.[36]

As noted in chapter 2, imperial officials generally regarded the Zhongjia as the scourge of Guizhou. Ethnographic accounts from the late Ming and early Qing periods never failed to mention the ethnic group's penchant for banditry and violence. Like all stereotypes, these unflattering portrayals carried a certain element of truth, but did not tell the entire story. The wan-

ing years of the Kangxi period did see an increasing number of Zhongjia
raids on villages in the Ding-Guang region as more and more Han immigrants settled in their midst and seized what little good land existed.[37]
Although imperial officials could only see these predatory behaviors as
threats to social stability, banditry and violence provided an important
way for the impoverished Zhongjia to supplement their livelihoods. Not
surprisingly, the Han residents of Ding-Guang did not view Zhongjia
activities in such a compassionate light. Members of the local gentry
lodged numerous complaints with provincial authorities during the last
years of the Kangxi reign, but the apathetic officials usually ignored these
pleas for help. The officials posted to Guizhou at this time were a sorry lot,
so demoralized by the dank climate and lack of cultural amenities that
they were unwilling to exert themselves even when crises arose.[38]

However, the rise of the Yongzheng emperor infused the provincial
administration with new vigor. Soon after assuming the throne, the monarch made it clear to Guizhou officials that he would not tolerate the las-
situde so prevalent during the last years of his father's reign. In a 1724 edict
to Mao Wenquan, his first appointee as Guizhou governor (*xunfu*), Yongzheng blamed the previous administration for the recent spate of raids in
Ding-Guang and other areas. By failing to relieve the grinding poverty in
the Guizhou countryside, local officials had effectively driven people to
illegal pursuits like banditry and raiding. Yongzheng ordered Mao and his
colleagues to govern with more compassion and rigor than their predecessors.[39] The emperor's decree showed that he understood why the Zhongjia
behaved as they did, but his insight did not mean he would allow this
behavior to continue. It was up to Governor Mao to alleviate the conditions that spawned criminal behavior, and to end any illegal activities
already in progress.

Unbeknown to the emperor, Mao and his colleagues had already
launched a military campaign in central Guizhou with humiliating
results. Acting in concert with the Guizhou provincial commander-in-
chief (*tidu*) Zhao Kun and Yunnan-Guizhou governor-general Gao
Qizhuo, Governor Mao had targeted a gang of bandits who had been
terrorizing villages throughout the Ding-Guang region. The ringleader
was a Zhongjia strongman named A Jin who had proclaimed himself
"king of the Miao" (Miao *wang*). From his headquarters deep in the

mountains near Dingfan, he commanded a network of kidnappers and robbers who had forced many nearby villages into submission. In the spring of 1724, A Jin's band raided several market towns. Without first seeking authorization from his superiors, Colonel Chen Yuanxun of the Ding-Guang garrison had ordered a force of two hundred troops to launch an attack on A Jin's lair. Three Qing soldiers were injured in the ensuing skirmish. A Jin escaped with all of his followers, and the imperial troops were forced to retreat to their base without capturing a single bandit.[40] To make matters worse, one of Colonel Chen's sublieutenants had needlessly burned down a Zhongjia village that had never offered overt assistance to A Jin's band. In his analysis of the events, written several months later, Governor-General Gao Qizhuo stated that Chen's men should have asked the villagers to help capture A Jin, offering assurances of clemency to those who cooperated. Instead, the troops had resorted to extreme measures that only provoked the Zhongjia to turn against the Qing and join the bandits.[41]

Colonel Chen tried to redeem himself with another unauthorized attack on A Jin, but further disaster ensued. Early in the autumn of 1724, he set out with three hundred troops and marched toward A Jin's base. The Zhongjia shot arrows at the Qing soldiers, wounding several. Once again, Colonel Chen was forced to beat a hasty retreat.[42] His repeated debacles called for a more aggressive plan to control the Zhongjia. If the Qing were to have any credibility in the region, they would have to attack the Zhongjia with more than two or three hundred troops. Accordingly, Governor-general Gao authorized a 2,400–man expedition against A Jin's stronghold in November of 1724. Instead of relying solely on men from the Ding-Guang garrison, the Qing force also included troops from units in northwestern Guizhou.[43]

This time, the Qing expedition succeeded. The sheer size of the Qing army made resistance impractical, and many Zhongjia collaborators served as guides and translators. The imperial troops easily made their way from Dingfan to A Jin's base. A Jin set up a roadblock and fled into the nearby forest, but Qing troops quickly rounded up all of his subordinates. Within a week, they caught A Jin himself and delivered him to Guiyang for trial and subsequent execution. Eventually, Qing troops withdrew from the area, leaving behind small units to guard strategic points.[44]

The Overthrow of the Kangzuo Chieftain

Several months after capturing A Jin, Qing officials in Guizhou scored another modest victory. In early 1725, Governor Mao informed the emperor that he had decided to depose the Kangzuo native chieftain, Xue Shiqian. Xue's family had controlled this small fiefdom just northeast of Dingfan since the early years of the Ming dynasty.[45] According to Mao, Xue had long engaged in brigandage, eluding capture by slipping into his mountain lair. In Mao's estimation, Xue was more evil than the other native chieftains. If the authorities allowed him to persist in his depredations, then other native chieftains in Guizhou might emulate his behavior.[46] Implicit in Mao's report was the concern that Xue might threaten the hard-won peace in nearby Ding-Guang.

Much wiser and warier after the long battle against A Jin, Mao felt it best to avoid another large-scale military expedition. In the hopes that friendly overtures would suffice, he sent a local magistrate to offer Xue life imprisonment in another province rather than capital punishment if he went to Guiyang without protest. Xue surrendered, and the government placed him in jail, garrisoned Bailaohu, and in 1727 placed that area under the direct jurisdiction of Zhenning department.[47] Kent Smith suggests that Xue's easy capitulation was a direct response to the show of force in Ding-Guang, which had begun to "lend new credibility to the power of provincial officialdom."[48] Xue probably also calculated that exile to a faraway region was preferable to certain death in battle or by execution if he resisted.

The Standoff at Changzhai

During the last year of his tenure as governor-general, Gao Qizhuo formulated a program for the final consolidation of Qing rule in central Guizhou. In the spring of 1725, he put forth a plan to greatly increase the military presence in the Ding-Guang region. Rather than increase the province's troop quotas, Gao planned to redeploy some of the units already stationed elsewhere in Guizhou.[49] The plan encountered numerous obstacles along the way, and it fell to Gao's successor, Ortai, to bring it to completion. The official with immediate responsibility for executing Gao's plan was Shi Liha, the newly appointed acting governor of Guizhou.[50] After surveying the Changzhai region in the autumn of 1725, Shi Liha voiced his intention to establish a substantial military force in the area. He planned to increase the number of troops in Dingfan by 340 men, and to add 431 troops to the garrison in Guangshun. In addition, provincial authorities planned to build seventeen guardhouses and stations in each of these departments, and eventually to construct a grand total of 370 new offices and military compounds. Workers would first build guard posts and stations near the administrative centers at Guangshun and Dingfan and continue the construction on a line gradually moving toward the interior of Zhongjia territory. Shi Liha hoped that this gradual penetration into the Zhongjia heartland would forestall any resistance from the local population.[51]

In spite of Shi Liha's precautions, Qing plans soon encountered a major stumbling block. When the line of new military outposts approached the Zhongjia stronghold near the hamlet of Changzhai, just south of Ding-Guang, local residents blocked all entrances to the construction site, and prevented workers from entering with building materials, thus halting construction.[52]

The standoff at Changzhai persisted for the better part of 1725. In the meantime, the Yongzheng emperor made a pivotal decision for the people of Ding-Guang, and indeed for the whole of southwestern China. He appointed Ortai as governor of Yunnan, charged concurrently with the responsibilities of the governor-general of Yunnan and Guizhou. Immediately after assuming office in February of 1726, Ortai turned his attention to the crisis in Changzhai. Other provincial officials were divided on how best to deal with the Zhongjia. Some advocated a military strike, while others were reluctant to pursue such an aggressive policy. Among those clamoring for a military solution was the recently appointed provincial commander-in-chief Ma Huipo, but the Yongzheng emperor had thus far refused permission for armed intervention. He urged Ma to consult with Ortai before taking any action. Accordingly, soon after Ortai assumed office, Ma Huipo reported to him that Changzhai residents were burning the few structures the Qing workers had managed to build and were frequently blocking access to the construction sites. He suggested that troops from northwestern Guizhou already designated for permanent transfer to Ding-Guang might be sent to guard the construction work near Changzhai.[53] Ortai readily accepted Ma's suggestion, adding that he was by no means averse to using military force to break the stalemate.[54]

Matters on the ground in Changzhai further convinced Ortai of the need for an armed solution. During the first week of May, local officials informed him that the local Zhongjia, having rejected numerous attempts at negotiation and reconciliation, had set fire to Qing military buildings. Adding insult to injury, the Zhongjia had also flogged and released naked a Qing sublieutenant sent to remonstrate with them. Local officials also reported that the Zhongjia had stationed 50 to 60 men at each of the heavily barricaded passes leading to the Changzhai area. In addition, the local rebels had also stockpiled a large cache of war materiel, including poison arrows, spears, armor, and helmets. Shi Liha and Ma Huipo dispatched 2,700 troops to support those in the Ding-Guang battalion. Ma also mobilized several units of non-Chinese auxiliary troops and ordered the combined forces to assemble at a strategic point just south of Changzhai. Shi Liha and Ma Huipo then asked Ortai for permission to attack the Zhongjia and pacify the region before the hot, rainy season set in at the end of May.[55]

In his reports to the emperor, Ortai made it clear that he wholeheartedly supported the military solution. He also hinted at his intention to use Ding-Guang as a testing ground for policy in other non-Han regions of the southwest. He declared that if the government did not suppress the Zhongjia, "all the Miao will notice and become even more intractable. This suppression is not just calculated to exterminate the [Zhongjia] rascals. It is designed to pacify all of the Miao."[56]

Ortai won approval for a military engagement, and in June of 1726, the first skirmishes broke out between Qing troops and Zhongjia gangs. The Qing army enjoyed overwhelming logistical superiority. Their army numbered between four and five thousand regulars, along with more than a thousand native troops. The Zhongjia were at a distinct disadvantage. They had no firearms and relied on an arsenal consisting chiefly of knives, armor, helmets, and spears. Most villages fell within a few days, although some held out for up to two weeks. In due course, however, Qing troops were able to subdue the entire region.[57]

Consolidating the New Order

The military victory only marked the beginning of the government's job. Now it remained for Ortai to secure the region's long-term stability and prosperity. To begin, he arranged for a larger permanent military presence in the area, with new units stationed at both Changzhai and Zongjiao, another strategic town. An additional 350 troops would be deployed in the area, evenly distributed between the two new command posts.[58]

Ortai's next order of business was to rebuild the local economy. Following a personal visit to the region in the autumn of 1726, he devised a program to encourage the Zhongjia to resume normal agricultural activities, and to secure orderly conditions by imposing Chinese social, economic, and cultural patterns. He extended tax amnesties and a monthly grain allowance as incentives for Zhongjia to return to the area. Ortai's plan also called for the establishment of a new resident official, the subprefectural magistrate (*tongban*) of Guiyang.[59]

Kent Smith notes that the physical presence of this official signified the region's formal entrance into the imperial orbit. The government took additional steps to affirm this transition. Indigenes were urged to shave their heads and wear the queue, the distinctive hairstyle that signaled loyalty to the Qing. Local officials also prepared population registers, issued surnames to those who had none, and arranged the villagers into public security (*baojia*) units.[60] By assigning surnames to local residents, encouraging them to wear the queue, and enrolling them on tax registers, the Qing state furnished itself with a means to identify its subjects, or, to explain the project in Scott's terms, "to create a legible people."[61]

A NEW ORDER IN SOUTHWESTERN GUIZHOU: THE CREATION OF NANLONG PREFECTURE

The land lay athwart the boundaries of Qian [Guizhou] and Yue [Guangxi]. Disputes and murders were frequent, and they were most difficult to adjudicate. When there was a crisis in Qian, the criminals fled to Yue; when there was a crisis in Yue, the criminals fled to Qian. When a crisis arose in the territories that belonged to neither Qian nor Yue, this created profound difficulties.

—*Xingyi fuzhi* (Gazetteer of Xingyi prefecture), 1851, 46: 10b

The next major undertaking in Guizhou involved the annexation of the Sicheng native prefecture (Sicheng *tufu*).[62] This area, which extended from the northern banks of the Hongshui River in southwestern Guizhou to the

You River in central Guangxi, had long been ruled by native officials of the Cen, a lineage with deep but obscure roots in southwestern China.[63] Ethnohistorians usually classify the Cens as Zhuang, but it is unclear when and how they became Zhuang, and whether or not they were ethnic Han at some point in the distant past. The matter is complicated by the need to rely on genealogies designed to enhance the clan's prestige and legitimacy by creating ancestral ties to Han Chinese personages from the central and eastern provinces.[64] Some genealogies establish descent from the Han dynasty (206 B.C.E.–220 C.E.) general Cen Peng.[65] Genealogies from the Ming and Qing periods list the family's founding ancestor as Cen Zhongshu, a Song dynasty hero from Zhejiang who supposedly helped the general Di Qing quell a mid-eleventh century rebellion in Guangxi.[66] The Song court rewarded Cen Zhongshu for his services by granting his family hereditary control over several native districts in northern Guangxi. In the centuries that followed, a succession of native officials surnamed Cen—who may or may not have been Cen Zhongshu's direct descendants—expanded the clan's domains through military conquests and rewards from the Song and Yuan governments.[67] In 1340, the Yuan granted an official named Cen Shumuhan hereditary control over the Sicheng region. The Ming government renewed his charter soon after the Ming assumed power in 1368.[68] By the fifteenth century, Cen rulers had conquered lands north of the Hongshui River, including a number of communities in present-day Guizhou. Territories south of the river in present-day Guangxi were known as inner dependencies (*nei shao*), while those north of the river were called outer dependencies (*wai shao*). Wherever the Cen acquired new lands, the original rulers became their vassals. Local rulers who already held titles as native officials were required to pay tribute to both the Ming court and to the Cen ruler.[69]

The Cens maintained cordial relations with the imperial government throughout the Ming period. The government periodically asked Cen native officials for military support in campaigns against non-Han rebels in the southwest. In return, the Cen rulers could rely upon imperial troops for assistance when they were harassed by other native officials, or when renegade vassals within their own domain needed a firm hand.[70] When the Qing troops entered southwestern China in pursuit of the Southern Ming, the Cen rulers transferred their loyalty to the new dynasty.[71] The Qing throne subsequently reaffirmed the Cens' hereditary claim to the title of Sicheng native prefect and allowed them to retain control over their territories on both sides of the Hongshui River.[72]

After this auspicious beginning, the Cens' relations with the Qing court gradually soured. Eighteenth-century writers often depicted Sicheng as a bumptious region of fuzzy boundaries, ambiguous jurisdiction, and frequent bloodshed. Numerous chieftains (*tingmu*), the landowning elite described in chapter 2, controlled small fiefdoms within the Cen domain. They were notoriously warlike, frequently engaging in land disputes and blood feuds. To make matters worse, these chieftains operated in a jurisdictional no-man's-land, answerable to neither the provincial officials in Guangxi nor those in Guizhou. The Sicheng native prefect was responsible for disciplining wayward vassals and sending the more recalcitrant ones to provincial authorities, but he seldom did so. However, even if he had been more proactive in handling these disputes, he would have been hard-pressed to find an imperial official to help resolve them. Government offices in and near the Cen domains were widely scattered and poorly staffed. Magistrates assigned to the region often chose to live elsewhere for at least six months out of the year because northwestern Guangxi was a breeding ground for malaria and other tropical maladies. Officials decamped to healthier climes during the warmer months and returned to their posts only when cooler temperatures reduced the possibility of disease.[73]

The administrative presence was equally thin in Guizhou. The Ming government had established a department (*zhou*) at Pu'an; and in 1687, the Qing court had created a subprefecture (*ting*) at Nanlong in southwestern Guizhou, near the northern edge of Cen territory. These administrative units had little influence over affairs within the native prefect's domain, and they were too remote from Qing political centers to function effectively. Both were jurisdictional subunits of Anshun prefecture, which lay 120 kilometers (75 miles) east of Pu'an and 160 kilometers (100 miles) northeast of Nanlong. Poor roads and rough terrain made it difficult for the local officials in either town to communicate with their superiors in the prefectural seat, or in the provincial capital at Guiyang.[74] If a real crisis erupted, local officials could not depend on military assistance. During the Kangxi period, only 1,500 troops were stationed at the garrison in Huangcaoba, a small town in the southwestern corner of Guizhou.[75]

In the mid-1720s, Yongzheng's reform-minded officials in southwest

China resolved to impose order on the chaotic landscape of the Guizhou-Guangxi borderlands. The catalyst for this decision was a longstanding feud between two chieftains, one in northern Guangxi and the other in Guizhou, with contesting claims to a group of hamlets on both banks of the Hongshui River.[76] Cai Chenggui, the highest-ranking military official in the region, reported the matter to Gao Qizhuo, who was then governor-general of Yunnan and Guizhou. Gao ordered the magistrates of Pu'an and Sicheng to conduct a joint investigation to determine the rightful owner of the disputed hamlets. When more than a year passed with no action on the magistrates' part, Cai sent the emperor a lengthy memorial describing the sorry state of affairs in southwestern Guizhou. He explained that although he had some troops at his disposal, he was reluctant to use military force until he determined whether the hamlets in question belonged to Guizhou or Guangxi. He suggested that provincial officials jointly investigate the region to ascertain which chieftain governed the villagers, and to which province the chieftains paid taxes. Cai went on to decry the lack of civilian administration in the region. (The highest-ranking civil officials were the subprefect of Nanlong and the district magistrate in Pu'an; and although there was a small military presence in the area, army figures like Cai himself generally preferred not to get involved in civilian matters.)[77] Cai ended by imploring the emperor to appoint more regular officials in southwestern Guizhou. The Yongzheng emperor responded by ordering the other high-ranking officials in Guizhou and Guangxi to assess the situation.[78]

The first report on the matter came from Ortai, who had by now assumed office as governor-general of Yunnan and Guizhou. In his view, the solution to the problem lay in the establishment of a clear boundary between Guizhou and Guangxi. As he wrote:

> The Miao fight and plunder endlessly, and the local officials are lax, letting matters drift until they ferment into severe upheaval. . . . Only because [the provinces] adjoin each other along a jagged line do these disputes reach such an extreme. Now if we use the river to create order, with territory south of the river belonging to Guangxi and that north of the river going to Guizhou, then the boundary will be orderly and natural, military defense and criminal investigations will be greatly expedited, and clashes . . . between the two provinces will be forever resolved.[79]

Several days later, Guangxi governor Han Liangfu weighed in on the crisis. He opined that the two warring chieftains were not the real source of trouble in the Guangxi-Guizhou borderlands. The worst culprit by far was the native prefect, Cen Yingchen, Governor Han charged that Cen had repeatedly failed to deliver criminals to local officials, and that he was generally incapable of governing his people. Despite Cen's many transgressions, Governor Han was reluctant to depose him, stating, "Only if this native official [Cen] acts in an outrageous and brutal manner . . . should we consider enacting *gaitu guiliu*." The governor contended that the changes wrought by the sudden introduction of direct imperial rule might be too extreme for indigenous peoples who could not read or speak Chinese. To ease the transition, he suggested that the Qing court establish a subprefect for managing the "Miao" (*li Miao tongban*) at Sicheng. With the guidance of this new official, Han argued, native populations would "have the imperial way bestowed upon them and slowly reform their hearts and minds."[80] However, Han's proposal was completely out of step with the activist policies that now carried the day. In his responding edict, the Yongzheng emperor approved Ortai's proposal to use the Hongshui River as a natural boundary between the two provinces and summarily rejected Governor Han's proposal to install a new subprefect at Sicheng. He also warned Han that military action might well be necessary if Cen resorted to rebellion. He ordered Governor Han and Ortai to proceed to Yunnan for a meeting with other high-ranking officials in the region.[81]

The conference in Yunnan ended with a resolution that all parties found reasonable. Because Cen Yingchen had never shown any inclination to mount an armed insurrection, military action would be premature at this stage. Everyone agreed, however, that Cen could not remain in power because he controlled both the northern and southern banks of the Hongshui. Ortai's plan to use the river as a hard boundary between Guizhou and Guangxi could be implemented only if Qing authorities deposed Cen and annexed his territories. The officials at the Yunnan conference decided to give Cen the opportunity to surrender peacefully. Governor Han agreed to visit him in Sicheng and to extend a personal invitation to a meeting with Ortai at the Huangcaoba garrison in the summer of 1727. Han would travel to Sicheng with an entourage of no more than fifty soldiers in order to avoid arousing Cen's suspicions. If Cen showed signs of resistance, Han would summon troops from nearby battalions in Guangxi. Once Cen reached the garrison in Guizhou, Ortai would invite him to resign from office. If Cen accepted, the boundary setting would proceed smoothly; if he resisted, Ortai would order military action.[82]

Although Governor Han remained skeptical about *gaitu guiliu*, this was a plan he could live with. He also agreed wholeheartedly with the decision to establish a firm boundary between Guizhou and Guangxi. As he told the emperor in a memorial from the spring of 1727:

> As for using the river to delineate the Qian-Yue border, I think this is not only natural for [Guizhou] but also what ought to be for [Guangxi]. When Sicheng's land is registered [as Guizhou's], it will create more tax revenue for Guizhou. . . . Once we set Guangxi's border according to the natural boundaries . . . these regions will no longer be beyond the reach of Guangxi soldiers when disturbances occur. . . . No more will there be the calamity of the strong bullying the weak. The winds of enmity, murder, and feuding may cease. Great indeed will be the benefits to the two provinces.[83]

The plans eventually came to fruition, but only after a few twists and turns. Upon receiving Governor Han's invitation to Huangcaoba, Cen Yingchen sent out spies to determine the provincial officials' true intentions. His informants came back with the news that Ortai and his colleagues planned to attack Cen in the hopes of forcing him to surrender his official title. Upon learning this, Cen sent three thousand of his personal troops across the river to Guizhou in advance of his visit to Huangcaoba. After Cen himself had crossed the river into Guizhou, he once again dispatched spies to investigate the situation in Huangcaoba. This time, his spies returned with the news that the Qing officials had no intention of taking military action against Cen unless he attacked first. Cen hastened to send a petition to the officials assembled in Huangcaoba, begging for clemency. He then ordered his troops to return to Sicheng. Once the soldiers had retreated, he prostrated himself before the provincial officials and relinquished his seal of office. Cen and his family were subsequently exiled to Zhejiang.[84] Although puzzled by Cen's actions, Ortai and his cohorts were pleased with the results, for the Guizhou-Guangxi borderlands were now under direct imperial rule.[85]

Over the next several months, Ortai carried out his plan to establish a new administrative order in the region. He suggested that the court create a new prefecture to consolidate control over the lands newly annexed to Guizhou. On Ortai's recommendation, the old subprefecture of Nanlong was elevated to a prefecture, with jurisdiction over the Guizhou territories of Pu'an department and Annan county (Annan *xian*). Nanlong also governed two additional subunits that consolidated the newly acquired lands from Guangxi: Yongfeng department (Yongfeng *zhou*), and Ceheng subprefecture (Ceheng).[86] The localities south of the Hongshui River were placed under the jurisdiction of Sicheng prefecture, which was now fully incorporated into the regular imperial administrative system. For better or worse, the Qing had asserted sovereignty over a land that had been part of China's territory for centuries, but where no previous dynasty had ever successfully asserted direct political control.

CONCLUSION

When Qing officials decided to depose Cen Yingchen, they risked provoking an armed conflict much larger than the one in Ding-Guang. The native prefect commanded a sizable personal army, and other *tusi* were sure to offer assistance in the event of a Qing attack. The worst-case scenario could have involved a coordinated revolt by all of Cen's allies in Guangxi, plus, perhaps, a few in neighboring areas of Guizhou and Yunnan—in other words, this could have been a regional war only slightly smaller in scale than the Southern Ming insurrection or Wu Sangui's rebellion. However, this did not come to pass. Neither the Qing troops nor the native officials' soldiers fired a single shot. Sicheng stands out as one of the few regions in southwest China where *gaitu guiliu* was achieved through a bloodless coup d'état rather than a protracted military struggle. Kangzuo was another region where *gaitu guiliu* involved a peaceful transfer of power, but there the stakes were lower because Xue Shiqian was less powerful and his domain was much smaller.

It is also worth noting that resistance to *gaitu guiliu* came not from the native officials, but from the commoners in Ding-Guang. Xue Shiqian and Cen Yingchen both capitulated readily because they stood to lose too much if they did not. The terms of surrender were favorable; the Qing would resettle the native rulers elsewhere in the empire, in areas where they could continue to enjoy lives of privilege. Resistance, on the other hand, meant certain death for the native rulers, if not in battle, then by execution at the hands of imperial officials who would surely judge them guilty of treason. Villagers in Ding-Guang, however, saw no such benefits in surrendering to the Qing. The arrival of direct rule threatened to constrain their livelihood choices. The increased administrative oversight meant that the raiding and banditry they relied upon to supplement their family incomes would now be criminalized. Faced with this knowledge, many local residents recognized that they could either submit meekly to the new order, which guaranteed only a life of continued hardship, or they could die fighting the Qing authorities. Thus, when local officials began erecting administrative buildings and army garrisons in Dingfan-Guangshun, these physical symbols of the imperial presence became easy targets for the people's outrage.

Commoners in the newly constituted Nanlong prefecture did not initially protest the arrival of direct imperial rule because it had little immediate impact on their daily lives. Indeed, the changes might have been too subtle for them to notice. Even after additional Qing functionaries were installed throughout the region, indigenous social and economic structures remained largely intact. Most Zhongjia villagers continued to live as tenant farmers on the estates of *tingmu*.[87] The main difference was that the *tingmu* were now answerable to Qing authorities rather than the do-nothing Cen Yingchen. If disputes or feuds erupted, local officials could put a stop to them before they escalated into drawn-out conflicts. In theory at least, all of the mechanisms were in place for Nanlong to become a full-fledged state space. The Qing government had succeeded in increasing its capacity to "see like a state"—to carve out new administrative units and project legibility into them. As chapters 4 and 5 will illustrate, however, local residents soon exhibited an equal capacity for perseverance, adaptability, subversion, and sometimes outright resistance. Their livelihood choices transformed the Yongzheng-era templates for standardization and centralization into a shifting matrix of conflict and compromise.

Chapter 4

LIVELIHOOD CHOICES IN THE
MID-EIGHTEENTH CENTURY

※

Imperial authorities hoped that the reforms of the Yongzheng reign would transform the Zhongjia into compliant subjects. Instead, local residents continued to make decisions based on the flexibility and pragmatism that had sustained them for centuries. Rather than submit uncritically to the state's demands, the Zhongjia made livelihood choices that best suited their needs. This chapter explores the nature and consequences of these choices by examining three money-making schemes recounted in palace memorials (*zhupi zouzhe*) from the mid-eighteenth century. These schemes typically revolved around the sale and purchase of good-luck charms, sometimes embossed with slogans like "the Qing will fall next year," or "a new king will rise up in northern Guangxi." Itinerant salesmen traveled from village to village, spreading prophesies of natural disasters and plagues, or even predictions of the end of the world. These vendors promised salvation and eternal prosperity for those who bought the charms, and certain death for those who did not.

Qing officials generally viewed these schemes as precursors to rebellion and thus acted with all possible speed to prevent local unrest from escalating into widespread insurrection. The government's response followed a template with slight variations according to the timing and location of an incident. As soon as local authorities caught wind of suspicious activities, they launched an investigation and rounded up participants and witnesses. The resulting testimony would eventually point to the ringleaders. After further inquiries, the authorities would distinguish the guilty from the innocent, punish the former, and allow the latter to go free. Once the local officials had neutralized the most recent threat, they would express dismay over the frequency of such events in their region. But their reports usually concluded that such incidents could be expected in a place like Guizhou, given the province's large population of indigenes mired in poverty, ignorance, and superstition.[1]

As far as Qing authorities were concerned, the participants in these schemes were foolish rustics who had failed to embrace the benefits of Confucian culture. Zhongjia participants, however, were more likely to see themselves as creative and flexible individuals who seized opportunities as they arose and made the best possible use of all the religious, social, and economic resources at their disposal. In other words, they opted for livelihood choices that made perfect sense to them, even if imperial authorities considered these choices to be wrong-headed.

To review the definition set forth in chapter 1, livelihoods encompass not just the activities that people use to make a living, but also the social, ethnic, and religious resources available to them, and the ways livelihood decisions relate to local conditions and external forces. These decisions entail "a range of reactions from acceptance, reluctant compliance, to diverse forms of everyday resistance."[2] Although the discussion in this chapter focuses primarily on individuals whose activities fell into the category of everyday resistance, it also turns an occasional spotlight on local residents who accepted—or who at least reluctantly complied with—Qing legal norms. Law-abiding peasants make less colorful research subjects than their more daring counterparts, but their actions must be given due attention in any discussion of livelihood choices. It seems reasonable to assume that the overwhelming majority of Zhongjia behaved within legal bounds. Indeed, the cases discussed in this chapter found their way into the historical record thanks in large part to the villagers who first observed and reported suspicious doings.[3] Illicit activity in remote corners of Guizhou often came to light only when and if local residents alerted community leaders, such as chieftains or Han local elites, who then notified the nearest provincial authorities. What impelled these men to report the illegal doings instead of turning a blind eye or even joining in? The palace memorials do not include direct testimony from the informants, but we can hazard some educated guesses about their motivations. Perhaps they acted out a genuine sense of civic duty, or even out of loyalty to the dynasty. Perhaps it was a simple instinct for self-preservation. Failure to report questionable activities was tantamount to aiding and abetting the perpetrators; and if someone else notified the authorities of such activities, the consequences could be deadly for a person who had turned a blind eye. In other words, it was safer to stay on the side of the law than to appear complicit with criminal elements. Perhaps, as Jean Michaud says, they were "keen to give the appearance of conformity simply to avoid problems."[4] Whatever the case, the decision to follow the law was as much a livelihood choice as the decision to break the law.

Why, then, might someone decide to break the law? In the estimation of Qing officials, many criminals were drawn to illegal activity because they lived in "abject poverty with no source of income" (chipin wulai). However, this was little more than a "documentary signpost" meant to assure higher officials that a crime was economic rather than political in nature.[5] It also failed to account for the range of livelihood choices that might or might not have been available to the criminal. In central and southwestern Guizhou, these choices were quite limited. Farming was the predominant economic activity, but as noted in chapter 2, unfavorable environmental conditions made agriculture a precarious livelihood choice at best. Mining offered another possibility, although Guizhou's metal and mineral reserves could not compare to those in neighboring Yunnan. Moreover, many of the jobs in mines went to immigrants from other provinces rather than to local Han or indigenes.[6] It is true that small pockets of commercial activity flourished throughout central and southwestern Guizhou. Salt was probably the most important commodity, as the province lacked reserves of its own and relied on imports from Yunnan, Sichuan, or Guangdong.[7] Small markets were held at regular intervals throughout the region—here, indigenes could barter forest products, medicinal plants, and livestock for salt, fish, cloth, and tools from Han merchants.[8] For most local residents, commercial activities provided little more than a means to supplement household incomes and acquire necessary goods; but the markets themselves did not constitute a viable livelihood.[9]

Returning to the notion of chipin wulai, many Zhongjia criminals did live in poverty, though not necessarily in abject poverty, and many did have sources of income, though perhaps not enough for all their needs.

Farming and commercial activities most likely provided only a bare subsistence, with few opportunities for social or economic mobility. Zhongjia who wanted more from their lives had to use a little ingenuity to carve out their own niches. The three cases examined in this chapter revolve around individuals who did precisely this. The first case, recorded in two sets of palace memorials dating from 1743, centered on an intricate transprovincial network of religious practitioners and self-styled magicians who devised an assortment of schemes to extract silver from caves or to transform base metals into precious ones.[10] The second case occurred near the central Guizhou town of Langdai in 1766 and centered on a Daoist monk who swindled money from Miao and Zhongjia villagers by purporting to ensure aid from the spiritual realm and protection from harm.[11] While local authorities were investigating this case, another plot came to light in Guiding, just south of the provincial capital of Guiyang. In this third case, an educated Zhongjia villager extorted money from his illiterate neighbors by enticing them to attend an audience with a man posing as the Son of Heaven.[12]

THE HUANG SAN CASE (1743)

The first case is the most complex of the three, and arguably the most interesting from an ethnohistorical standpoint. [13] This study refers to it as the "Huang San case," after the man whose arrest alerted provincial officials to an intricate web of plots involving vague millenarian notions and a variety of schemes to find or fabricate silver. More than the other two cases, it illustrates how Zhongjia culture and religion shaped local livelihoods and responses to Qing rule. It is also the only instance of cross-border crime examined in this chapter. Whereas the other two cases were mostly confined to small areas within Guizhou, this one spilled into Guangxi and Yunnan, thus highlighting the free flow of people and ideas across a permeable tri-provincial frontier.[14] Not coincidentally, perhaps, the criminal activities originated in the newly constituted prefectures of Nanlong and Sicheng, a sign that ethnic and religious networks were far more important to local residents than administrative boundaries.

The story began in the winter of 1743, when a Zhongjia farmer named Lu Quan provided lodging to five peddlers passing through his hamlet near the southwestern Guizhou town of Yongfeng. The leader of this small gang was Huang San, a Nong from Xilong, in northern Guangxi.[15] Two of Huang San's companions were also Nong and the other two were Zhongjia.[16] In today's ethnic terminology, Lu Quan and the other Zhongjia would most likely be classified as Buyi, and Huang San and the other Nong would probably be considered Zhuang. As noted in chapter 1, the Buyi of southwestern Guizhou share many linguistic and cultural traits with the Zhuang of northwestern Guangxi. Huang San and his fellow Nong would have fit easily into a Zhongjia community where the dialect, customs, and religious beliefs were similar to their own.[17] Before long, the quintet was conducting a brisk trade in good-luck charms. As a self-proclaimed master of the magical form known as *duangong*, Huang San personally guaranteed the efficacy of every amulet he sold. For the right price, he would also chant spells and perform rituals that were supposed to provide additional good fortune or further protection against disease or natural disaster.[18]

If his guests' activities had stopped here, Lu Quan might have been content to let them stay with him indefinitely. Many of his neighbors put great faith in good-luck charms, spells, and incantations, so it seemed natural for Huang San to tap into this ready market. Lu Quan became concerned only when he learned of a mysterious new twist in Huang's sales pitch. Huang San began telling customers that he knew where to find silver in the nearby forest. When Lu Quan pressed for an explanation, Huang San gave a cryptic reply: "I pasted a sign on the entrance of an old cave so that I'll know where to look. When I find the silver, I'll share it with whoever supplies the new king with weapons and money. Everyone who helps will enjoy good fortune in the end."[19] The reference to a "new king" led Lu Quan to the unsettling realization that he might be harboring a criminal gang, or, even worse, members of an incipient rebel movement. He decided to report his suspicions to the nearest local authority, a Zhongjia chieftain (*tingmu*) named Wang Ling. For good measure, Lu Quan brought along one of the good-luck charms.[20]

At first, Wang Ling did not consider the charm anything out of the ordinary. The front was printed with the modified Chinese characters that practitioners of the Mo religion used to write prayers and poems.[21] Although Wang Ling could not decipher the texts—only Mo priests and their disciples could—he assumed that they were the usual prayers for good fortune.[22] However, when he turned over the charm to inspect the reverse side, he found an unwelcome surprise. There, written in a bold hand, were the unmistakable ideographs for "son of heaven" (*tianzi*), one of the Qing emperor's many titles. Wang Ling's suspicions deepened as Lu Quan described Huang San's talk of a "new king." He agreed that the visitors might be engaged in criminal activities, perhaps even a plot to challenge the dynasty and proclaim their own "son of heaven" or "new king." He urged local residents to use all means necessary to capture Huang San and his gang. Wang Ling also reported his concerns to a member of the Han local gentry named Wang Li, who duly notified the Yongfeng department magistrate.[23] Several weeks later, villagers waylaid the gang and staged a citizens' arrest. Two suspects were beaten to death when they tried to escape; but Huang San and the other two were captured alive, and were escorted first to the Yongfeng prison, and then to the prefectural seat at Nanlong.[24]

Lu Quan, Wang Ling, and Wang Li all exit the story at this point, but it is worth pausing to discuss their roles in the capture of Huang San. As noted above, all three men were alert to the possibility that Huang San might be involved in anti-Qing activities. Even so, notifying imperial authorities was not their only option. They could have aided or abetted Huang San, or simply turned a blind eye to Huang's activities. When Lu Quan heard of Huang San's plans to prospect for silver in the forest and wait for a "new king," Lu might have decided to join in the scheme. Instead, Lu Quan went to the *tingmu,* Wang Ling. When Wang Ling learned of Huang San's peculiar doings, he might have looked the other way—or even joined the scheme himself—but instead, he reported the matter up the chain of command to Wang Li. For his part, Wang Li, a member of the Han local elite, could have dismissed the whole affair as foolishness typical of the Zhongjia "barbarians," but instead, he notified district officials in Yongfeng.

What, then, impelled Lu Quan, Wang Ling, and Wang Li to report the suspicious activities instead of turning a blind eye or even joining in? The answer may lie in the positions the three men occupied within their respective communities and their desire to preserve a status quo that worked to their advantage. Although Yongfeng district was administered by regularly appointed Qing officials, governance at the village level remained in the hands of indigenous elites like the *tingmu,* Wang Ling.

Although they enjoyed some degree of autonomy, they were also expected to function as adjuncts of the Qing state and thus bore responsibility for maintaining stability in their communities. If Wang Ling had failed to report Huang San to higher authorities at the first sign of trouble, he would have been held responsible for any ensuing unrest and would have been punished accordingly. The *tingmu* also commanded great respect and loyalty within their fiefdoms. Lu Quan was probably a farmer, or *sizhuang baixing*, on Wang Ling's estate.[25] In exchange for his fealty to Wang Ling, he received a small parcel of land to farm. Any transgression on Lu Quan's part would have threatened this arrangement. It is possible that he flirted with the idea of joining Huang San's scheme, but decided against it. His livelihood, although hardly luxurious, was at least stable, and perhaps, in his eyes, preferable to the life of a vagabond like Huang San. Equally important, Lu Quan did not want to risk punishment for harboring a criminal. Wang Li represented a liaison between rural residents—Han and non-Han alike—and the imperial state. Therefore, Wang Li found common cause with the *tingmu*, Wang Ling. The desire to preserve stability took precedence over ethnic distinctions. Wang Li also had to consider his own reputation and status. The palace memorials identify him as a student-by-purchase fourth class (*jiansheng*). This title was reserved for men who contributed grain or money to gain admission to the National University (*Guozijan*) and who became eligible for low-ranking government positions without passing any level of the civil service exams.[26] It was in Wang Li's best interests to support the state that had awarded him a degree and the commensurate prestige. Thus, for Lu Quan, Wang Ling, and Wang Li, anything less than cooperation would have undermined their entrenched livelihoods.

A closer look at the actions taken by the three Zhongjia men, Lu Quan, Wang Ling, and Huang San, also yields further insights into Qing-era portrayals of this ethnic group. Taken as a whole, the activities of this trio support the contradictory portrayals of the Zhongjia found in Qing-era ethnographic writings. That is, contemporary observers characterized the Zhongjia both as sinicized and as intractable, depending on the circumstances. Huang San and his gang embodied the notion that the Zhongia (and the Nong, their ethnolinguistic kin) were rotten to the core. Lu Quan and Wang Ling, by contrast, lent credence to the idea that some Zhongjia had "advanced toward culture" (*xianghua*) and had "developed awe and respect for the law." However, compliance with Qing legal norms should not be mistaken for acculturation, let alone uncritical or reflexive obedience to the imperial state.[27] The decision to cooperate was a rational and conscious one for these Zhongjia men. It was a livelihood strategy in its own right, founded in the understanding that each action carried consequences.[28]

The narrative returns to the prison in Nanlong, where Huang San now faced the consequences of *his* actions. Prefectural officials in Nanlong interrogated him for several days until his story came together in a series of rambling confessions. Huang San's adventures had begun five years earlier, when he began hearing rumors of "spirit silver" (*gui yin*) buried in caves and disused mines. Everyone he encountered near his Guangxi hometown seemed to know about the silver, but no one knew exactly where it was, or how to get it. After several months of fruitless searching, Huang San met a man called Wang Zuxian, who boasted of great expertise in finding spirit silver. Wang Zuxian claimed to know of a vast silver reserve in a defunct mine in Guizhou, and he invited Huang San to join him on an expedition there. Huang San urged him to go ahead and promised to catch up later.[29]

By the time Huang San arrived in Guizhou several months later, Wang Zuxian was nowhere to be found. Huang San hunted for the silver on his own, only to meet with the same frustrations he had experienced in Guangxi. Once again, he encountered many local residents who knew about the "spirit silver," but had no idea how or where to find it. He finally enjoyed a minor breakthrough when he met a Zhongjia ritual specialist (*bumo*) named Baomu Bai, who boasted of exceptional skill in *duangong* magic.[30] Huang San visited Baomu Bai's home to watch the magic in action, and he was impressed enough to ask if he could stay on as a disciple. Baomu Bai readily agreed.[31]

At this point, it is helpful to supplement the Qing sources with more recent work on Zhongjia religion. The palace memorials offer little information on the role of the *bumo* in Zhongjia society, or how the Daoist-inflected practices of *duangong* fit into Mo beliefs and rituals. To begin with, the *bumo* generally fell into two categories: those who acted on behalf of the dead, and those who acted on behalf of the living. *Bumo* in the former category performed ceremonies at funerals to expiate the sins of the deceased, while those in the latter category prayed for good fortune or conducted rituals to stave off natural disasters and drive away evil spirits and pestilence.[32] *Duangong*, with its emphasis on prayers to dispel evil and bring good fortune, seems to fit comfortably into the second category. But to complicate matters slightly, *duangong* has often been associated with Maoshan Daoism, a sect that entered Guizhou from Sichuan at least a thousand years ago.[33] Maoshan Daoist priests have traditionally worked alongside the *bumo*, and although some of their functions overlap, they play distinct roles in their communities.

In light of this, it is not clear if Baomu Bai was a *bumo* whose repertoire included Daoist rituals, or if he was a Daoist priest who embraced Mo practices. Perhaps he was both, or perhaps such distinctions were not finely drawn in his community.[34] Even more to the point, it appears that Baomu Bai walked a thin line between legitimate religion and chicanery. He was one of many *bumo* involved in the region-wide quest for "spirit silver." Some *bumo*, like Baomu Bai himself, relied exclusively on prayers and incantations to lead them to the right spot, while others dabbled in alchemy and crude forms of cupellation in their attempts to transform base metals into precious ones.[35] Huang San was eager to learn all the tricks of the trade. If any of the magico-religious methods proved effective, he might find the silver, or even learn how to conjure it up from a long-abandoned pit or lonely forest cavern.[36] If the magic failed, he would at least acquire the textual knowledge and persuasive powers needed to convince others of the same rumors that had enticed him.

After several disappointing attempts to find silver, Baomu Bai and Huang San received some exciting news. A man in Luoping, just over the border in Yunnan, had discovered a way to transform copper into silver. His alias was Huang Zuxian, and he had recently established a smelter at the home of a *bumo* named Baomu Lun.[37] Huang San and Baomu Bai pooled their resources with three friends, Wang Bujiang, Wang Bujiang's son Wang A Jiang, and Bao Changding, and the group set out for Yunnan.[38] When they arrived, local residents pointed them to Baomu Lun's house, where they awaited instructions. Eventually, two assistants named Yi Gen and Yi Bao came to collect copper from Huang San and his friends for Huang Zuxian's alchemy.[39] Huang San and his companions were invited to watch as the purported alchemist poured the coins into a charcoal-fired brazier. After some time, Huang Zuxian reached into the brazier and came up empty-handed. The copper had disappeared into the brazier without producing a trace of silver. Huang Zuxian explained that the unusually large audience had rendered his magic ineffective. He offered to try again if Huang San and his friends had more copper. The visitors arranged to borrow some copper from a local resident on the condition that they would share some of the resulting silver.[40]

By this time, however, Wang A Jiang and Baomu Bai had had already begun to doubt Huang Zuxian's abilities. They consulted with his assistant Yi Bao, who confirmed that his boss had never once succeeded in transforming copper into silver. Huang Zuxian relied upon sleight of hand for the ruse. On previous occasions, Yi Bao had watched Huang Zuxian place fake silver—probably chunks of lead alloy—into a cup, which Huang hid in a corner of the brazier until after the copper had been added. After a suitable interval, he withdrew the fake silver from the furnace and presented it to his customers.[41]

Wang Bujiang, Wang A Jiang, and Baomu Bai did not want to be cheated again, so they asked Yi Bao to help them spy on Huang Zuxian. Yi Bao agreed, and the four of them stood outside the smelter and watched through a window as Huang Zuxian buried silvery nuggets under a pile of charcoal in the brazier. Yi Bao whispered to his companions that the hidden pieces were made of the same lead alloy Huang Zuxian had used before. Soon afterward, Huang San and Bao Changding arrived with their newly acquired copper, which they handed over to Baomu Lun and Yi Gen. The two assistants passed the coins to Huang Zuxian, who dropped them into the brazier with a great flourish. After some time, Huang Zuxian dug out the concealed decoy silver and presented it to Huang San. A Jiang and Yi Bao stormed into the room and announced that Huang Zuxian was a fraud. Moments later, they were joined by Wang Bujiang, who demanded that Huang Zuxian repay him for the copper already lost in the brazier. Bao Changding soon added his voice to the chorus. Huang Zuxian responded to the attacks on his credibility by punching Wang Bujiang. A Jiang rushed to his father's aid, and Baomu Bai and Bao Changding quickly joined the fray. Huang San, Yi Gen, and Baomu Lun all stood aloof from the melee. Huang San and Yi Gen had not witnessed the deception firsthand and may have preferred to go on believing in Huang Zuxian's abilities. As Huang Zuxian's host, Baomu Lun was probably well aware of the scam, but he was sharing in the profits and had a vested interest in keeping mum.[42]

Soon, the ruckus in the smelter attracted the attention of passers-by. One of them happened to be the villager who had loaned Huang San and his friends the copper coins. He demanded immediate compensation, and another fracas ensued. This time, Wang Bujiang, A Jiang, Bao Changding, and Baomu Bai took advantage of the chaos and slipped away, eventually making their way back to Guizhou. Huang Zuxian disappeared, seemingly without a trace. Huang San stayed at the home of Baomu Lun, scratching out a meager existence as a farm worker (*bang gong du ri*).[43]

Huang San remained in Yunnan until late 1742, when he decided to take to the road again. His wanderings landed him in Ceheng, a town near the Guizhou-Guangxi border. There, he had a chance reunion with his old friend Wang Zuxian, who had never given up his own quest for spirit silver. Wang Zuxian told Huang San that he knew of a promising cave near Yongfeng, a few days' walk to the north. He also had new predictions for Huang San: Not only did the cave contain silver, but it was also where a new king would emerge. Wang Zuxian also told Huang San that on the fifteenth day of the seventh month of 1743, the skies would turn black for seven days and seven nights, everyone would fall ill, and a new king would rise up. Wang then gave Huang San several yellow paper charms inscribed with the characters "Son of Heaven."[44]

After this encounter with Wang Zuxian, Huang San befriended four other men who were interested in prospecting for silver near Yongfeng. The group set out shortly before the Chinese New Year in 1743. Huang San began making good-luck charms to sell along the way. On the front, he inscribed the prayers that he had learned from Baomu Bai. Taking inspiration from Wang Zuxian, he added the characters "Son of Heaven" on the back. The good-luck charms provided a viable livelihood while he and his friends searched for silver. It was thus that the quintet landed on Lu Quan's doorstep.[45]

After listening to Huang San's confession, the authorities were satisfied that his only aims had been to find silver and sell good-luck charms. His ramblings about a "new king" were nothing more than a garbled and diluted version of Wang Zuxian's ideas. He had been drawn to crime because he lived in "abject poverty with no source of income" (*chipin wulai*). Any wrongdoing had been an unintended consequence of his greed and ignorance. His worst offenses had been spreading false rumors and cheating a few dozen villagers in southwestern Guizhou.[46]

Although Huang San himself was relatively harmless, it appeared that he might have brushed shoulders with more dangerous criminals, especially Wang Zuxian. Provincial officials throughout the southwest launched a manhunt for Wang and eventually captured him in a town along the Guizhou-Guangxi border. After several days of questioning, the authorities determined that he had no more intention of challenging the Qing dynasty than Huang San did. His millenarian ideas were a product of an encounter many years earlier with two long-dead criminals.[47] Like Huang San, Wang was motivated primarily by a desire to find easy riches. The case might have ended right here, but officials continued to receive disturbing reports about further attempts to find "spirit silver." It appeared that Huang San and Wang Zuxian had inspired many imitators throughout the Zhongjia and Nong regions of Guizhou, Guangxi, and Yunnan. The net result was not one, but several overlapping schemes that crisscrossed Guizhou's borders with Yunnan and Guangxi. One scheme centered on rumors that it was possible to extract silver from disused mines or ordinary caves. An ancillary scheme involved the sale and distribution of good-luck charms embossed with anti-Qing propaganda, millenarian messages, and magical spells. These talismans not only protected their owners against misfortune, but also served as entrance tickets to ceremonies in caves or mines where self-proclaimed alchemists would attempt to transform various substances into precious metals. The ceremonies themselves represented another business venture, for the attendees were expected to provide either a financial contribution or some of the raw materials deemed necessary for the production of gold or silver. These materials ranged from the relatively mundane, like copper coins, to the more exotic, like semi-precious stones or the dried saliva and excrement of the Himalayan blue sheep, also known as the bharal.[48] Because some of these items were not readily obtainable in southwestern Guizhou, a lively traffic in counterfeit goods also developed.

In short, Qing officials in three provinces had their hands full with this case. False leads and red herrings further complicated the investigation. In the summer of 1743, Guizhou officials arrested a Nong wanderer found carrying charms printed with anti-Qing slogans. When questioned, the man insisted that he was distributing the charms on orders from his landlord, who was organizing an armed insurrection in northern Guangxi. This accusation prompted Guangxi officials to raid the landlord's home, where they found not a single weapon. Subsequent interrogations confirmed that the landlord had never asked anyone to sell charms, anti-Qing or otherwise, and that he had no plans to rebel. The focus of the investigation shifted back to the vagabond, who confessed that he had run away from the landlord several months earlier. The two men had a long history of animosity, culminating in the vagabond's attempt to impersonate his landlord in an important commercial transaction. When the landlord threatened to hand him over to the authorities, he slipped over the border into Guizhou, where he eked out a hand-to-mouth existence. At some point, the vagabond acquired the anti-Qing charms, and he planned to resell them for some extra cash. When arrested, he made a desperate attempt to take revenge on his landlord by laying false charges against him. The attempt backfired, and he was imprisoned for slander and a host of other charges.[49]

The Huang San investigation concluded after six months with the arrest and imprisonment of several dozen criminals found guilty of "concocting fallacies with intent to instigate trouble" (*yaoyan xitu shanhuo*). The official verdict categorized the affair as a case of "mutual bullying and deception (*huxiang qikuang*), nothing more than a plot to earn money through unlawful means (*wufei piancai zhiyi*). There was no seditious intent (*bingwu mouni zhixin*)." Huang San and Wang Zuxian remained in jail. Huang Zuxian, the man who tried to turn copper into silver, was eventually captured in Yunnan.

Even after declaring the case closed, Qing authorities were unsatisfied with the outcome and its broader implications for imperial ambitions in the region. They remained unconvinced that they had caught all of the miscreants, or even the right ones. When interrogated, witnesses often claimed affiliation with criminals from much older cases. Sometimes they mentioned individuals who had died or gone to prison years earlier, and sometimes they identified men whose names matched those of long sought-after fugitives. It was rarely clear if the informants had in fact brushed shoulders with these criminals, if they had encountered men who had assumed the criminals' aliases, or if they had simply heard the criminals' names through local rumor mills and offered them up under interrogation. To further complicate matters, witnesses and suspects alike had multiple nicknames that varied with local dialects. As one Guangxi official wrote, "It is difficult to distinguish truth from falsehood, or to deter-

mine the names and hometowns of the criminals. . . . Even when [wit-
nesses] recognize a face, the names and hometowns do not match."[50] More
discouraging still was the knowledge that the Huang San case was not an
isolated occurrence. Officials in the region had seen many cases like it
before, and they could expect to see many more in the future.[51] Even Yunnan governor Zhang Yunsui, a veteran of southwest China affairs, seemed
to concede defeat when he wrote, "The Miao are poor and foolish, and
easy to lure from the correct path. Each criminal starts rumors. . . . The
disorder arising from the sale and distribution of charms began years ago,
and we continue to deal with it today. It is like a wind that never stops, but
lingers and spreads . . . [and] the Yao and Zhong suffer its ill effects."[52]

Although the Huang San case stopped short of rebellion, local residents did not have to take up arms to tell Zhang and his cohorts what
they already knew: The Nong and Zhongjia residents of this region had
their own social, economic, and cultural priorities, cemented by linguistic
and religious ties that transcended provincial boundaries. There was little
the Qing could do to reorient these priorities.

LANGDAI, 1766

Langdai, a subprefecture attached to Anshun prefecture, occupied a key
strategic position in central Guizhou. Situated only about 80 kilometers
(50 miles) from the provincial capital of Guiyang, Anshun was the headquarters of the Guizhou provincial military commander (*tidu*) and home
to five military units. Anyone who stirred up trouble in this area would
have to confront one of the highest concentrations of Qing civil and military authority in Guizhou. The ethnic composition of Langdai's population represented a microcosm of the entire province, with Han living
interspersed among the Miao, the Lolo, and the Zhongjia. Each group
tended to live in segregated, compact communities, but members of the
different ethnic groups did mingle freely in public places, especially in the
region's many periodic markets.

In May of 1766, Guizhou Governor Fang Shijun learned of suspicious
doings in the countryside around Langdai.[53] Villagers had informed local
authorities that five non-Han men[54] were going from hamlet to hamlet
ordering people to give them money. Some households gave only a few

coins, but others gave up to three or four ounces, or taels, of silver. Those
who did not pay were warned that they would face mortal injury in a
deadly hailstorm. Officials quickly tracked down the men and found a
variety of mysterious items in their possession, including small red flags,
a bolt of fabric, turbans, a woman's scarf, a red gown, a flowered skirt, and
fifty multi-colored flags. When interrogated, two of the co-conspirators[55]
averred that a Daoist priest named Dong Zhengyuan and his disciples,
Ran Jing, Ran Hua, and Ran Lang had conspired to spread falsehoods and
swindle the guileless Miao. Officials hastened to the Daoist temple, where
they arrested Dong Zhengyuan and confiscated twenty-eight taels from
him. A thorough search of the temple revealed no traces of unlawful
activity, and the three disciples were nowhere to be found. When authorities interrogated Dong Zhengyuan, he confessed that poverty had driven
him to hatch a scheme with Ran Jing (one of his disciples) some months
earlier.[56] In desperation, he had asked Ran Jing to spread the word from
hamlet to hamlet that a terrible hailstorm would strike the region the following summer. If people were willing to donate money for a sacrifice,
they would be spared from harm. Ran Jing was the ideal person to carry
out this scheme because he was well known to villagers as an itinerant
medicine man, and he spoke several Miao dialects. After agreeing to Dong
Zhengyuan's scheme, Ran Jing bought a piece of red cloth and had eighty
triangular flags made from it. He set out for the Yongning area, southwest
of Langdai, and began to spread rumors of the disaster to come. Ran Jing
had recruited two Zhongjia villagers to collect money for him.[57] These two
then recruited three more Zhongjia men.[58] Eventually, the five men collected ninety-nine taels on Ran Jing's behalf. Ran Jing then gave his first
two recruits twenty-five taels to share.

Asked about the flags and articles of clothing, the suspects stated that
these belonged to Ran Jing. He had given the red flags to each of his money
collectors as protection against the calamity. The bolt of fabric would be
made into talismans for the people who had paid protection money. With
the proper spells and incantations, the suspects had claimed, these talismans would ward off disaster. As for the turbans, scarves, and skirts, the
suspects stated that a tailor from Jiangxi had made them for Ran Jing.
Authorities then hastened to interrogate the tailor, who confessed that
Ran Jing had planned to use the skirts and turban when he impersonated
Nacha, a mountain-dwelling immortal. Thus disguised, Ran Jing intended

to extract more money from people who asked him to chant incantations on their behalf. The tailor also stated that Ran Jing had promised him a ten percent cut of the profits, but he had yet to receive any money.

Governor Fang next sent urgent messages to provincial authorities in Sichuan and Yunnan encouraging them to find the three chief male-factors—the disciples Ran Jing, Ran Lang, and Ran Hua. Soon thereafter, the governor received word that the three Daoists had escaped to Sichuan.[59] In a separate memorial, Sichuan governor Aertai reported on the three-some's capture and interrogation. One of the miscreants was discovered with 184 taels of silver and two horses, and his personal effects included a variety of clothing, turbans, silver-plated hairpins, and paper charms. When questioned, the three criminals confirmed that they were all dis-ciples of the impoverished Daoist, Dong Zhengyuan, who frequently sent the trio to Miao and Zhongjia hamlets to sell medicines that Dong had concocted. As a result of their travels, the three disciples were well acquainted with all the headmen in the area. About four months earlier, Ran Jing had fallen into a casual conversation with two Zhongjia head-men, who remarked that the area was in the midst of a drought. Poverty had driven many villagers to raid and plunder households in neighbor-ing villages. One headman reasoned that after all, death was probably inevitable, so why not die trying to better one's circumstances rather than die of starvation? He confided that he planned to gather a crowd of two hundred men for a massive raid on the prefectural seat of Anshun. Ran Jing warned the headman that he could not hope to get away with this, for Anshun had five military battalions (*ying*) and four guard posts (*shao*). The two headmen asked Ran Jing for suggestions, and it was thus that he began to spread fantasies of invincibility. He said that he belonged to a blood brotherhood of two or three hundred men in the large town of Zhaotong, several hundred miles away in Yunnan province. He also said that he knew of a spirit named Siniang, whose magical powers could be invoked to help the raiders. To bolster his own credentials, Ran Jing also boasted that he had studied magic. The two headmen invited him to visit their hamlet for a demonstration. Ran Jing accepted the invitation and apparently gave a satisfactory performance, for the headmen and the vil-lagers accepted the veracity of his claims. They asked him to call upon the spirit and the blood brotherhood to come forward and protect them dur-ing the raid. Ran Jing agreed, but said that he would need four or five hundred taels of silver to complete the deal. The two gullible headmen talked him down to two or three hundred taels, and they arranged to meet a few weeks later.

When the rendezvous took place, the headmen gave Ran Jing 140 taels of silver, 60 of which Ran Jing turned over to Dong Zhengyuan. Within a few days, Ran Jing collected another 110 taels and acquired two horses. On the twenty-fourth day of the second month, as previously arranged, Ran Jing, Ran Lang, and Ran Hua set out for Yunnan and then fled to Sichuan, where patrolling troops captured them and extradited them to Guizhou. After faithfully recording the confessions in his memorial, Governor Aertai wondered if the raid on Anshun had truly been the headmen's idea, or if Ran Jing had given a false confession.

The Qianlong emperor and his grand councilors wondered, too, and they expressed their thoughts in an edict to Governor Fang:

> If Ran Jing and the others have fabricated evidence and laid a charge in a false confession, it should not be difficult to get the truth from them in a thorough investigation. If it was really the Miao headmen's idea, he will be prosecuted according to the laws of the empire. . . . This may not amount to more than an ordinary case of raid and plunder, but we must raise our voices and assume a stern expression (*dong shen se*). Failure to make an exhaustive investigation, and to punish the criminals to the fullest extent of the law, may give rise to widespread and serious unrest.[60]

With these words in mind, Governor Fang interrogated Ran Jing upon Ran's return to Guizhou in June of 1766.[61] The story that emerged was slightly different from the confession extracted in Sichuan. In this version, Ran Jing admitted that he had used the headmen as scapegoats. Ran said the raid had been his idea, but he had planned to target the small market town of Dayanjiao, not the prefectural seat of Anshun. He explained that villagers around Langdai had believed his weather predictions and had spread his warnings far and wide to collect money on his behalf. Households that paid were given talismans for protection against the coming disaster. After about a month, Ran Jing returned to the temple with his earnings. He went to a tailor and asked for a padded coat, a robe, and a flowered skirt. These garments were to provide his costume for his reincarnation of the Nacha Immortal, who would save everyone from disaster.

Ran Jing made the rounds of several other villages near Langdai and continued spreading rumors about the hailstorm. Wherever he went, people took him at his word and agreed to collect money on his behalf. As before, whenever the collectors turned in their money, Ran Jing gave them small red flags to protect their homes from harm.

One day, a Zhongjia villager visited Ran Jing's temple seeking medical treatment for his son. After providing the requested treatment, Ran Jing tried to entice the man to join his scheme. The other two monks, Ran Hua and Ran Lang, happened to overhear, and, when they saw how easily Ran Jing deceived the visitor, they went to Dong Zhengyuan. It is not clear whether they wanted Dong Zhengyuan to stop Ran Jing, or if they wanted to share in the profits. In any event, several days later, the threesome paid a visit to the Zhongjia petitioner at home. After listening to the man lament his poverty, Ran Jing suggested that the villager gather a mob to raid a local periodic market to be held on the third day of the third month. When the man expressed concerns about local authorities, Ran Jing assured him that spiritual protection and aid from a blood brotherhood in Zhaotong could be arranged. The men then set a day to go to Yunnan to make a personal request for the brotherhood's help. Ran Jing also announced that everyone who desired the brotherhood's services would have to pay for them. Once again, his followers went from village to village collecting money on his behalf. In due course, Ran Jing had amassed slightly more than 228 taels.

Determined to give everyone a good show for their money, Ran Jing presided over an initiation ceremony for the prospective raiders about ten days before the planned event. He ordered someone to slaughter a chicken and mix the blood with wine. One by one, the raiders drank while Ran Jing murmured incantations. He promised everyone that the blood wine and the spells would protect them during the raid. When the ceremony ended, Ran Jing announced that he would go ahead to Zhaotong to arrange everything with the blood brotherhood. He told the crowd: "You go on to Dayanjiao and raid the market. Divide the cloth and rice among yourselves. In this way, you can all avoid poverty. Everyone must stand ready to do this." Because the men had all taken the blood oath, no one uttered a word to prevent him from leaving. After borrowing two horses, Ran Jing and his two fellow monks slipped away and dallied in Yunnan for several days before they were finally apprehended in Sichuan.

In sum, Ran Jing capitalized on the villagers' fear and desperation. For their part, the villagers probably felt they had nothing to lose. The raid represented their last, best hope. Ran Jing's ceremony allowed them to nurse the fantasy that they could elude the authorities entirely, or, if pursued, that they would be invulnerable to the bullets and arrows of government troops. Perhaps Ran Jing nursed his own fantasies of invincibility. After learning of the case from subordinate officials, Governors Fang and Aertai maintained a steady correspondence with Beijing on the progress of the investigation. Every civil and military official in Guizhou, Sichuan, and Yunnan was on the alert. To put it simply, Ran Jing's fantasies were no match for the eyes, ears, and brushes of officialdom.

Nor, in the end, were fantasies a match for the penal code. Ran Jing, along with Dong Zhengyuan, Ran Hua, most of the money collectors, and even the tailor, were all found guilty of "concocting books or sayings of sorcery involving prophecies" (yaoyan yaoshu), "with the intention of plotting rebellion" (moufan).[62] The penalty was immediate decapitation.[63] Governor Fang also ruled that the heads of Ran Jing and Dong Zhengyuan should be transported from hamlet to hamlet and displayed on city walls. The Zhongjia villagers who had willingly paid Ran Jing were treated with leniency, for, as Governor Fang pointed out, they did not know they were being cheated. It should be noted that although several money collectors are identified as Zhongjia, they were all prosecuted according to the Qing penal code rather than native laws because they resided in areas long subject to regular administration.[64]

GUIDING, 1766

In 1740, the Qianlong emperor ordered the establishment of charitable schools (shexue) throughout Guizhou to provide non-Han students with a basic education in the Confucian classics. The schools quickly foundered, however, as provincial officials were hard pressed to find scholars and teachers willing to live and work in Miao territory. After only eleven years, the emperor ordered the closure of the shexue, convinced that their influence had been more harmful than beneficial. In a 1751 edict, Qianlong proclaimed that the few teachers who were willing to venture into Guizhou's minority areas were "not only unable to lead [the Miao] toward good, but tended . . . to entice them into evil." In the emperor's view, the "Miao" were moreover stupid by nature and thus incapable of comprehending the Confucian classics. Even worse, after learning to read, many students perused novels and other "vile books," which merely led them to depravity and villainy. Transformation through education was thus a practical impossibility, and the emperor thought it prudent to dismiss all *shexue* instructors and gradually disband the schools.[65]

It is difficult to say whether or not the teachers truly enticed Guizhou's non-Han residents into evil, or if those who acquired literacy did indeed end up reading so-called vile books. The final criminal case to be examined in this chapter does indicate, however, that traditional Chinese education for non-Chinese populations had some unintended consequences. In 1766, Wei Xuewen, a Zhongjia man with some education, induced illiterate villagers to participate in a moneymaking scheme with a strong anti-Qing flavor. Although his scheme never escalated into an armed insurrection, Wei Xuewen did speak of overthrowing the Qing, and the idea seemed to hold considerable appeal for the Zhongjia in his hometown of Guiding. Equally important, he encouraged his adherents to participate in rituals which effectively—if only temporarily—negated state authority.

As a child, Wei Xuewen had learned to read and work an abacus. In spite of his education, he had few employment opportunities. During the fall of 1765, he met up with two of his friends, and they sat around lamenting their poverty.[66] One of the friends asked Wei Xuewen to come up with a moneymaking scheme, but Wei was unable to think of anything. After mulling over the problem for several months, Wei Xuewen realized that he and his friends could capitalize on the Miao fear of future disasters and their reluctance to pay taxes. He gathered his friends again and suggested they make talismans to sell in Miao villages.[67] He proposed they tell villagers that the "son of heaven" himself had commissioned the charms to bring the Miao peace and prosperity. Wei Xuewen's friends liked the plan and asked him to make a prototype of the talisman. By the beginning of 1766, Wei Xuewen had produced several rough drafts, all of them inscribed with characters prophesying the fall of the Qing.

Wei Xuewen showed the talismans to his friends, and they were pleased. The group decided to test their scheme on a local villager, a young man named Luo Shirong, who had recently profited from the sale of his deceased father's land. Wei Xuewen approached the youth and identified himself as a provincial examination candidate, thereby bolstering his credibility in the eyes of the illiterate young villager. He said that Luo Shirong had been chosen to overthrow the Qing dynasty and become the next "son of heaven." When Luo Shirong demanded proof, Wei Xuewen told him to listen at his father's grave. He would hear a tremendous roaring sound, evidence that a dragon had taken up residence there. This, Wei Xuewen averred, would offer conclusive proof that Luo Shirong was a member of the imperial lineage. Wei also sold him a bronze seal and a wooden seal to use in his new capacity as the ruler. Luo Shirong was immeasurably happy with his new prospects for wealth.[68]

But when Luo Shirong went to the grave and tried to listen for the dragon's roar, he heard nothing. Realizing he had been cheated, he went back to Wei Xuewen and demanded his money back. Wei Xuewen then told Luo Shirong that they wanted him to impersonate the Son of Heaven in a ceremony to swindle money from the local Miao. They also explained the scheme to sell talismans to Miao villagers. After being promised a share of the profits, Luo Shirong agreed to join the scam. One of Wei Xuewen's co-conspirators ordered his son and a friend to play the "heavenly spirit" (tianshen) and the "general" (jiangjun), respectively. Wei Xuewen dubbed himself "heavenly generalissimo" (tianshuai xiangzhu).[69]

Wei Xuewen commissioned a carver to produce enough talismans to sell to villages in a wide area near Guiding. When the work proceeded too slowly, he pitched in and made some himself. Once the talismans were completed, Wei Xuewen instructed two of his friends to recruit people to sell the charms. Wei's two friends convinced three other people to assist them, saying: "The son of heaven will emerge into the world through a cave. . . . He will be accompanied by his protector, the heavenly spirit. The [son of heaven] has sent forth these charms. Miao who buy them and keep them in a safe place will enjoy peace and prosperity. A charm costs but one tael. Those Miao who wish to see the heavenly spirit in person must pay us four or six taels."[70]

During the winter and early spring of 1766, Wei Xuewen and his assistants earned eighty-one taels from the sale of eighty-seven charms. Some of the profits were used to buy ceremonial garb for the upcoming pageantry in the cave. After a dress rehearsal, Wei Xuewen pronounced the performance ready for general audiences. Late one night, one of his assistants led a group of eight Miao men into the cave for their audience with the "son of heaven" and his attendants. Four nights later, another five men attended, and nine nights later, another ten. The audiences were short affairs, during which Luo Shirong and the others would utter incantations promising the fall of the Qing dynasty and lifelong prosperity for all those in attendance. The miscreants earned one hundred and fifteen taels from the pageantry.

The audiences continued for about a month before a local resident realized that something illegal was afoot. This man went to Luo Shirong's home and tried to blackmail him for information. Luo Shirong gave him a small amount of hush money and then, fearing that the entire scheme would be revealed, burned all the paraphernalia from the audiences in the cave. Wei Xuewen and all of his conspirators soon agreed to cancel any further appearances in the cave.

But some of the talismans, inscribed with anti-Qing slogans, were still circulating in the villages near Guiding. An illiterate villager named A Ji, curious about the writing on his talisman, showed it to a literate friend named Pan Youlin, who immediately recognized the words "heavenly commander" (*tianshuai*), "emperor" (*huangdi*), and "jade son of heaven" (*yu tianzi*). Pan realized that they had stumbled upon a case of lèse-majesté and warned A Ji that this was a very serious matter. They hastened to turn in the talismans to the local headman, who reported the matter to the district magistrate. Following a comprehensive investigation, Wei Xuewen and his conspirators were apprehended and brought before Governor Fang.[71]

In one of his reports on the case, Fang noted in despair that Zhongjia were often identical to Han in their clothing and eating habits, and many could speak, read, and write Chinese. In extreme cases, he wrote, Zhongjia even behaved like wicked Han (Han *jian*).[72] In a responding edict, the emperor indicated that any Zhongjia who behaved like a wicked Han was to be punished like a wicked Han: "The Miao are simple-minded and childish. If not for the wicked Han inciting and deceiving (people), matters would not reach the point of such disorder. The case of Wei Xuewen ranks among the crimes of wicked Han. It must be treated as a heavy crime."[73] Literacy had, in effect, transformed a Zhongjia into a wicked Han. Wei Xuewen's education, however rudimentary, had equipped him with the cultural and cognitive tools to resist the Qing state.

Governor Fang meted out punishments accordingly. In his estimation, the statute on disloyalty (*moupan*) was too light for Wei Xuewen and Luo Shirong.[74] He ordered them punished under the statute on high treason (*mou dani*).[75] Fang ordered that Wei Xuewen and Luo Shirong be decapitated, and that their heads be displayed in every hamlet. Other conspirators were prosecuted under the statute on rebellion, the punishment for which was also decapitation with the heads to be displayed in every hamlet.[76] Lesser participants faced one hundred lashes and exile.

As for the Miao villagers involved in the case, Governor Fang ruled that those who purchased talismans were unaware of their seditious content. Because they were illiterate, they had been unwittingly duped. Most Miao involved in the case were ordered to wear the cangue for a month and received forty lashes on the day of their release from this yoke. A Ji, the illiterate man who had taken the suspicious charms to his literate friend, Pan Youlin, was exempted from punishment. For his part, Pan Youlin received all the major criminals' property as a reward for bringing the case to light.[77]

CONCLUSION

The masterminds behind these three cases had no pretensions to power, no plans to mount armed insurrections, and no intention of challenging Qing rule in Guizhou. Their goals were expressly economic rather than consciously political. Yet many of their actions carried political import in their flagrant disregard for Qing authority. Moreover, if anti-Qing sentiments were indeed brewing in the region, then these swindlers might have inadvertently spurred them on. Men like Huang San, Wang Zuxian, and Wei Xuewen—all of whom possessed varying degrees of literacy in Chinese and at least a passing familiarity with imperial institutions—represented a unique threat to the Qing state. They had "advanced toward [Chinese] culture," only to seize upon elements that best served their interests and to twist these elements into a mockery of the Qing state. The Wei Xuewen case in particular suggests that literacy and education carried a certain economic value, although hardly the sort envisioned by Qing authorities.

Zhongjia individuals like Wei Xuewen viewed Confucian schooling as a strategy to protect and promote their own economic interests, and not as a means to advance toward the state-imposed ideal of civilization.[78] Wei capitalized on his literacy in order to take advantage of his illiterate neighbors. By posing as a provincial examination candidate, he gained the trust of Luo Shirong and other uneducated members of his community. He also appropriated symbols and rituals of imperial authority in such a way that suggested a lack of respect for—if not an outright rejection of—Qing rule. In this way, he engaged in a variation of what James Scott calls "state mimicry."[79]

The Huang San case also carried an insidious message for Qing authorities. Until his arrest, Huang operated within a sphere of autonomy defined by his own interests and needs, bounded not by Qing provincial borders, but by the fluid, transregional matrix of his master-disciple network. In many respects, Wei Xuewen and Huang San prefigured leaders of the Nanlong Uprising, who built their rebel movement on a similar foundation of religious networks and indigenous traditions shot through with reinterpretations of Chinese culture. This rebellion will be the subject of chapter 5.

Chapter 5

THE NANLONG UPRISING OF 1797

※

In February 1797, members of the Zhongjia ethnic group launched an uprising against the Qing state. Rallying under the battle cry, "Heaven will exterminate the Han Chinese, native headmen, and imperial troops" (*Tian jiang mie Hanren, bing mie Miaomu bingyi*), the rebels laid siege to the prefectural seat of Nanlong and sacked neighboring villages. Provincial and central government officials initially dismissed the Zhongjia as undisciplined bandits incapable of sustaining a coordinated rebellion.[1] This proved a grave miscalculation. Within weeks of the first assault on Nanlong, as provincial officials scrambled to shore up defenses, the Zhongjia attacked every major town in southwestern Guizhou and seemed poised to strike the provincial capital of Guiyang.

Far from being undisciplined bandits, the Zhongjia were well-trained guerilla fighters who drew strength from a potent combination of charismatic leadership and magical beliefs. Their movement had evolved from a cult surrounding two Zhongjia religious leaders, a young woman called Wang Niangxian, "Immortal Lady Wang" and a man nicknamed Wei Qiluoxu, or "Seven-whisker Wei."[2] Wang Niangxian, a mysterious personage known to all but seen by few, was the spiritual head of the rebellion, while Wei Qiluoxu, a magician and martial arts expert, was the self-appointed political and military leader. Aware that the Qing armies possessed superior weaponry, he instructed his followers to use magical charms and rituals to neutralize their adversaries' technological advantages.[3] Rebel troops advanced into battle "with a white fan in one hand and a white scarf in the other, dancing and bobbing atop their horses," or beating on bronze drums as they chanted "Stop the bullets! Stop the arrows!"[4]

The rebels' success was short-lived. After a sluggish start, the Qing suppression campaign rapidly gained momentum in April of 1797. Although the Zhongjia continued to frustrate imperial troops with surprise maneuvers and delaying tactics, they could only hope to postpone their eventual defeat. Rebel morale and popular support declined as scores of Zhongjia soldiers suffered mortal wounds at the hands of the imperial troops, demonstrating to even the most fervent believers that their charms and incantations were no match for Qing armaments. During the spring and summer of 1797, Qing armies secured a series of important victories. By early autumn, they had captured both Wei Qiluoxu and Wang Niangxian; and Qing forces reestablished control throughout southwestern Guizhou before the end of the year.

This chapter presents the first Western-language analysis of this rebellion, which is usually called the "Nanlong Uprising" (Nanlong *qiyi*) in post-1949 Chinese historiography. By utilizing both Qing archival materials and Buyi (Zhongjia) folk literature, the analysis gives equal voice to the imperial officials who sought to contain the rebellion and to the indigenous men and women who faced an enemy they knew to be much stronger. The Qing government materials—namely, correspondence between provincial officials and the imperial court in Beijing—provide a chronological account of the major battles in the rebellion and reveal the missteps that nearly undermined the early phases of the Qing campaign against the Zhongjia.[5] These documents are treated as more or less historical fact, or at least the version of events that imperial officials wanted to preserve. On the other hand, the Zhongjia folk narratives, "Immortal Maiden Wang" (*Wang Xiangu*) and "Song of the Nanlong Resistance" (*Nanlong fanbing ge*), represent not historical facts, but rather selective historical memory, or the way Zhongjia chose to perceive and remember the rebellion. The events depicted in these accounts run the gamut from slightly exaggerated to categorically implausible, all with an eye to casting the rebels in a heroic light and softening the psychological blow of their ultimate defeat.[6]

"Immortal Maiden Wang" is a narrative poem (*changshi*) from the southwest Guizhou town of Anlong.[7] In 1958, Buyi ethnographers recorded a folk tale about Wang Niangxian, the young Zhongjia woman commonly regarded as the rebellion's spiritual leader. Researchers who returned to the area twenty years later learned that the tale was based on a folk song. Further inquiries led to three elderly Buyi men, who performed the version featured in the collection used in this chapter. The song recounts the life and heroic deeds of Wang Niangxian, who uses her supernatural abilities to relieve Zhongjia poverty. Greedy officials thwart her at every turn until she becomes enraged and mounts a popular uprising. Throughout the rebellion, she performs a number of miracles to assist her troops in battle against the Qing. Ultimately, however, her magical skills prove insufficient; imperial armies invade her hometown and whisk her off to Beijing for execution.

"Song of the Nanlong Resistance" strikes a different tone.[8] Throughout the narrative, oratorical talent—particularly the ability to give Qing officials a sound tongue-lashing—seems to take precedence over magical powers or even martial skills. Once again, Qing armies eventually quell the uprising, but this narrative casts the rebels' final defeat in a less tragic light than does "Immortal Maiden Wang." The message is that the Qing defeated the Zhongjia on the battlefield, but could not quash their sharp wit or defiant spirit.

Although the two narratives are more fanciful than factual, they play an important role in this analysis of the Nanlong Uprising. The Buyi rarely, if ever, have had the opportunity to speak for themselves about the Nanlong Uprising or other pivotal events in their past. Their history has largely been controlled by Qing officials and, more recently, by communist scholars.[9] It is a history that reflects the goals and priorities of the dominant political group, not those of the Buyi themselves. When subordinate groups appear in the official record, their presence, behavior, and motives are mediated by the interpretation of dominant elites.[10] The analysis in chapters 3 and 4 "read against the grain" of the official record to find the voices and motivations of participants in anti-government movements or illegal schemes. In this chapter, the indigenous narratives provide rare glimpses of Buyi views on their own history—albeit with the occasional imprint of PRC ethnohistorians and editors bound to the Chinese Communist Party's political agenda.

PREVIOUS SCHOLARSHIP ON THE NANLONG UPRISING

No scholar outside China has examined the Nanlong Uprising in any detail.[11] However, the rebellion has garnered far more attention in China. General histories of Guizhou province or the Buyi ethnic group all include brief discussions of the rebellion. More detailed analyses may be found in a 1991 issue of the journal *Research in Buyi Studies* (*Buyi xue yanjiu*) devoted to the Nanlong Uprising. This volume includes articles on such topics as the causes of the rebellion, the role of folk religion, and the reasons for the rebels' defeat. These articles provide important background on the Nanlong Uprising, and also reveal much about the principles guiding Chinese scholarship on ethnic minorities. Most of the scholarly contributors are themselves members of the Buyi minority nationality: at once representatives of their own nationality and participants in a hegemonic state project. Their primary responsibility is to write the history of their own ethnic group in a way that glorifies and legitimizes the People's Republic of China.[12] Buyi scholars are therefore obligated to depict the Nanlong Uprising not as a pivotal event in the history of their own ethnic group, but rather, as an episode in the larger history of the People's Republic of China.

Accordingly, some Buyi writers take pains to point out that "the Han" targeted in the rebels' battle cry—"Heaven will exterminate the Han" (*Tian jiang mie Hanren*)—signified only Han *landlords* (*Hanzu dizhu*).[13] (This is somewhat misleading, for although the rebels did target Han local gentry and landlords, their animosity extended to ordinary Han peasants as well.)[14] The Buyi scholars who make these claims undoubtedly consider it prudent to qualify any suggestion that their ancestors wanted to exterminate the Han—by far the largest and most powerful ethnic group in China. More importantly, if Qing landlords can be seen as the primary Buyi enemy, then the Nanlong Uprising must be a peasant rebellion, a product of "class contradictions" (*jieji maodun*) rather than ethnic tensions.[15] In this respect, the Nanlong Uprising can be seen as virtually the same as every other peasant rebellion in Qing China: in other words, the Uprising becomes nothing more and nothing less than a small step in the country's march toward socialism.

Several articles by modern Buyi scholars elaborate on the notion that Han landlords were the primary enemy, and these articles all follow a similar thread: After the reforms of 1727, when Yongzheng-era officials deposed the native ruler and Nanlong became a regular administrative unit, Zhongjia peasants endured more oppression than ever before. Han immigrants from China's central provinces purchased native lands and then rented these lands back to the original owners at exorbitant rates, forcing the Zhongjia to become tenants on their own ancestral fields. Han landlords also demanded occasional payments of rice, wine, or meat, euphemistically termed "gifts," and ordered their Zhongjia tenants to perform unpaid manual labor. At the same time, the Zhongjia also had to pay taxes to the central government and were subject to corvée and military service. In these narratives, after decades of oppression, the Zhongjia people took up arms in 1797, thus becoming one of the many peasant groups to wage war against the landlords. They fought valiantly, but it was not until the rise of the Chinese Communist Party that feudal oppression ended, and peasants of all ethnicities came to enjoy peace and prosperity.[16]

This rhetoric also informs the scholarship on "Immortal Maiden Wang" and "Song of the Nanlong Resistance," scant though it is. A lone journal article and a few scattered references in other works comprise the entire body of PRC writing on the indigenous narratives.[17] Tian Yuan's brief article applauds the two poems for expressing the "beautiful hopes" of the Buyi people in their struggle against feudal oppressors, namely Han landlords and Qing officials.[18] And in a chapter on Buyi literature, Huang Yiren cites the two narratives as examples of folk stories that arose from "the exacerbation of class contradictions and ethnic contradictions" and the Buyi people's "nonstop struggle against the feudal system and class oppression."[19]

Another scholar, Jin Anjiang, singles out one verse from "Immortal Maiden Wang" as a paean to pan-ethnic unity, and he uses this verse to support his assertion that the Nanlong Uprising marked a step forward in strengthening solidarity and cooperation among the many ethnicities cohabiting in Buyi regions. Jin Anjing's argument relies on the lines, "Tens of thousands of Buyi, along with [their] Miao, Yao, and Zhuang brothers . . . joined Wang Xiangu [Wang Niangxian] to single-mindedly exterminate the imperial troops."[20] Jin concludes that the harmonious ethnic relations in Guizhou today are a legacy of shared historical experiences like the Nanlong Uprising. He is quick to add, however, that the Qing government's "cruel suppression" of the Nanlong Uprising militated against pan-ethnic unity by exacerbating inequalities among the different ethnic groups. This in turn gave rise to "estrangement and enmity among the ethnic groups." It was only after the rise of the People's Republic of China that Guizhou's minority nationalities began to enjoy true equality and unity: "Only by upholding the leadership of the Chinese Communist Party and upholding the socialist road, can the universal development and prosperity of the minority nationalities be realized."[21]

Clearly, authors like Jin Anjiang, Huang Yiren, and Tian Yuan zero in on aspects of the indigenous accounts that can be used to glorify the Chinese Communist Party and ignore the rest. Issues such as the narratives' actual content, literary merit, and possible significance for today's Buyi populations remain unexplored. Perhaps these scholars feel that the narratives rely too heavily on primitive religion and superstition to be of any historical value—or perhaps these magico-religious components simply make the narratives too sensitive for deeper examination.[22] Indeed, folk religion and magic are delicate topics for Buyi scholars of the Nanlong Uprising. Most authors seem inclined to ignore them altogether, or else to roundly denounce the rebels' reliance on charms and incantations. Leng Tianfang, for example, acknowledges that folk religion played an important role in mobilizing the Zhongjia masses to rise against their oppressors. However, Leng states that during the later stages of the rebellion, the deleterious effects of the rebels' blind reliance on charms and incantations became more and more apparent and that this ultimately hastened the rebels' defeat. In a final rebuke, Leng calls the rebels' practices "truly stupid and primitive."[23] The message is clear: Unscientific beliefs and unsound tactics undermined the Nanlong Uprising and prevented the Buyi peasants from triumphing over their class enemies. Only by eliminating superstition can the Buyi and other minority nationalities move forward.

This chapter, unfettered by a political agenda, offers a very different interpretation of the Nanlong Uprising. It views the rebellion as the most elaborate and fully articulated expression of the livelihood choices described throughout this book. As demonstrated in chapter 4, local residents developed sophisticated money-making ventures that combined local superstition and anti-Qing slogans to gain popular support. The masterminds behind these schemes enticed impoverished villagers with promises of instant wealth, lifelong immunity from taxes, and protection from natural disasters. That such promises never came to fruition was of little consequence. It was the hope of overcoming Guizhou's ecological and economic constraints that repeatedly impelled local residents to put their faith in charlatans whose promises, however far-fetched, were still much more enticing than what local officials either offered or delivered. In short, by the end of the eighteenth century, many villagers of southwestern Guizhou exhibited a clear propensity to reject imperial authority in favor of charismatic figures who extended the slightest hope for a better life. The Nanlong Uprising marked the first time this propensity found expression in armed rebellion.[24]

THE NANLONG UPRISING
AS RECOUNTED IN QING DOCUMENTS

Wang Niangxian, née Wang Acong, hailed from Dongsa, a hamlet near the prefectural seat of Nanlong.[25] She was born into a family of Mo ritual specialists who began teaching her spells and incantations as soon as she could talk.[26] Wang Niangxian specialized in a ritual called "crossing the darkness" (*guoyin*) that enabled her to serve as a mediator between the spiritual and terrestrial realms.[27] Her most prized possession was a set of five-colored stones that she believed to represent her covenant with heaven. She traveled from village to village telling people that the stones endowed her with a magic so potent that a mere moment in her presence could cure any ailment. She also announced that heaven had sent down an order forbidding every type of magic but her own.

Wang Niangxian was not above using trickery to attract followers. On one occasion, she secretly planted rice in a grotto. She told villagers to pray to the rice spirit for food, and then led them to the grotto. When they saw rice shoots flourishing there, they believed that she must be an immortal (*xian*). It was thus that the common people began to call her Wang Niangxian, or Immortal Lady Wang. Day after day, they asked her to cure their illnesses and predict the future. Many gave her money, wine, pigs, and rice in exchange for her services, although she never asked for payment.[28]

As a local cult grew around Wang Niangxian, her half-brother Wang Huaming and his friends began to see the potential for a lucrative venture.

They persuaded her to cease all public audiences; and they built her a temple at a location where they promised she would enjoy even better communication with the spirits. Wang Huaming and his friends invited villagers to visit the temple but would allow the villagers only to stand outside the building, where they could call up to Wang Nianxian, burn incense, and kowtow. Worshippers were required to bring contributions of food and wine, which Wang Huaming and his friends collected.[29]

In late 1795, some villagers grew concerned that Wang Niangxian and her followers might be planning a rebellion. They filed a complaint with the acting prefect of Nanlong, Zeng Tingkui, who authorized an investigation that resulted in the arrest of several cult members. After several days of interrogation, local officials determined that fears of rebellion were unwarranted. Wang Niangxian's followers were not distributing suspicious seals or woodcuts, or spreading anti-Qing slogans. As a precaution, however, Prefect Zeng decided to keep the cult members in jail. Several months later, a local headman, He Zhanbie, voiced fresh complaints about the Dongsa cult. Prefect Zeng dismissed the complaints as nonsense, but to be on the safe side, he did file a report with provincial authorities. His superiors in Guiyang supported his initial conclusion that the Zhongjia were merely practicing their traditional form of magic, not plotting rebellion. They also ordered Prefect Zeng to release the prisoners detained after the first investigation.[30]

This decision was a sound one. Nothing in this account suggests that Wang Niangxian or her handlers had any intention of mounting a rebellion. Most likely, they were engaged in a scheme similar to the ones described in chapter 4. Wang Niangxian's activities did not seem to have a seditious component, and Wang Huaming and his friends seemed interested only in the booty they could gain by taking advantage of Wang Niangxian's devoted followers. All in all, the Dongsa cult was a self-contained organization that posed no real threat to social stability. It might have remained so if not for Wei Qiluoxu.

Wei Qiluoxu lived in the nearby hamlet of Dangzhan. Like Wang Niangxian, he seems to have been a Mo practitioner who frequently "crossed the darkness" on behalf of his fellow villagers.[31] People who benefited from his services often tried to reward him with cattle, wine, and other goods, but he never accepted their gifts. Because of his generosity in providing free spiritual services, Zhongjia villagers called him "Great

Master Wei" (Wei Da Xiansheng) and many became his followers. Wei also claimed to possess a strong social conscience. As a local healer, he observed firsthand the poverty and despair of his fellow Zhongjia, and he took it upon himself to help them. As he explained in his confession:

> Throughout history, we . . . have been oppressed by the Han. They cheated us out of our land and then rented it to us. They made us slaves. It was unbearable. Every Miao had a mind to kill the Han, but no one dared raise a hand. When the Miao in eastern Guizhou and Hunan rebelled [in 1795], all of the soldiers near us were transferred out. At that point, I decided to gather the Miao to rise up against the Han, to burn and kill them. My will was strong, and people knew I was also skilled in the martial arts. I went everywhere in search of followers, and I found many willing to join me.[32]

It appears, then, that Wei Qiluoxu's organization began as a magico-religious group with a mandate that soon extended to social banditry.[33] He began to build a small army in 1796, using simple recruiting tactics: that is, he sent some of his adherents into the countryside to invite Zhong-jia peasants to burn and loot Han villages. For many Zhongjia, this was enticement enough to join up. It was an easy way to obtain money, grain, and other goods, and offered an exciting alternative to growing rice and tending cattle. As one Zhongjia man said later, "If we could raid Han houses, we could leave the bitterness of farming behind." But many Zhong-jia joined only reluctantly, after Wei Qiluoxu's henchmen warned that anyone who refused to participate would face certain death.[34]

Wei's initial battle strategy was as simple as his recruiting strategy. He planned to invade a Han village and seize all the grain and guns he could find, killing anyone who dared to resist. He would also gather new Zhong-jia recruits from villages throughout southwestern Guizhou, using coer-cive means if necessary, and then he would move on to the next town to repeat the process. In this way, his army would increase in size and strength with each successive raid. He targeted Puping, a relatively prosperous town in the northern part of Nanlong, for the first attack. From there, his men would fight their way to the prefectural seat and beyond. He com-posed a slogan to sum up his ambitions: "When the clouds rise, we will burn Puping, eat breakfast in Nanlong, and kill our way to Kunming" (*Yun tengteng, shao Puping, Nanlong chi zaofan, sha shang Yunnan cheng*).[35]

The Social Bandit Becomes Emperor

On January 31, 1797, Wei Qiluoxu's army attacked Puping and rampaged through neighboring villages. When they reached Dongsa, Wei Qiluoxu's ambitions took a new turn. After surveying the area, one of his men reported that many local residents were adherents of the young priestess Wang Niangxian. Wei Qiluoxu realized that a strategic alliance with Wang Niangxian would enhance his appeal and credibility among Zhongjia peasants. He sought out Wang Huaming, her brother and public representative, and tried to strike a deal, saying, "I, too, can 'cross the darkness.' During my last crossing, I saw the great jade emperor (*da huang yudi*). He told me, 'The Miao [Zhongjia] will conquer all under heaven.' Wang Niangxian is to be the immortal empress (*huangxian niangniang*), and I am to be her husband." Wang Huaming agreed that he and his sister would cooperate, although it is not clear if he did so willingly, or if Wei Qiluoxu threatened to kill him if he refused. Wang Niangxian was not consulted.[36]

On February 1, Wei Qiluoxu ordered Wang Niangxian's followers to join his men in an assault on the prefectural seat of Nanlong. The rebels entered the city with no resistance and proceeded to burn and pillage as they moved through the streets. No longer just bandits, the rebels now believed they were on a mission sanctioned by Heaven. The terrified residents of Nanlong tried to defend themselves with whatever came to hand—kitchen utensils, hunting knives, or sticks. Several hundred rebels encircled the city walls to prevent anyone from leaving or entering. Nanlong now belonged to the Zhongjia, and they would use its riches to finance their next conquest.[37]

In the afterglow of this first victory, Wei Qiluoxu moved to consolidate his authority. He proclaimed himself emperor and assumed the reign title "Heavenly Compliance" (*tianshun*), and he bestowed the reign title "Realized Immortal" (*xianda*) on Wang Niangxian. This act of proclaiming a reign title was significant in at least three ways. First, it undoubtedly satisfied Wei Qiluoxu's own delusions of grandeur. Second, as a public relations tactic, it may have increased his legitimacy in the eyes of the Zhongjia. And third, as a political symbol, it represented an act of lèse-majesté and a declaration of independence from the dynasty, because only the emperor himself could take a reign title. By claiming his own reign title, Wei

Qiluoxu put himself on equal footing with the monarch. Now it remained to capitalize on this new title and build his own empire in Guizhou.

The Qing Response: A Desultory Counteroffensive

While Wei Qiluoxu and his followers celebrated his victory at Nanlong, the town's prefect, Zeng Tingkui, was plunged into despair. He died two days after the attack on Nanlong, although it is not clear whether he committed suicide or succumbed to illness. Before Zeng's death, he relayed a hasty communiqué to Guizhou governor Feng Guangxiong, who at this point was overseeing troops on the Hunan-Guizhou border. Zeng's message was terse, indicating only that one thousand Zhongjia bandits had laid siege to Nanlong.[38]

The news must have filled Feng Guangxiong with alarm. The Zhongjia attacks coincided with the two major rebellions of the late eighteenth century—the White Lotus uprisings in Hubei, Sichuan, Shaanxi, and Gansu, and the Miao Rebellion in western Hunan. With its military and financial resources already stretched to the limits, the embattled dynasty could ill afford another crisis.[39] Indeed, the White Lotus and Miao Rebellions had already siphoned so many provincial troops from Guizhou itself that only a few thousand men were available to respond to the violence in Nanlong.[40] Even worse, just weeks before the Zhongjia insurrection, southwest China's highest-ranking civil and military official, Yunnan-Guizhou governor-general Le Bao, had been ordered to Hubei to assist with the ongoing campaign against White Lotus rebels.[41] With so few troops in the Nanlong region, the chaos could easily spread throughout southwestern Guizhou and into neighboring Yunnan and Guangxi. A few thousand soldiers were available in Anshun, one hundred miles northeast of Nanlong, and Feng hurried to arrange their transfer to the new battlefront. He then contacted the Guizhou provincial military commander Zhulonga and the Nanlong regional military commander (*zongbin*) Zhang Yulong, both of whom were on the front lines in Hunan, and ordered them to proceed to Nanlong without delay. Finally, Feng sent Beijing an urgent request for permission to follow Zhang and Zhulonga to Nanlong as soon as possible. As he pointed out, hostilities on the Hunan border were drawing to a close, and reconstruction (*shanhou*) was already under way in some areas.[42]

The emperor's responding edict approved Feng's request and ordered Le Bao to leave Hubei for Nanlong as soon as he could. The court also instructed Feng to diagnose the nature of the disturbances in Nanlong. Were the instigators merely bandits whose only goal was to burn and plunder, or were they bona fide rebels, cut from the same cloth as the Miao in Hunan?[43]

Feng replied to this edict before he set out for Nanlong. Based on the original communiqué from Zeng Tingkui, he wrote, he did not think the disorder in southwestern Guizhou would reach the scale of the Miao Rebellion. Only one thousand or so Zhongjia had attacked Nanlong, little more than an angry mob. Feng reasoned, moreover, that it was not in the Zhongjia character to rebel:

> Although the Zhongmiao possess a fierce nature, their clothing and customs are no different from those of ordinary people (*yu qimin wu yi*). Their perversity cannot be compared to that of the Hunan Miao. It was only because the military presence [in Nanlong] was weak that they dared to create a disturbance. They amount to little more than an unruly and undisciplined mob. They assemble like crows, gathering suddenly and then dispersing just as suddenly. . . . They specialize in burning and looting, and lack cunning and astuteness. I fear that these Miao bandits will assemble over and over again, spreading trouble to surrounding areas. Thus, I have ordered the officials in nearby towns to determine how many "village braves" (*xiangyong*) are available, and encourage the local militia to shore up their strength and defend crucial areas.[44]

Feng acknowledged that the Zhongjia posed a potential threat to social order, but he did not believe that additional Qing troops were needed in the Nanlong region because *xiangyong* local militia, who were recruited and organized by Han villagers, would be able to contain the threat. Also striking is Feng's assertion that the Zhongjia were, in appearance at least, "no different from ordinary people"—that is, they were no different from the Han.[45] In this case, acculturation did not signify any degree of identification with the Han or loyalty to the Qing Dynasty. But at this early juncture, Feng lacked adequate information about the rebels and could assess the situation based on only received wisdom about the Zhongjia.

Also noteworthy is Feng's characterization of the rebels as "an unruly and undisciplined mob." Only much later would he realize how badly he had underestimated the rebels' organizational capabilities. The movement continued to grow in strength and number after the attack on Nanlong, as Wei Qiluoxu continued to consolidate his small empire. Shortly after declaring himself emperor, Wei set up his own state with two capital cities. His hometown of Dangzhan became the administrative and military seat, and Dongsa became the ceremonial capital. Each capital had a government that included generals, ambassadors, generalissimos, and prime ministers. Wei Qiluoxu personally oversaw the officials in Dangzhan, while those in Dongsa governed in Wang Nangxian's name. Wei Qiluoxu's second-in-command was a Zhongjia man known by the nickname Da Wang Gong, who assisted with military recruiting, troop mobilization, and local administration. Also among Wei Qiluoxu's most trusted officials was a Han renegade named Sang Hongsheng who was responsible for managing the rebels' treasury, granary, and weapons supply, and who also advised Wei Qiluoxu on military strategy.[46]

Wei Qiluoxu's recruiting techniques also became more elaborate. With Wang Niangxian on his side, he could now tap more fully into local superstition and magico-religious inclinations. Male warriors called "realized immortals" (*xianda*) and women called "immortal maidens" (*xiangu*) enticed villagers to join the rebellion with promises that Heaven would reward the rebels with a lifetime supply of rice.[47] On occasion, recruiters also invoked Wang Niangxian's name to attract new recruits. As one rebel recalled:

> After the attacks on Nanlong, two men came to my village and told me that Wang Xiangu [Wang Niangxian], the priestess from Dongsa, had conferred upon me the title of "brilliant immortal" (*guangxian*). They said this was a higher rank than Xianda. I could transmit the 'ways of the immortals' (*xianfa*), distribute grain, and command troops. I subsequently gathered more than two thousand Miao from nearby hamlets to resist the imperial troops."[48]

When such inducements failed, Wei Qiluoxu's followers resorted to coercive measures. The message was simple: Join the rebellion or die as an enemy of the Zhongjia.

Whether recruited voluntarily or under duress, the rebels soon numbered far more than Zeng Tingkui's original estimate of one thousand. Within six weeks of the attack on Nanlong, they laid siege to every major town near Nanlong: Xincheng and Yongfeng to the northeast; Ceheng to the southeast; Pu'an and Annan to the northwest; and Huangcaoba and Bangzha to the southwest. Wei Qiluoxu's followers also rebelled in Yongning and Zhenning on the southwestern edge of Anshun prefecture.[49] In short, by the time Feng Guangxiong, Zhulonga, and Zhang Yulong arrived on the scene in mid-February, the rebels already controlled the entire southwestern quarter of Guizhou.

The three Qing commanders first proceeded to Anshun, where they tried to determine the quickest path to Nanlong.[50] It was decided that Feng would station himself at Guanling, strategically located between Anshun and Annan, to oversee the campaigns and to wait for Le Bao. Feng also planned to set up a granary in Guanling to provision troops in the field. Feng Guangxiong ordered Zhulonga to take a westerly route through Yongning and Annan. Zhang Yulong was to travel due south through Angu, Yongfeng, and Xincheng. Zhulonga and Zhang Yulong would receive support from the Weining regional military commander Qi Ge and the Changzhai assistant brigade commander (shoubei) Cui Lin.[51]

Conditions were far from ideal when the four field commanders (Zhulonga, Zhang Yulong, Qi Ge, and Cui Lin) struck out for Nanlong in early March. It was raining, and the slick, muddy roads slowed troop movements to a cautious crawl. To make matters worse, the Zhongjia had set up roadblocks everywhere. Only Zhang Yulong made any headway against the rebels during the first month of the suppression campaign. On March 11, his troops captured Angu, a small but strategic town on the way to Nanlong. Even this marked only a minor victory, for countless rebels escaped into the nearby mountains, and constant fog made it impossible for the Qing troops to give chase. The one bright spot was that a number of loyal villagers had assisted Zhang in the attack on Angu, which suggested that not all Zhongjia in the region had sworn allegiance to the rebels.[52]

The other three commanders also met with numerous difficulties. When Zhulonga and his men reached Annan on March 14, they managed to break through the roadblocks and chase Zhongjia rebels into the mountains. Zhulonga's forces held the town briefly before the Zhongjia returned and encircled the city again, trapping the Qing troops inside for several days. Qi Ge and his men had planned to meet up with Zhang Yulong at Angu, but after several unsuccessful attempts to break through the road-blocks, they were forced to retreat into the surrounding mountains. Unluckiest of all was Cui Lin, who stopped in Yongning on March 16 to help local officials shore up the town's defenses. He suffered fatal wounds when some old ordinance exploded as he moved it to a storehouse.[53]

The Qing court was understandably displeased with these early ventures. Feng and Zhulonga soon received an imperial reprimand for taking too long to bring the situation under control. Nanlong remained under siege, yet none of the Qing commanders seemed to be within striking distance of that town. True, Zhang Yulong had secured Angu, but he had allowed too many rebels to escape. If, as Feng had insisted, the Zhong-jia bandits were nothing more than an unruly mob, why were they so difficult to suppress? The court noted with obvious relief that Le Bao would soon reach Guizhou with additional troops. The Yunnan-Guizhou governor-general was a much better tactician than Feng Guangxiong, and campaigns would surely gain momentum under his command.[54]

Le Bao was still miles from Guizhou, however, and in the weeks before he arrived, the situation continued to deteriorate. In mid-March, Yunnan governor Jiang Lan reported that the rebels had made numerous incursions into the eastern part of his province, where they were likely to receive aid and comfort from Zhongjia and other non-Han villagers. He also feared for the safety of Han Chinese living in the border area. The rebels had already raided several Han settlements on the Yunnan side. On one occasion, after seizing all the money, guns, and grain they could find, they tied up Han men, women, and children, and carried them off into the mountains. Provincial soldiers pursued them and eventually apprehended the rebels and freed the captives. In a separate incident, a gang of Zhongjia bandits had forced their way into another Han village, although local militia had chased the rebels out of town before anything untoward happened. The local braves even managed to capture and decapitate one of the invaders. These incidents had worried Jiang Lan so much that he ordered an expeditionary force of five hundred provincial soldiers to enter Guizhou and investigate. The report of the expedition leader described an encounter with two columns of Zhongjia cavalry. Two women warriors rode near the front, both of them dancing and bobbing in their saddles. The rebels were clad entirely in white, and most of them clutched a white scarf in one hand and a white fan in the other. They had no firearms, only heavy sticks and hunting knives. Two Zhongjia men shouted a command to attack, and the mounted rebels rushed forward. The Yunnan soldiers promptly opened fire. The rebels chanted "Stop the bullets! Stop the bullets!" But the incantation failed to deliver the desired effect. Qing bullets struck first one of the female warriors, and then the other, killing them instantly. Before the battle ended, Yunnan forces had killed several hundred rebels and captured more than a dozen alive.[55]

Beijing's response to Jiang Lan suggests that the court took heart from the rebels' apparent stupidity:

> According to the confessions [of the ringleaders], the Miao bandits wear white turbans around their heads, and carry white scarves and fans to deceive the stupid Miao into believing that knives and bullets could not harm them. In view of this, the Miao criminals do nothing more than stir up trouble and deceive people. They lack cunning and ability. . . . As for the "immortal maidens" and "realized immortals" [that is, rebel soldiers] who say it is possible to use turbans and fans to shield themselves from harm, many [of them] were shot and killed in battle. Certainly this proves that their words cannot be trusted. This is obvious and simple to understand. It will make it easier to admonish and disband the rebel gangs. Those who call themselves "realized immortals" and "immortal maidens" to deceive the foolish Miao are truly despicable and must be captured. . . . Moreover, there must be leaders above these "Immortals." Once these leaders are caught, it will be even easier to capture the followers.[56]

The optimism in this court letter masked Beijing's mounting impatience with the officials in Guizhou. Once again, if the Zhongjia rebels were so foolish and superstitious, so lacking in cunning and ability, why were they so difficult to contain?

Indeed, the court's frustration increased as the Guizhou troops continued to lose ground in a series of bloody but inconclusive battles. After capturing Angu, Zhang Yulong learned that the rebels had taken Paishakou, another strategic point on the road to Nanlong. Zhang and his men climbed a steep, heavily forested path to reach the rebels' mountain lair. When they arrived, they found close to a thousand angry Zhongjia with guns.[57] Qing soldiers fatally wounded several rebels and burned their huts to the ground. The rebels fled, but imperial troops gave chase and killed them by the score. Two days later, Qing troops used cannons to bombard the rebels, killing several hundred. When several Zhongjia tried to flee, Zhang Yulong's men chased after them and hacked them to death. The Qing troops also set fire to trees and houses, leaving a burned landscape behind. The surviving rebels fled into the mountains, and the following day, close to two thousand rebels attacked the imperial army. Qing troops fired on the rebels with cannons and did not count the number killed. Zhang's men managed to capture a few rebels, but none of them could provide any useful information. For all the destruction, this battle brought few tangible results. The roads to Nanlong remained blocked, and Zhang Yulong could not see a way forward.[58]

As the imperial troops' southward progress slowed, the rebels' northward march proceeded apace. On March 22, rebels attacked and occupied Guansuling, an important mountain pass between Yongning and Guanling, thereby gaining control of the main westward route to Yunnan. A day later, they laid siege to Guanling and killed the officials whom Feng Guangxiong had placed in charge of the granary there. At this point, Feng was on his way to meet Le Bao in Anshun, or else he too might have perished in the fighting.

The disorder soon spread into three other towns—Guangshun, Dingfan, and Changzhai— all of which were dangerously close to the provincial capital of Guiyang. The rebels in Guangshun barricaded themselves in two walled villages, Bachang and Jichang. On March 23, local officials urged Zhongjia living near these two rebel encampments not to join the insurgency. Evidently, his admonitions had some effect, for these Zhongjia villagers agreed to remain loyal to the Qing state.

Feng Guangxiong, who was still en route to Anshun, apparently received faulty or incomplete information about Guangshun. He learned only that the rebels had taken Guangshun, but somehow did not find out that many local Zhongjia still remained loyal to the Qing. At any rate, when provincial troops marched into Guangshun, they did not attempt to distinguish the loyal Zhongjia from the rebels. They torched numerous hamlets where the residents had already promised not to join the insurrection. The needless slaughter undoubtedly pushed many surviving Zhongjia into the rebel ranks.[59]

By the end of March, after a series of increasingly dire reports from the field, Beijing was thoroughly disgusted with Feng Guangxiong and delivered this stinging rebuke in a court letter:

> Earlier, [Feng] reported that the Zhongjia bandits numbered no more than a thousand. How is it, then, that large bands of rebels now occupy every town and road in southwestern Guizhou? Recent communiqués would suggest that the rebels number in the tens of thousands, not [in the] thousands! It is plain to see that Feng's reports were not reliable. It is equally plain that the disorder in Guizhou is indeed comparable to the Miao Rebellion in Hunan. Thousands of soldiers will be needed to eradicate the [Zhongjia] rebels.

The court letter went on to note that Feng was a scholar, not a soldier, and that he was perhaps too advanced in age to take on heavy responsibilities. Once Le Bao arrived, Feng was to resume his civilian duties in Guiyang. He would manage administrative matters relating to the suppression campaign but take no further part in military strategy.[60]

Le Bao arrived in Anshun on March 31 for a debriefing from Feng Guangxiong. On his way to Anshun, Le Bao passed through the Guiyang region, where the rebels were using coercive tactics to gain new recruits. Le made personal visits to several Zhongjia hamlets to convince the villagers not to join the resistance. He told them that Qing armies had summarily crushed the Miao rebels in Hunan, and warned that the Zhongjia upstarts in Guizhou would soon face a similar fate. Le Bao also urged the villagers to stay on the lookout for anyone engaged in suspicious activities. Anyone who arrested such troublemakers, he said, could expect rich rewards.

Le Bao was confident that he had persuaded the Zhongjia of Guiyang to remain loyal to the Qing. But any good feelings that Le may have obtained from his success in this small mission probably evaporated during his meeting with Feng Guangxiong. Feng had just completed a tour of the Anshun region, where conditions were much bleaker than in Guiyang. The rebels had already taken many towns in the Anshun area, and the people were panicked. Feng was deeply apprehensive. If the rebels seized Anshun and Guiyang, what would stop them from pressing eastward or southward to other strategic points in Guizhou?[61]

Clearly, the rebels had to be stopped, and soon. Qing troops had made no real progress up to that point. In Le Bao's estimation, Zhang Yulong's assaults on Angu and Paishakou did not constitute real victories. They were a success only in terms of the number of rebels killed. But they were not successful from a tactical standpoint because the road to Nanlong remained blocked. Guanling, Yongning, Yongfeng, Xincheng, Huang-caoba, and of course Nanlong all remained under siege. Now the main road from Zhenning to Yunnan was also blocked, making it difficult to transport firearms, grain, and other supplies to the troops. Le Bao decided that he would mount an offensive on Guanling as soon as additional troops arrived from Hunan. Once Guanling was secure, he would go on to liberate Yongning and finally Nanlong. He also ordered Yunnan troops to mount an attack on Huangcaoba from the west.[62]

Le Bao set out for Guanling when the reinforcements arrived on April 8. The combined forces advanced about twenty miles to Huangguoshu, only to discover that the rebels controlled the road all the way to Guanling. Le Bao's soldiers pressed ahead toward Huangguoshu, although the rebels continuously harassed the troops along the way. Shouting and waving their flags, the rebels swarmed like bees around the Qing troops. As Le Bao's forces moved forward, more Zhongjia emerged from their hiding places in the stone caves of Huangguoshu and fired on the Qing troops. Undaunted, the troops advanced, capturing and killing many rebels.

Late that night, the government troops scaled Dapoling, a mountain peak opposite Guanling. Le Bao surveyed Guanling from atop the summit and noted that the surrounding terrain included a thick forest, with a wide gully traversed by a stone bridge. There were Miao settlements on either side of the forest, and Le Bao estimated that at least one thousand rebels were hiding there. The Zhongjia had also set up numerous sentry posts on the road to Guanling. Le Bao recognized that a direct attack on Guanling would be impossible. He found a circuitous route using mountain paths that the rebels did not yet occupy, and two days later, he launched a three-pronged attack on Guanling. The rebels put up stiff resistance, but Le Bao's men killed scores of them and seized the rebels' grain and gunpowder to redistribute among themselves. More importantly, through these successful attacks, Le Bao had reopened the main artery from Guizhou to Yunnan.[63]

Le Bao next set his sights on Balongtun, a strategic town between Guanling and Yongning. After a full week of fighting, Le Bao and his troops subdued the rebels in a series of coordinated attacks. Soon, some two thousand Zhongjia from neighboring villages went to the Qing encampment to surrender in person. Le Bao then ordered his men to charge into Yongning while he brought up the rear. After a few skirmishes, Le Bao and his forces arrived in Yongning. There, Le Bao met up with Zhulonga, who had finally managed to extricate himself from Annan. On April 16, Le Bao summoned all the Qing troops in the area and staged a massive attack on Yongning. When the Yongning magistrate heard the gunfire and saw explosions outside the city wall, he knew that imperial troops had arrived to end the month-long siege and he sent local militia members to help. Realizing they were outnumbered by government troops, the rebels surrendered by the score.

With Guanling, Yongning, and Annan under Qing control again, Le Bao and other Qing military leaders could begin planning the next campaigns. They decided that Zhulonga would proceed to Yongfeng, and after liberating the siege of that town, Zhulonga would continue to Nanlong. At Nanlong, he would meet up with Le Bao, who intended to go by way of Angu, Paishakou, and Xincheng. In that way, the Qing forces would approach Nanlong along two routes, liberate the city, and quickly exterminate the rebels.[64]

On April 26, Le Bao's men did break the siege of Xincheng, but in the weeks that followed, nothing else went according to plan. Once Xincheng was under Qing control, Le Bao ordered brigade commander (*youji*) Chang Shan to lead a few hundred men to Huangcaoba, where Yunnan troops had been mired for several weeks. The plan was for Chang Shan to relieve the Yunnan troops, recapture Huangcaoba, and then push his way eastward to Nanlong. There, he would meet up with Le Bao and Zhulonga, who would arrive by way of their planned itineraries through rebel territory.[65] However, both Zhulonga and Le Bao ran into immediate difficulties. Zhulonga and his troops made only limited progress before heavy rebel attacks prevented them from going any farther. Le Bao eventually ordered Zhulonga to abandon Yongfeng for the time being and to find an alternate route to Nanlong.

Pockets of rebel resistance also slowed Le Bao's progress from Xincheng. The rebels in the area all knew that Le Bao had recently captured Xincheng, and they were determined to prevent further Qing advances. They set up numerous roadblocks and erected high wooden barriers on the road leading to Wangchengpo, a key mountain pass on the way to Nanlong. Le Bao searched for alternate routes, and, finding none, hatched a strategy to destroy all of the rebels' roadblocks on the way to the pass. On the night of May 9, he ordered his troops to march toward Wangchengpo and throw torches at the wooden barriers. When the Qing troops did so, the barriers promptly ignited. The rebels scattered in panic as Qing troops fired on them. Many Zhongjia died, and others fled under cover of darkness. The Qing troops then took control of the Wangchengpo pass.

Even after this victory, Le Bao could only make slow progress toward Nanlong. The morning after the midnight capture of Wangchengpo, he surveyed the landscape and saw that the rebels had regrouped at a mountain several kilometers away. There was no effective way to attack these rebels, for they had set up encampments on the mountain at many elevations. Le Bao ordered his men to ascend this neighboring peak and to burn as many encampments as they could. Hundreds of rebels died in the fires, but countless others simply escaped by climbing to a higher elevation. It was a maddening impasse for Le Bao, but after nine days, Qing troops lured the remaining rebels into an ambush, vanquished them, and seized control of the mountain.[66]

While Le Bao was fighting for Wangchengpo, Chang Shan met his demise near Huangcaoba. The rebels apparently found out that Guizhou troops were on their way and laid an ambush. In order to reach Huangcaoba from the east, Chang Shan's troops had to cross the Mabie River.[67] Wei Qiluoxu personally led his rebel troops to the river's edge and destroyed the sole wooden bridge spanning the water. The rebels then jumped into waiting boats and sailed to the opposite bank to set booby traps on the road to Huangcaoba. When Chang Shan and his Qing troops arrived, they could not cross the river and were forced to set up camp, opposite Huangcaoba. The rebels sailed across the river and attacked the Qing troops in the dead of night, killing the entire battalion. Wei Qiluoxu heralded the massacre as "The Great Victory at Mabie," and it became one of the most celebrated pieces of Zhongjia lore.[68]

A Change in Momentum: Qing Armies Seize the Upper Hand

After so many campaign setbacks, Le Bao finally had a breakthrough in early June. He planned to press to Yangchang, the next important town on his slow march to Nanlong. For days, heavy rains and rough terrain conspired against him, and as usual, the rebels had erected roadblocks at many points along the road. As Le Bao and his men inched forward, he began to consider the possibility of taking an alternate route to Nanlong.

Several days later, a solution emerged when two brothers[69] appeared at Le Bao's headquarters and presented themselves as "loyal Miao" (*shun Miao*). The brothers complained that the rebels had seized their farmland and implored the Qing general to help them recover it. After listening with great interest, Le Bao invited the men to serve as spies for the imperial army, promising large rewards if they could provide good intelligence on rebel movements in Yangchang. Not only would they regain their own lands, they would also receive the lands now claimed by the rebels in Yangchang.

The men readily agreed and hurried to Yangchang. Two days later, the elder returned to report that he and his brother had feigned surrender to the rebel commander of Yangchang.[70] The commander had initially rejected them because he suspected they were already sworn allies of the Qing. When he threatened to kill the brothers, they hastily explained that their surrender to Qing troops had only been a ruse to keep their farmland. The rebel commander seemed to accept this and ordered the two men to seal their loyalty by drinking the blood of a freshly slain chicken. He then asked them to stand guard by the village gate. The elder brother had managed to sneak away just long enough to inform Le Bao of the progress of the plan.

Le Bao stated his intention to attack Yangchang that night, and ordered the two brothers to continue acting as spies throughout the assault. The ensuing battle ended in a decisive victory for Qing troops, with countless rebels killed and thirty-eight rebels captured alive. Le Bao directed the brothers to identify each captive; and then Le Bao personally interrogated them one by one. In this way, Le Bao learned about the cult that had taken hold in Nanlong the previous year, and also gained some understanding of the rebels' organizational structure. The rebel commander at Yangchang held the title "realized immortal" and oversaw local administration and troop mobilization. Every area under rebel control was placed under the jurisdiction of a different "realized immortal." A shadowy figure by the name of Da Wang Gong selected the "realized immortals," but the captives could not say with certainty who this man was, or where he might be.

They were also not sure if Da Wang Gong was the primary leader of the rebellion, or if he was subordinate to a higher authority figure. Nevertheless, Le Bao was satisfied to have even these small kernels of information. As he pressed on toward Nanlong, he believed he could continue to gather intelligence on this Da Wang Gong.[71]

Le Bao's success at Yangchang was the first of several important victories that summer. In late July, Yunnan governor Jiang Lan reported his province's troops had finally broken the siege at Huangcaoba, thus clearing the western approach to Nanlong.[72] Guizhou troops met up with the Yunnan armies outside Huangcaoba and launched a coordinated attack on Bangzha. The combined forces captured and interrogated numerous rebels, who revealed that Wang Niangxian of Dongsa and Wei Qiluoxu of Dangzhan were the true leaders of the rebellion.[73]

Armed with this knowledge, Le Bao decided to capture the two leaders before launching the final assault on Nanlong. On October 5, he sent five columns of troops into Dongsa and another three into Dangzhan. Thousands of Zhongjia had assembled in Dongsa to protect Wang Niangxian. When the rebels saw the imperial troops approaching, they felled trees to block the roads. However, Le Bao's men pressed on, burning everything in their path, killing anyone who dared resist.

At last, the Qing troops reached Wang Niangxian's fortress, a multi-storied tower encircled by two stone walls. Rebels fired at the soldiers and hurled stones from the fortress windows, so the imperial troops could not go forward. Several men attempted to scale the wall, but the rebels stoned them to death. Another group of soldiers tried to set fire to the gate, but the rebels promptly extinguished the flames with water. Le Bao finally hit upon the idea of digging tunnels underneath the wall to move his soldiers behind enemy lines. Soon after Le Bao's troops began digging, a large section of the wall collapsed, allowing the men to rush into the enemy rebel stronghold. The rebels sprinkled gunpowder throughout their fortress and ignited it, apparently preferring self-immolation to capture. The Qing troops rushed into the town and pulled Wang Niangxian from the flames.

A similar scenario unfolded in Dangzhan. When the Qing troops approached, Wei Qiluoxu and his followers barricaded themselves in a building and set themselves on fire. Imperial troops arrived just in time to pluck them from the fire. Wei Qiluoxu's hands were severely burned, but he was still able to speak and move about.[74] After the attacks on Dongsa and Dangzhan, Qing troops recaptured Nanlong and Yongfeng with little resistance. Beijing subsequently changed the names of both towns to honor the citizens who had survived the long sieges. Nanlong became Xingyi, meaning "flourishing virtue," and Yongfeng was renamed Zhenfeng, meaning "loyal and prosperous."[75] Wei Qiluoxu and Wang Niangxian were escorted to Beijing and summarily executed.[76]

THE NANLONG UPRISING AS RECOUNTED IN BUYI (ZHONGJIA) NARRATIVES

'Immortal Maiden Wang'

"Immortal Maiden Wang" is the more fanciful of the two indigenous accounts.[77] It portrays Wang Niangxian, not Wei Qiluoxu, as the mastermind behind the uprising. The first few stanzas establish her credentials as a priestess and rebel leader by recounting her remarkable childhood. She could climb and crawl as soon as she emerged from her mother's womb, and learned to speak before she was a month old. When she and her mother went out on sunny days, the spirits provided a red parasol to shield them from the heat; when she and her father went out on rainy days, the spirits provided a green umbrella to keep them dry. People took these unusual occurrences as signs that the young girl enjoyed protection from the spirits, and possessed strong magical powers.[78]

Soon, her abilities became manifest in even the most mundane tasks. Like all Zhongjia girls, she tended her family's cattle and horses and collected firewood in the forest. While her friends struggled to control their animals, hers were unfailingly placid and obedient. When she went into the forests, the wood chopped itself and piled into a heap at her side, while she sat under a tree and worked on her embroidery. Soon, her unique powers became apparent to others. When she was walking home from the forest, onlookers noticed that she was being carried on a sedan chair of flowers. From that point forward, everyone believed she was an immortal who enjoyed protection from the spirits, and they began calling her "Immortal Maiden Wang."[79]

As she grew older, Wang Niangxian became aware of the poverty and oppression around her, and she used her magical powers to improve the lives of her fellow Zhongjia. While grazing her cows one day, she remarked to a friend, "The officials are truly despotic and hateful! They occupy the mountains, the forests, and all the land. They will not even relinquish the most barren rocks. We have no fields to till, and every year we suffer famine. We have no land to plant. Season after season, we have not been able to cultivate cotton. . . . I demand lands for the poor people to till! Everyone must have food and clothing." So saying, she turned clumps of dirt into cultivable land. Thereafter, people called these lands "immortal dry land" (*shenxian di*) and "immortal paddies" (*shenxian tian*). It is interesting to note that Wei Qiluoxu's concerns for the public welfare are here attributed to Wang Niangxian, but instead of resorting to social banditry, she used her conjuring powers to create new farmland.[80]

Before long, however, imperial officials and native officials seized the fields Wang Niangxian had just created. "Outrageously wicked and corrupt were the officials. People were dying of hunger and could not tend the lands. The officials came and took them [the lands] by force." When Zhongjia villagers expressed their despair, Wang Niangxian announced her intention to fight the imperial officials and local despots to the death. The people rallied around her and said, "The officials have crowds of soldiers and horses. . . . You alone cannot accomplish much. We have deliberated and decided to fight."[81] Wang Niangxian also confronted officials about one of the Zhongjia people's most serious grievances against the Qing authorities. Like many other non-Chinese residents of Guizhou, the Zhongjia tried to earn money by selling firewood to Qing officials. More often than not, the officials would refuse to pay. Wang Niangxian spoke out against this injustice:

The officials are wealthy, with storehouses full of grain. The common folk starve to death on the side of the road. Officials and gentry have meat and wine every day while the poor people subsist on chaff and bran. Officials occupy the fields; native officials seize the land. The common people have nothing to eat and must sell firewood in order to buy rice. In the forest, there are white birds and black, none blacker than the crow. In the human race, there are good people and evil, none more evil than the officials! When they come to procure firewood, they offer no money![82]

At first, Wang tried to reason with the officials, but they beat her with heavy sticks. Enraged, she threw herself into hand-to-hand combat with

Qing troops for three days and three nights. She seemed invincible, even though she was just one small woman, single-handedly fighting thousands of men. After she killed scores of imperial soldiers, they retreated to their garrisons, and she returned to her home village. Her martial skill and ruthlessness struck fear into the hearts of the local officials. They pasted up announcements proclaiming her a "devil" (yaoguai) who was protected by evil spirits. Wang Niangxian responded with harsh words about the officials' behavior: "In daylight and in darkness, they harm people. When they buy firewood, they do not pay for it. Then they return to beat people. How can such injustice exist in the world? Everything must be set right!"[83]

In order to set things right, Wang Niangxian now determined to organize a rebel movement. She gathered followers by reminding them of her magical ability to "cross the darkness" and to communicate directly with the spirits. Wang Niangxian told the villagers, "The spirits have ordered me to transmit the following message to you: Why do we suffer? Only because of the officials and the gentry. . . . If we want food, we must rise up and resist the officials and gentry. If we want peace, we must rise up with our knives and axes and kill the officials of Nanlong. . . . Only after we bring oppression to an end will the people have security. Only when extortion is wiped away will the hamlets and mountains know peace."[84]

Wang Niangxian's words inspired people to take action. Tens of thousands of Zhongjia joined her cause and resolved to exterminate the officials and the gentry. Although it is difficult to determine whether Wang Niangxian actually uttered these words, in all likelihood, the creators and transmitters of this narrative used her character as a mouthpiece for the injustices endured by the Zhongjia. Once again, in this narrative it is Wang Niangxian and not Wei Qiluoxu who mobilizes the masses. Her rebellion is divinely inspired from the start and skips the social banditry phase described in the Qing accounts.

Wei Qiluoxu does enter the story soon, but in a subordinate role. During the planning phases of the rebellion, Wang Niangxian joined forces with Wei and two other local men, Da Wang Gong and Sang Hongsheng. Da Wang Gong and Wei Qiluoxu both wanted to rise up against corrupt officials and greedy landowners. Sang Hongsheng, a Han Chinese man identified as a "guest" (kejia),[85] also wanted to lead a rebellion. Once the four established an alliance, they began planning their first major attack. Wei Qiluoxu was to attack the north gate of Nanlong, Da Wang Gong the south gate, and Wang Niangxian the west gate.

On the day of the attack, Wang Niangxian and her troops laid siege to Nanlong. The officials and citizens could only look on in horror, and the imperial troops stationed in the city realized they were no match for the rebels:

> Although the soldiers were numerous, they could not defeat Wang Xiangu [Wang Niangxian]. The soldiers who died were many. Their blood flowed like a river. They fought for seven days and seven nights, until their corpses were numerous enough to fill a dike. The soldiers closed the [Nanlong] city gates. Xiangu [Wang Niangxian], closed in tight. Her troops besieged the city for three days and three nights. The magistrate was terrified. He notified the capital, and the emperor, too, was frightened . . . and sent a panicked edict ordering the transfer of troops from Yunnan and Guangxi. Soon, the dirty hound of a Governor-general Le Bao led ten thousand troops toward Nanlong. He burned villages to the ground as he rampaged through Guizhou like a rabid dog.[86]

The rebels went on to seize the Guizhou towns of Xincheng, Yongfeng, and Huangcaoba in rapid succession.[87] Soon, the rebels seemed poised for a direct attack on Guiyang and the emperor became nervous and fearful. "By day, he [the emperor] dispatched soldiers (to Guizhou), and by night he panicked. The dog of a Yunnan-Guizhou governor-general, Le Bao, received an edict ordering him to proceed directly to Nanlong. The soldiers were like jackals and wolves, rampaging along the roads."[88] They burned and pillaged every town and hamlet in their path. It is interesting to see Le Bao referred to as a hound or a rabid dog, given the Qing propensity to label non-Chinese peoples with pejoratives using the dog character component. Here, the creators and transmitters of "Immortal Maiden Wang" turned the linguistic table on the Qing.

After sketchy descriptions of some battles with the Qing armies, the narrative turns to a vivid account of the greatest rebel victory, the ambush at the Mabie River. Upon learning of Le Bao's plans to cross the river, Wei Qiluoxu led his troops to the Mabie and ordered them to destroy the bridges spanning the waterway. Next, Wei's men seized every boat in the vicinity and moved the vessels to the opposite bank, where Le Bao's men could not reach them.[89] When Le Bao and his men reached the riverbank, they were furious to see the ruined bridge and the boats on the far bank. To make matters worse, a violent thunderstorm struck. Lightning split the sky, and huge waves roiled the water's surface. Le Bao sought out some local craftsmen and ordered them to build rafts for his troops. This proved a foolish move on his part. Unbeknown to him, the tribesmen were loyal to the rebels and seized the opportunity to sabotage the vessels. Normally, when the craftsmen made rafts, they lashed wooden planks together with thick rope, but this time, they used thin vines to bind rough-hewn logs. When the rafts were finished, the unsuspecting Le Bao ordered his soldiers to pole the rafts across the river. The watercraft broke apart immediately, leaving hundreds of Qing troops spluttering and thrashing about in the water—including Le Bao, who could not swim. A soldier saved him from drowning and carried him to shore. Many others were not as fortunate and lost their lives in the turbulent Mabie.

After this debacle, yet another ambush lay in store for the Qing troops. While Le Bao tried to gather his wits, Wei Qiluoxu prepared an ingenious attack. He set up camp on a mountain, where he stockpiled logs and large stones in preparation for his next assault on imperial troops. At this point, Le Bao's foremost concern was self-preservation. Two important generals had lost their lives in the ill-fated attempt to cross the Mabie. After losing so many of his crack troops, Le Bao needed reinforcements. He retreated several miles to join forces with Guizhou governor Feng Guangxiong and his troops. After conferring, the two generals agreed to try crossing the Mabie once again. This time, they would descend from a nearby mountain and make their way across the river with each soldier holding fast to the shoulders of the man in front of him. Feng would lead the charge, and Le Bao would bring up the rear.

The path at the foot of the mountain was extremely narrow. As the Qing troops squeezed through, they heard a deafening noise. The entire mountain seemed to shake. Suddenly, giant objects rained down on them like hail. Wei Qiluoxu and his men stood at the top of the mountain, showering the Qing troops with rocks and logs. As in the ill-fated attempt to cross the Mabie River, many Qing troops were killed or injured. Many lost their legs or were smashed to death. Those whose legs remained intact retreated to safety.[90] Le Bao once again managed to avoid death or injury, but Feng Guangxiong was slightly wounded. Wei Qiluoxu hurried to tell Wang Niangxian about his victories, and Wang spread the news to Zhongjia throughout Guizhou.[91]

This episode of "Wang Xiangu" contains a healthy dose of poetic license and exaggeration. In fact, neither Le Bao nor Feng Guangxiong was anywhere near Mabie. Le Bao, of course, was fighting at Bifengshan, and Feng Guangxiong was overseeing administrative work in Anshun. By incorporating these high-ranking Qing officials into the poem, the original creators and transmitters of the narrative probably hoped to heighten the importance of this final rebel victory. They may have also wanted to soften the blow of later episodes, which had to recount Wang Niangxian's final defeat. Lingering images of Le Bao's near-drowning might have provided some comfort as, later in the poem, listeners learned of the young heroine's capture by Qing forces. At the same time, this Mabie episode represents a sharp departure from the rest of "Wang Xiangu." The events arise from the application of human ingenuity, not of magic, which suggests the influence of PRC compilers and editors. In other words, to attribute the Zhongjia triumph at the Mabie River to spiritual intervention might give credence to the religious beliefs that Communist officials sought to discredit.

The narrative continues by describing the Qing officials' panic in the wake of the Zhongjia victories. Le Bao and his colleagues sent numerous, frantic reports to the emperor, who also grew alarmed. He ordered soldiers to be transferred to Guizhou from other provinces (Yunnan, Guangxi, Guangdong, and Hunan). Soon, these imperial troops overran Guizhou "like packs of wolves" and marched toward Nanlong. Wherever they went, they behaved "like wild animals," killing people on sight.[92] As soon as the Qing forces came upon a house, they would burn it to the ground.

At the same time, the rebels also incurred serious losses. They were greatly outnumbered, and knew they could not defeat the imperial troops. Once again, Wang Niangxian used her magic to help the rebels. Chanting a spell, she "sprinkled beans on the ground to produce soldiers" (*sadou chengbing*).[93] One bean became one thousand soldiers; ten beans became ten thousand. The "bean soldiers" (*doubing*) took up weapons and battled with the imperial troops. Wang Niangxian also provided food for the troops. She uttered a spell, and rice poured down from heaven. The grains of rice formed a small mountain, more food than the thousands of troops could ever finish. The rebel soldiers called it "spirit rice" (*shen fan*). It was infused with magic, so that whenever a soldier ate it, he became even braver. After fighting with the "bean soldiers," the imperial troops were even more frightened of Wang Niangxian.[94]

Before long, however, thousands of Qing troops descended on Nanlong in search of Wang Niangxian, whom the emperor had branded "a demon" (*yaojing*) and "the root of the trouble" (*huogen*).[95] The emperor dispatched still more soldiers to Nanlong, whereupon Wang Niangxian led the rebel army to Dangzhan and set up an encampment. Everywhere, towns and hamlets in this area were surrounded by rebel soldiers. For many days, Qing troops could not break through the rebel lines, but at last they overwhelmed the rebels and stormed Nanlong. Once inside the city, Le Bao captured and interrogated dozens of people, including Wang Niangxian's mother and sister. Le Bao tortured these Zhongjia to extract information. When Wang Niangxian learned of her family's fate, it "pained her like a crown of thorns."[96] In the dead of night, she led three armies into Nanlong, determined to rescue her mother and sister. She entered the gates unaware that the city was full of Qing soldiers. As soon as they spotted Wang Niangxian, they opened fire, wounding her in seven places. She crumpled to the ground. Evidently, the "Immortal Maiden" was not immortal after all, and the narrative does not explain why her magical powers did not protect her from the Qing bullets. In any event, imperial soldiers tied her up and carted her off to Beijing in a heavy wooden basket.

The narrative concludes on a mournful note: "Today the sky is a slice of blackness. The sun sets early. Our Immortal Maiden was captured by imperial troops and sent to the capital. The river grows murky and the sparrows cease their song. Our Immortal Maiden was killed by the immeasurably evil emperor." After her death, a five-colored cloud appeared in the sky. There, Wang Niangxian continues to live on as a spirit who watches over the terrestrial realm. The last few lines of the poem urge the listeners not to despair, for the Immortal Maiden never really died: "She will forever live on by our side. . . . She remains in the sky, preparing for war. She still intends to kill the officials and the gentry [in order] to wipe everything clean and help the impoverished."[97]

'Song of the Nanlong Resistance (Nanlong fan bing ge)'

In many respects, "Song of the Nanlong Resistance" hews closely to Qing accounts of the rebellion, though it exaggerates Zhongjia victories. This poem also seeks to turn the rebels' battlefield defeats into moral victories. In this version of events, Wei Qiluoxu and Wang Niangxian emerge as equal partners in the planning and execution of the rebellion. This creates an interesting middle ground between the Qing accounts, which find Wang Niangxian playing a passive and not altogether voluntary role in the actual rebellion, and "Immortal Maiden Wang," which portrays her as both mastermind and martyr.

"Song of the Nanlong Resistance" does not provide detailed accounts of major battles, and even glosses over the victory at the Mabie River. Instead, it relies on a series of dialogues between the rebel leaders and Qing officials, which highlight Zhongjia defiance in the face of defeat.[98] In this account, when imperial troops descended on Dangzhan and captured Wei Qiluoxu, they took the rebel to see Le Bao. The Qing general swore at him: "Damn you, Wei Qiluoxu! You incited the people to rebel and killed my general, Chang Shan. Today, I captured you. Do you have anything to say for yourself?"

Wei Qiluoxu replied, "The officials of Nanlong oppressed the common people, pushing them to the point of rebellion. When I led the people to rise up, I complied with Heaven's will and the people's sentiment. Today I was captured. If you want to kill me, then kill me. If you want to hack me to pieces, then hack me to pieces. What more need I say?!"

Le Bao retorted, "Your crimes are as high as a mountain! You incited the people to rise up and attack a prefecture. You killed an imperial general [Chang Shan]. Even to skin you like a slaughtered animal would not lessen your crimes. I will have you escorted to the capital, where the emperor himself will decide your fate!"[99]

After capturing Wei Qiluoxu, Le Bao set his sights on catching Wang Niangxian. He ordered his troops to block access to Dongsa hamlet on three sides, leaving only one road clear for Wang Niangxian when she descended from her mountain stronghold to return to Dongsa. He made an announcement: "Barbarian soldiers who are willing to die should come out and fight! Those unwilling to die should come down the mountain and surrender!" Le Bao stationed himself at the foot of the mountain and kept watch. Wang Niangxian hid in a fortress, readying her soldiers for battle. Eventually, she spied Le Bao and his men preparing to attack, and she was infuriated. After ordering her troops into battle formation, she taunted Le Bao: "Today the shields and daggers move. So you have more soldiers than I do. I am not frightened! I will send you to see the king of Hell (*yanluo*)! I will peel off your skin and use it for a drum, and gouge out your eyeballs to use as lanterns! I will knock out your teeth and use them as nails for the drum, and cut off your hands to use as hammers!"

Le Bao interpreted Wang Niangxian's song as a declaration of war, and he responded with the following challenge: "I am leading an expedition to Nanlong to slaughter the barbarian troops. . . . Your corpses and skulls will be reduced to ash! Quickly! Quickly! Come down the mountain and submit to our knives. Do not use clever words. Come fight!"

Wang Niangxian then led her troops down the mountain and fought three battles with the imperial troops. Her men were "as fierce as wolves and tigers," but they were unable to ward off Le Bao's soldiers. They fought "knife to knife, gun to gun, soldier to soldier, general to general" (*dao dui dao lai qiang dui qiang, bing dui bing lai jiang dui jiang*).[100] In the end, however, the imperial troops were too numerous for the rebels, and Wang Niangxian's troops were forced to retreat. She took advantage of the chaos and hid herself among the local population.

By this time, Le Bao had also lost five of his battalions in the fighting, and he, too, was forced to retreat.[101] The Qing general returned to his headquarters to regroup, but the following day, his troops stormed Wang Niangxian's headquarters with flaming arrows in readiness. When Le Bao gave the command, each soldier shot his arrow into the compound, and fire engulfed the building. Satisfied that he had exterminated his enemies at last, Le Bao led his troops to Nanlong.

But Le Bao had not seen the last of Wang Niangxian, for she was still very much alive. The narrative does not make it clear whether she actually perished in the fire and came back to life—rising from the ashes, as it were—or if her supernatural powers enabled her to escape injury. Whatever the case, she cut her hair and disguised herself in men's clothes in order to hide among the Zhongjia peasants of Nanlong. For several days, she wandered around, lamenting the recent turn of events:

I weep for my soldiers who died in battle. I weep for my father and elder brother. I weep for the soldiers who died in the fire. The villages and hamlets are deserted, empty of people. Qing soldiers gored my parents to death and plunged knives through my sisters' hearts. Detestable are the imperial troops—criminals, every one of them! They destroyed my home and murdered my kinfolk and friends.[102]

Wang Niangxian's disguise was not fail-safe, however. A sharp-eyed farmer recognized her and reported her to members of the village association, who then made a citizen's arrest and began dragging her off to Governor-General Le Bao. En route, they met another Qing general. We are told that this General Jia was on his way to Nanlong when he encountered five men escorting a sixth person.[103] The general asked the men to identify their companion, and they replied: "She is none other than the rebel leader, Wang Niangxian. She . . . plans to raise another army and engage in mortal combat with the emperor's troops yet again. Fortunately, someone came and secretly reported on her. We saw her without a guard and arrested her. Now we will turn her in to Governor-General Le Bao." General Jia took a look, and at first, he could only see a handsome young man. On closer inspection, he realized that it was indeed Wang Niangxian, disguised in male clothing. The general said with a smile, "At Nanlong, you killed many of the emperor's soldiers. . . . You are truly formidable! I never thought that capturing you would be so effortless!"[104]

Jia and Le Bao sent gleeful reports to the emperor recounting the capture of Wang Niangxian. The two generals then had a great celebration, and spoke of Wang in admiring terms, calling her "a heroine, the likes of whom we rarely see."[105] In all likelihood, this conversation between the Qing generals never occurred, but perhaps it eased the sting of defeat for the original Zhongjia composers of this narrative and their descendants.

Le Bao and Jia escorted Wang Niangxian and Wei Qiluoxu to Beijing and presented the two prisoners to the emperor.[106] All of the civil and military officials at court were in attendance. They saw a handsome, dignified couple with a regal bearing. The Jiaqing emperor asked if the prisoners were husband and wife. Le Bao replied that they were not, and added:

This woman is Wang Niangxian. The man is Wei Chaoyuan, nicknamed Wei Qiluoxu. The barbarian masses took the woman to be their supreme leader. The man was their main military leader. These two could be called heroes. Their troops besieged Nanlong for three months, killing countless imperial soldiers. They also attacked Puping and Yongfeng, and in those battles, they slaughtered three thousand of our troops. Thereafter, they fought several more battles in which they killed [the soldiers of] five of our companies altogether. General Chang Shan was also killed at their hands. I have therefore brought them before Your Majesty and await your verdict.[107]

The emperor ordered that the two prisoners be immediately executed. As soon as he delivered the verdict, a huge group of soldiers and palace officials pushed Wei Qiluoxu and Wang Niangxian to an execution ground outside the Forbidden City. Undaunted, Wei Qiluoxu and Wang Niangxian lifted their chests, their eyes bright and sharp as arrows, fiery anger gushing forth. With fierce scowls, they said, "After death, we shall return! You may expect us to attack you at any time." The soldiers charged with the execution dared not raise their swords and retreated in terror. Only after the commanding officers barked stern orders did the soldiers take courage and move forward again. They killed Wei Qiluoxu using a rack of fine iron teeth. They cut Wang Niangxian into five parts. No one could bear to watch.[108]

CONCLUSION: THE ENDURING CULTURE OF RESISTANCE

Ultimately, the Zhongjia rebels achieved only a temporary disruption of the existing order, not the total destruction they desired. In this respect, the uprising can be seen as a "historical achievement of popular imagination."[109] That is, local malcontents envisioned an end to their impoverishment and domination by overlords, and acted upon this vision when the opportunity arose. In the end, these rebels suffered defeat because they overestimated their own abilities and underestimated the might of the Qing state.

The three accounts discussed in this chapter illuminate different facets of the Zhongjia defeat. Interestingly, both the Qing sources and "Immortal Maiden Wang" point to a similar triumph of technology over popular imagination. To be sure, both accounts reflect realities on the ground during the rebellion, but certain aspects of the indigenous narrative seem tailor-made to fit the PRC's political agenda, particularly its emphasis on the primacy of science and reason over religion and superstition. In both versions, the rebels prove an unexpectedly formidable enemy, but the imperial troops' superior weapons and military capabilities ultimately give them the edge. In both versions, the final battle for Nanlong finds the rebels utterly without resources when Wang Niangxian's magical powers betray her during those last crucial hours—the triumph of science over superstition championed by PRC policy-makers.

In contrast, "Song of the Nanlong Resistance" appears to present the Zhongjia—and subaltern groups in general—as possessed with greater agency. In the final verses of the song, Wang Niangxian and Wei Qiluoxu literally have the last word, signaling the Zhongjia intent to rise up again at the next opportunity. Just because the Zhongjia had failed in this instance to overthrow the existing order, there was nothing to stop them—or another equally disenfranchised community—from trying again.

Leaving aside the modern-day political overtones, the final implied message of "Song of the Nanlong Uprising," became abundantly clear to Qing authorities after the Zhongjia uprising, and in the aftermath of the much larger Miao Rebellion in western Hunan (1795–1806). The final years of the eighteenth century found provincial and central governments actively seeking measures to alleviate the causes of possible unrest in southwestern China.[110] For example, in early 1798, the new Yunnan-Guizhou governor-general E'hui and Feng Guangxiong put forth elaborate new proposals to ease the poverty that had underlain the Nanlong Uprising. Han Chinese and Zhongjia were to live in segregated villages. Careful land surveys would be carried out to determine which fields belonged to Zhongjia farmers, and which fields belonged to the Han. Local officials were to mark boundaries with stones and strictly prohibit any encroachments by the Han. E'hui and Feng also wanted to provide the Zhongjia with occupations that might provide an alternative to crime, such as raising horses for postal station relays.[111]

However, such measures proved too little, too late. Local officials did not make much of an effort to enforce the new land regulations. There is no further information on the horse-raising scheme, but if the plan was implemented, few people took advantage of it. Thus, by 1801, trouble was brewing again in Guangshun, one of the many areas that had been affected by rebellion. In this case, yet another individual emerged with a money-making scheme that took advantage of the people's superstitious bent. A man claimed that after a fourteen-month pregnancy, his wife was about to give birth to the new Miao king.[112] This man attracted a small following before the officials could put a stop to his activities. Although Qing authorities managed to nip trouble in the bud this time, the potential for unrest remained undiminished.

Chapter 6

A LEGACY OF FRAGILE HEGEMONY

※

Qing China's Manchu rulers faced special challenges in legitimizing and consolidating their rule over Guizhou. In other newly acquired territories such as Mongolia, Tibet, Xinjiang, and even southern Yunnan, the foreign origins of the Qing ruling house offered certain advantages. The Manchus could adopt Ming institutions and bureaucratic procedures for ruling the Han population, and could employ a variety of techniques, inherent in their own tradition, to rule the vast amounts of territory and the non-Han populations that had been incorporated into the Qing empire.

The heritage of the Manchus, especially their practice of Tibetan Buddhism and their martial and nomadic tradition, opened many avenues for legitimizing the extension of Qing rule. The Qianlong emperor even had himself portrayed in artwork as a bodhisattva in order to improve relations with Tibetan and Mongolian Buddhists. Strategic marriages with rival royal families in the north and northwest helped to secure alliances on those frontiers.[1] In southern Yunnan, officials made an effort to understand and accommodate the traditions and institutions of the native Tai population. From the Qing perspective, the relationship of the Tai's Theravada Buddhism to their own school of Buddhism—as well as the Tai's sophisticated political organizations—made it possible to categorize the these southern people as "acceptable barbarians." For their part, Tai aristocrats could downplay their subservience while emphasizing the benefits of mutual accommodation.[2]

In Central Asia and southern Yunnan, common points of reference not only legitimized Qing territorial claims, but also served as the foundation for what has been termed the Qianlong emperor's "pluralist configuration of empire." That is, the Qing reached a kind of mutual accommodation with local populations by appropriating indigenous beliefs, symbols, and writing systems. The Manchus, Han, Mongolians, Muslims, and Tibetans constituted five culture blocs that comprised the principal domains of the Qing realm. Each enjoyed an equivalent position in the Qing imperial polity under a "universal Heaven" represented by the emperor himself. The equal status of the five groups was symbolized by multilingual inscriptions in Chinese, Manchu, Mongolian, Tibetan, and Uighur, which were found on steles, gates, and public edifices throughout the Qing realm.[3] Also symbolic were two major multilingual publications of the eighteenth century, the *Imperially Authorized Mirror of the Five Scripts of Qing Letters* (Wuti Qingwen jian) and the *Imperially Commissioned Unified-language Gazetteer of the Western Regions* (Qinding xiyu tongwen zhi). The latter, completed in 1763, is a geographical and genealogical dictionary of western-region place names and personal names (in Manchu, Chinese, two Mongolian languages, Tibetan, and Uighur). The work was intended primarily as an aid in the compilation of military histories and imperial gazetteers. It also helped standardize Chinese transliterations of these non-Chinese names, thus avoiding confusion in field reports to the court as well as in historiography. Even more importantly, this dictionary represented what Millward calls "an exercise in imperial scholarship and scholarly imperialism, a linguistic conquest to consolidate both practically and symbolically the military victories already achieved."[4]

In Guizhou, however, Qing rulers and officials confronted what must have seemed like a mind-boggling array of languages and traditions. Here, the Manchu heritage did not afford any particular advantage or status, and common points of cultural and religious reference were virtually nonexistent. Qing officials were unable to grasp any institutions or symbols upon which to build the relationships of mutual accommodation found in other frontier regions. Multilingual inscriptions and dictionaries were a practical impossibility, for most Guizhou ethnic groups lacked writing systems. So unfamiliar and so apparently uncivilized were the

Guizhou indigenes that most literati simply derided them as barbarians. However, barbarians or not, Guizhou indigenes had come under Qing jurisdiction, and officials needed a way to understand and control them. In this context, the production of knowledge about frontier areas and the peoples who inhabited them gained increasing importance.[5]

One product of the demand for information on Guizhou was Aibida's *Handbook of Guizhou* (*Qiannan shilue*). Aibida compiled this book for his own reference and for the benefit of future administrators while serving as Guizhou governor in the early 1750s. He condensed information from local gazetteers and other contemporary geographic writings into a single, handy volume, organizing his material according to geographic region. Each of the thirty-two chapters is devoted to the political history, economy, climate, and population of a single administrative unit.[6] Aside from its practical function, the handbook carried considerable symbolic value. To refer to the concepts introduced in chapter 3, the volume functioned as a catalogue of the state spaces the Qing had delineated within Guizhou. The very act of committing geographic information to paper signaled that these sections of Guizhou had become part of the world known to—and under the jurisdiction of—the Qing state.

Ethnographic accounts found in local gazetteers, the *Qing Imperial Illustration of Tributaries*, and especially the Miao albums, also became crucial administrative tools during the Qianlong reign. The Miao albums were illustrated manuscripts that described non-Han populations in the southern Chinese provinces. Each manuscript featured illustrations and texts that defined and categorized the different groups that inhabited a given province. The genre began as an administrative document designed by, and intended for the use of, officials responsible for governing the peoples therein. Each album entry featured a detailed illustration of a particular non-Han population with a caption noting the group's geographic location, economic activities, physical attributes, clothing and hairstyle, religious practices and festivals, and marriage and funeral customs. Some captions also described the dietary habits of a given group, commented on the extent of Chinese proficiency among its members, and even made pronouncements on the general "nature" of the population.[7] An entry on the Bulong Zhongjia, for example, highlights not only the group's funeral customs, but also points to a potential for unruliness: "At funerals, cattle are butchered and dressed, and relatives and friends are invited. Drinking from the 'ox-horn of happiness, the guests often get drunk and sometimes even wind up killing each other. . . . By nature, the Bulong are alert and fierce. When coming and going, they carry sharp knives. They will avenge even an angry look."[8] Such descriptions served a dual purpose. On a practical and administrative level, they provided valuable information to local officials dealing with non-Han populations.[9] On a cultural and ideological level, they helped establish where a given group fell on a continuum from "like the Han" (yu Hanren tong) to savage or in some way "other." However, this rubric went beyond a simple dualistic conception of barbarian versus civilized. It measured a group's distance from Sinocentric ideals by considering a variety of different criteria.[10] As a result, a group might be drawing closer to certain ideals even as it lagged behind on certain others. This complex formulary might help to account for the contradictory and ever-changing portrayals of the Zhongjia noted in chapter 2. At the same time, the depiction of various non-Han groups enabled the Qing to exalt the ethnic diversity within their realm.[11] In this respect, the Miao albums roughly paralleled the multilingual inscriptions and dictionaries employed in Central Asia. The albums also represented an exercise in imperial scholarship and scholarly imperialism, in this case an attempt at *artistic* conquest designed to consolidate both practically and symbolically the military and administrative goals achieved in Guizhou.

There was, however, a crucial distinction between the multilingual works and the Miao albums. Whereas the inclusion of a given Central Asian language in a gate inscription or dictionary affirmed that the ethnic group now ranked among equals with the other cultural blocs of China, representation in the Miao albums signaled that a given ethnic group was, in theory at least, subordinate to the Qing. The very act of ethnographic depiction signifies an unequal power dynamic. Those who do the depicting—writers and illustrators working at the behest of a colonial or imperial authority—control the process of defining or constructing the identity of the ethnic groups described. Those who are depicted—members of the ethnic groups described—do not have the chance to participate in this process, or to ensure that their own opinions and self-perceptions are incorporated into official depictions. [12] The governing logic, it seemed, was that even if the peoples described in the Miao albums had opinions about those who depicted them, they had only limited power to convey their views in ways persuasive to those in power.[13]

However, this logic suggests a hard binary of dominance and subjugation that did not exist in southwestern Guizhou. This book has explored the other side of the story—that of a people who refused to accept the subordinate status assigned to them and who found ways to communicate their resentment to those in power. The Miao albums codified the indigenes' inferior status for Qing authorities, but not for the indigenes themselves. As previous chapters have shown, many local residents found creative ways to circumvent Qing laws and norms, and thus preserve their own identities. The perseverance of local residents prevented the Qing from achieving a total monopolization of cultural, political, and economic space in Guizhou, and limited the imperial enterprise to what Peter Perdue terms a "hegemonic project with incomplete results."[14]

Qing domination, at least in the military, administrative, and geopolitical sense, was more or less a given: the Zhongjia were too small in number for real resistance, and they had only existed as semi-autonomous entities within the Chinese imperium, never as independent kingdoms. The Zhongjia never harbored illusions of breaking free and establishing an independent state.[15] The trick was to maintain as much room to maneuver as possible and, if possible, negotiate a little more.

LIVELIHOOD STRATEGIES

This book has explored the ways that the Zhongjia of Qing-dominated eighteenth-century Guizhou maintained—and sometimes expanded—their room to maneuver through their livelihood choices. Many Zhongjia faced poverty and a dearth of economic opportunities. However, a few Zhongjia with creative resources—that is, those who possessed literacy, religious training, martial arts skills, or supposed supernatural powers—found ways to make their own economic opportunities. Such individuals sometimes attracted the less fortunate (and more easily duped) and enticed credulous followers to participate in illicit activities with a strong anti-Qing flavor. This produced a temporary and fragile new social order, in which a few poor but resourceful indigenes gained some power, thanks to support from their poorer and less resourceful brethren. This new order pivoted on a relationship that was exploitative in the sense that the leaders preyed on their followers' desperation by manipulating their superstitious beliefs. At the same time, the relationship between leader and followers was also symbiotic because all parties benefited in one way or another. For example, ringleaders like Wei Qiluoxu and Ran Jing, described in chapter 4, were able to realize their own fantasies of wealth and power; at the same time, their followers also gained new wealth while imagining themselves as participants in an important social movement that would create a world free of oppression. Most important of all, ringleaders and followers alike shared the desire to negate the existing order.[16]

To be sure, there was an element of coercion in these movements, and many followers only joined under threat of death. Still others joined out of sheer gullibility. But for many followers, taking part in illegal schemes or rebellions represented a rational choice. The impoverished residents of central and southwestern Guizhou understood that they could either passively accept their straitened circumstances or pursue extralegal livelihood choices.[17] After weighing their limited options, many chose the extralegal route. This calculated disregard for the law persisted well into the nineteenth century in Guizhou, when residents persisted in growing and selling opium despite government prohibitions. Even after Qing officials tried to substitute other cash crops for poppy, peasants continued to grow opium because it was more profitable than other crops.[18]

The local Guizhou ethos that favored local livelihoods over imperial fiat undermined Qing plans in the region. As discussed in chapter 2, government officials of the Yongzheng period went to great lengths to impose order on Guizhou and its people. Qing policy showcased the Qing government's newfound ability to "see like a state," that is, to implement schemes of legibility and standardization that would enable the central government to extend its reach into the remotest areas.[19] Such policies gave the Qing state a firmer foothold in some areas of central and southwestern Guizhou, but instead of making the region more tractable overall, these policies only generated resentment and resistance from the local population. Even as the government showed an increasing capacity to "see like a state," the people of Guizhou exhibited an equal talent for throwing sand in the state's eyes.[20]

Clearly, then, Qing rule did not deprive indigenous communities of their voice or their agency. Frequent, creative resistance enabled local residents to maintain a continual dialogue with imperial authorities— an unceasing argument about power, authority, and legitimacy.[21] The instances of unrest examined in this book were, in essence, episodes in an ongoing dialogue between the Qing state and the people of Guizhou. On numerous occasions, the Qing state tried to end the argument by silencing local voices through punitive measures or military suppression. But new sets of local speakers continually emerged to resume the discussion, preventing the Qing state from ever gaining full control over cultural and political space. Qing rule was therefore not hegemonic, but rather a hegemonic project with incomplete results.[22]

The remainder of this chapter explores the unfulfilled hegemonic enterprise in Guizhou by returning to three larger issues raised throughout the book. First, I examine the nature of Qing colonialism and imperialism in Guizhou. As suggested in chapter 3, the attitudes and policies of Qing officials indicate that the imperial government viewed the Dingfan-Guangshun and Nanlong regions as something akin to colonial space—specifically as internal frontiers to pacify, civilize, and domesticate. Next, I locate a place for Guizhou's indigenes, particularly the Zhongjia, in the Qing vision of multicultural empire, elaborating upon Emma Teng's assertion that ethnic groups in Taiwan and southwestern China were superfluous to this vision. I suggest that this superfluity—that is, a position on the margins of empire—could confer a great degree of power and autonomy to an ethnic group, particularly in the case of the Zhongjia. Finally, I briefly discuss the legacy of Qing rule in Guizhou today. As in imperial times, local communities still manage to resist (or negotiate their way around) state directives to preserve indigenous livelihoods, and in some cases create new ones. State hegemony in Guizhou, therefore, remains at best incomplete.

THE COLONIAL CONCEPT IN GUIZHOU

Qing expansion in the regions of Dingfan-Guangshun and Nanlong had little to do with the resource extraction usually associated with colonialism. Instead, the annexation of indigenous lands was above all an attempt to ensure that the emperor's writ extended to all corners of the realm, and to create administrative order where none had existed before. Yongzheng-era policy envisioned the pacification of indigenous populations, reinforced by administrative, moral, and cultural transformations. Such measures amounted to what Stevan Harrell has called a "Confucian civilizing project."[23] That is, Qing authorities attempted to bring indigenous populations to heel by introducing the presumed benefits of Chinese moral and cultural standards.[24] In contrast, James Scott prefers to view civilizing projects as attempts at domestication, that is, "a kind of social gardening devised to make the countryside, its products, and its inhabitants more readily identifiable and accessible to the center."[25] I would argue that the Qing enterprise in Guizhou involved both civilizing and domestication. The aims of the Qing government included the moral transformations Harrell describes, as well as the social and administrative changes that concern Scott. Qing authorities believed that the twin processes of civilizing and domestication would reinforce each other, ultimately transforming the region's geopolitical and human landscapes.

Few if any of these transformations came to fruition. The Qing venture in central and southwestern Guizhou stands out as a project of civilizing and domestication with less than satisfactory results. In this context, a project refers to a set of objectives that may never be realized, with outcomes that may deviate wildly from the anticipated. When Peter Perdue and Stevan Harrell write of hegemonic and civilizing projects, we can infer that they mean goals articulated but incomplete in the face of resistance from targeted populations. Nicholas Thomas promotes a similar idea when he defines a project as a transformative endeavor that involves " . . . a particular imagination of the social situation, with its history and projected future, and a diagnosis of what is lacking, that can be rectified by intervention, by conservation, by bullets, or by welfare." Thomas also stresses that " . . . projects are of course often projected rather than realized; because of their confrontation with indigenous interests . . . [they are] frequently deflected or enacted farcically or incompletely."[26] The idea of goals projected but largely unfulfilled aptly describes the Qing attempts at civilizing and domesticating central and southwestern Guizhou.

THE ZHONGJIA IN THE MULTICULTURAL QING EMPIRE:
TOWARD A HIERARCHY OF PERIPHERAL PEOPLES

The Qianlong emperor envisioned the Qing Empire as a "great unity" (datong) of five domains: Manchu, Mongol, Han, Tibetan, and Muslim.

The status of these five "culture blocs," was signified through the use of Manchu, Mongolian, Chinese, Tibetan, and Turki/Arabic for multilingual imperial inscriptions on gates, stelae, and monuments. In this imperial ideology, which James Millward calls "Five Nations, Under Heaven," the emperor claimed to rule impartially over his diverse subjects. Millward provides a diagram for this model in which the five major culture blocs occupy parallel positions centered on the Qing imperial house. At the center of Millward's model is not an abstract "Chinese civilization," but the Qing emperor himself, who showed a different face to each of the five blocs, yet did not favor one above the other—at least not in the ideal system.[27]

Notably absent from the five blocs are the Guizhou indigenes—or indeed any of southwest China's non-Han populations. Far from enjoying the emperor's impartial benevolence, it appears that they were targets of official chauvinism. Although Qing authorities stopped using derogatory language to describe Mongols and Uighurs after their homelands were incorporated into the empire, derogatory terms continued to appear in government communications about Guizhou's ethnic groups. As noted in chapter 2, Qing officials made particularly liberal use of the "dog" character component when writing about the Zhongjia.

If the Qing emperor claimed to be an impartial ruler over diverse peoples, then why accord different status to different ethnic groups? Quite simply, it was because the Tibetans, Mongols, Manchus, Turks, and Chinese were, in fact, national political entities, at least in the pre-modern mode of being national. In contrast, most southwestern peoples were not such political entities, with the possible exception of some Tai polities, which were treated administratively like the Inner and Central Asian groups—although these Tai groups never reached the theoretical political level of the five nations under Heaven.[28] Given the limited role in the national polity available to these Guizhou outlier groups, was there a place in the Qing vision of multicultural empire for peoples who did not constitute national political entities? Some answers may lie in Emma Teng's work on Taiwan. She explains that a combination of cultural and political factors excluded the island's indigenes from the Qing concept of "great unity." Unlike the Manchus, Mongols, Tibetans, and Chinese, the Taiwan indigenes did not contribute to the creation and development of the Qing state.[29] Moreover, the Qing did not view Taiwan indigenes as a "nation" because they lacked centralized leadership. Without a king, a khan, or prince, these Taiwan residents appeared to be no more than a collection of primitive tribes. Teng also notes a vast difference in the cultural status the Qing accorded the Taiwan indigenes and the Five Nations. The indigenes had no written language, no genealogies, no history, no recognizable religion, and above all, no recognizable state. Without these key elements, Taiwan's indigenes could never rise to the level of the five culture blocs. Thus, the Qing made no effort to codify their language and culture in imperially sponsored dictionaries, or in vast multilingual gazetteers such as the *Imperially Commissioned Unified Language Gazetteer of the Western Regions*. Instead, Taiwan's indigenous people became the subjects of ethnographic writings on "savage customs."[30]

In every respect, then, the Taiwan indigenes were peripheral to Qing interests and occupied at best a secondary status in the multicultural realm. Accordingly, Teng creates a place for them in Millward's schemata by adding a second tier beyond the five major cultural blocs.[31] I would also place the Guizhou indigenes on this second tier, although the Zhongjia might be a fraction closer to the five major blocs than the various ethnic groups on Taiwan. I limit my comments here to the Zhongjia because they have received the most attention in this book.

If we look again at the political and cultural criteria Teng lists as prerequisites for inclusion in the "Great Unity," it appears that the Zhongjia came marginally closer to meeting them than did the Taiwan indigenes. First, as noted in chapter 3, the Sicheng native official played an important role in helping Qing generals defeat the Southern Ming remnants in Guizhou. In this way, the Zhongjia made a small contribution to the development and consolidation of the Qing Empire—a contribution that was certainly smaller than the Mongols or the Manchus but greater than the Taiwan indigenes. Secondly, although the Zhongjia did not constitute what the Qing viewed as a "nation," they did have readily recognizable leaders in their native officials, at least until the native official system was mostly dismantled in the 1720s. Moreover, native officials' families maintained genealogies to facilitate the succession process. This gave the Zhongjia a history of sorts, although the Qing would never grant this history the same legitimacy they gave the history of the Mongols, Manchus, or Tibetans. In addition, most Zhongjia communities maintained a clear political structure with easily identifiable leaders. These were usually village headmen who, in theory at least, were directly answerable to Qing authorities. Finally and most fundamentally, *gaitu guiliu* made the Zhongjia full subjects of the Qing Empire by bringing them under the emperor's direct authority. The Taiwan indigenes, by contrast, did not gain recognition as full subjects until late in the nineteenth century.[32]

These political and cultural factors combined to give the Zhongjia a slightly higher status than the Taiwan indigenes. This marginally higher position did not, of course, give the Zhongjia any special privileges. They would never be partners in empire, nor could they even attain the level of the Tai in southern Yunnan, whom the Qing accorded a special status for their role as a buffer between China and the powerful kingdoms of mainland Southeast Asia. These distinctions suggest that there was a hierarchy of peripheral peoples on Teng's proposed second tier, with the Tai on top, the Zhongjia somewhere in the middle, and the Taiwan indigenes and the Miao (Hmong) close to the bottom.

That such a hierarchy existed gives lie to the notion of the emperor's impartial love. Only those groups with a sufficiently high cultural and political level—the Han, Manchu, Muslims, Tibetans, and Mongolians—received imperial favor.[33] Those deemed culturally inferior—the Taiwanese aborigines and most southwestern indigenes—became the targets of Qing civilizing projects. However, participation in these projects was no guarantee of acceptance in the eyes of imperial authorities. Guizhou provincial officials occasionally remarked that some Zhongjia were "no different from the Han" because they had adopted Chinese clothing, spoke reasonable Mandarin, and had learned to read and write. But the simple fact that officials made such observations suggests that the Zhongjia were indeed still different from the Han in the eyes of Qing officialdom. If the Zhongjia were truly indistinguishable from the Han, then not even the most acute observer would have been able to differentiate between an acculturated Zhongjia and a true Han.

Moreover, being "no different from the Han" did not confer the same status as being Han. For a Zhongjia to be "no different from the Han" simply meant that he had assumed the trappings of Han culture, not that he had actually become Han.[34] In terms of Millward and Teng's schemata of the Qing multicultural world, this meant that a Zhongjia could not move from the second tier of peripheral peoples to the primary tier of the five culture blocs. The Qing world, then, appears not as a broadly inclusive multicultural realm, but rather a rigid two-tiered society. On the first tier were the partners in empire. On the second tier were the peripheral peoples of southwestern China and Taiwan. The peripheral peoples were encouraged and sometimes even forced to change, but not even total conformity to Han cultural norms would elevate them to the status of partners in empire.

The findings in this book suggest that the Zhongjia and other ethnic groups in Guizhou recognized and even embraced their marginal status. Unlike the Han, Manchu, Mongols, Tibetans, and Muslims, the Zhongjia had only a conditional stake in the Qing Empire. They could only become partners in empire if they advanced toward culture (*xianghua*) and effectively ceased to be Zhongjia. Faced with such a dilemma, many chose *not* to advance toward mainstream Chinese culture and instead to advance in their own way, by making the livelihood choices that best suited their economic and cultural needs. Their peripheral status gave the Zhongjia license to pursue their livelihood choices—and, when the state interfered, gave them more opportunities to rebel. By relegating these Guizhou indigenes to a marginal position, the Qing government effectively rendered them ungovernable—a great irony in view of the various Qing efforts to make the region more tractable. In the end, this peripheral status may have been the indigenes' greatest asset in their quest for cultural and economic autonomy.

GUIZHOU TODAY

It now remains to take a brief look at contemporary Guizhou. The province is still one of China's poorest, and for many of its inhabitants, living conditions have not improved appreciably since the eighteenth century. One mitigating factor is that current inhabitants now enjoy a wider range of economic opportunities and livelihood choices than did their ancestors during the imperial period. Instead of resorting to banditry and rebellion, young people in search of better prospects can leave Guizhou for the booming coastal province of Guangdong, where they can find work in manufacturing or construction.[35] Nevertheless, at the beginning of the twenty-first century, social discontent is not uncommon in Guizhou. In 2002, for example, retired workers from the state-owned Guiyang Steel

Factory blocked two major highways to protest their low pensions.[36] Six years later, during the summer of 2008, residents of the southern Guizhou town of Weng'an set fire to government buildings to protest an alleged police cover-up in the rape and murder of a teenage girl.[37]

It is true that such incidents are not unique to Guizhou and increasing numbers of people throughout China have taken to the streets to protest a variety of economic grievances and abuses of power. But some instances of Guizhou social unrest do carry echoes of the past. For example, the story of the Caohai Nature Reserve in northwestern Guizhou demonstrates that local residents still mount a vigorous response when the state interferes with indigenous livelihood strategies.[38] In 1972, Guizhou provincial officials drained Caohai Lake in order to create more productive farmland. Ten years later, these officials restored the lake after neighboring counties voiced concerns about microclimate changes. Farmers living nearby were never informed that officials planned to refill the lake; one day the farmers found their lands inundated. They assumed that the water would recede, but it never did. Left with only minuscule plots of arable land, many farmers could not grow enough to feed their families; they thus resorted to fishing and trapping waterfowl in the lake. In 1985, to protect the region's population of migratory birds and other wildlife, the Guizhou provincial government declared Caohai a national nature reserve. With the establishment of this reserve, the farmers' supplementary activities became illegal. Nonetheless, many farmers continued to fish and hunt waterfowl well into the late 1990s. Reserve managers enforced the prohibitions only intermittently, but when they did, they met with stiff resistance. On several occasions, reserve authorities destroyed fishing huts, burned nets, and confiscated poached fish. Villagers vehemently protested these actions, sometimes even physically attacking the reserve staff.[39] The Caohai farmers viewed the state's interdictions on fishing and trapping as a violation of their right to maintain a basic level of subsistence, and responded with violence.[40]

Other problems may arise from the increasingly large gap between rich and poor residents of Guizhou. When I visited the Xingyi region in May 2001, I had the opportunity to interview a rural Buyi family—the modern-day descendants of the Zhongjia. Eight people lived in a single-room stone house without running water or electricity. The youngest members of the family, two small girls, showed signs of undernourishment; I guessed their ages to be six and nine, but their father told me they were nine and thirteen. Everyone spoke the southwest variant of Mandarin, and the two girls proudly showed me their schoolbooks. No one in the family showed much interest in the history of their own ethnic group, although an elderly man did tell me that they maintained a genealogy dating back to the early Ming period.

The contrasts between this family's village and the city of Xingyi, only fifteen minutes away by car, were striking. Xingyi has a thriving downtown area with enticing restaurants and bright shops selling the latest in Western music and fashion. One evening, I had dinner with a family whose three-bedroom apartment would have been the envy of any Chinese city-dweller—and perhaps of many American urbanites, as well. The apartment was spacious, airy, and tastefully decorated, with a fully appointed kitchen, satellite television service, and a digital video disc player. The family, not surprisingly, was Han. Asked about the rural minority areas just outside Xingyi, they remarked only that the people there were extremely poor. Such socioeconomic disparities indicate that the Buyi and many of Guizhou's other ethnic groups are still largely peripheral to the Chinese world.

In more recent years, however, there have been signs of change, with new initiatives to bring tourist revenue into Buyi areas. This will present local populations with new challenges, as they seek to preserve their culture in the face of an increasingly market-oriented economy.[41] Ethnic minority culture has become a fundamental aspect of promotional activities. Officials actually consider tourism itself to be ideally suited for these regions because it capitalizes on the very conditions which make Guizhou so poor: the harsh but picturesque mountain landscapes, and the social and cultural distance from China proper. As geographer Timothy Oakes explains:

> The representations of minority culture which became ubiquitous features of promoting the province would not only make Guizhou more interesting to outsiders, but were meant to establish a model for the "cultural development" of minority groups themselves, conditioning them to articulate symbolic cultural practices with commercial projects. Tourism was thus seen not simply as a propaganda and marketing tool for Guizhou, but also as a process of development and integration encouraging minority regions to become more modern.[42]

During the first decade of the twenty-first century, this enterprise was producing uneven results. Some areas have benefited from it, while others, including the Buyi village I visited, have been bypassed altogether. Perhaps authorities simply do not see any commercial potential in the Xingyi region. If so, their reasoning is difficult to understand because the area's landscape of limestone hills and green fields rivals anything in Guilin or Shilin's Stone Forest in Yunnan.

Regions that have been targeted for modernization and development include Buyi areas near the famous waterfalls at Huangguoshu, Miao and Dong (Kam) villages in southeastern Guizhou, and, most recently, so-called Tunpu villages near Anshun. The Tunpu claim descent from the first Han settlers in Guizhou and trace their ancestry to thirteenth-century Jiangsu. Visitors to Tunpu villages apparently get a taste of old and "original" thirteenth-century Han culture in the form of rustic-looking buildings and an archaic-sounding dialect. The authenticity of this culture is questionable, but domestic tourists seem drawn to the region.[43]

Ethnic groups engaged in the tourism trade typically sell handicrafts such as batik and embroidery and participate in an assortment of performances and festivals. Crafts, songs, and dances are all carefully packaged for predominantly Han tourist-consumers. Ethnicity has, in effect, become a mass-produced commodity. Oakes has expressed concern that the standardization and commercialization of ethnicities may dilute the original cultures and ultimately result in a form of internal colonialism. As he explains:

> Cultural development and the preservation of "authentic *minzu* culture"
> legitimize a division of labor in which rural labor remains subordinated
> to urban modes of production. . . . The ideology of preservation, in this
> case, colludes with capital to fossilize rural modes of crafts production as
> a national cultural resource, and as a reservoir of skilled yet cheap exploit-
> able labor.[44]

In view of the state-society relations explored in this book, I look at the matter from a different point of view. The ongoing effort to develop tourism is in many respects similar to the Confucian civilizing project of the Qing period. It is above all a state-sponsored attempt to impose order and orthodoxy on Guizhou's indigenous populations. However, unlike the civilizing and domestication projects of eighteenth century Qing authorities, PRC efforts promise immediate and tangible benefits—namely cash infusions for poverty-stricken communities. From the standpoint of these communities, producing commodities for the state tourism enterprise represents a new type of livelihood strategy. In contrast to the illegal and extralegal strategies used during Qing times, these are state-sanctioned. But a common theme still unites present-day Guizhou with its past: People adopt only those strategies that serve their own interests. Moreover, minorities who participate in the tourism trade do not sacrifice their own agency. They find ample room to negotiate with the state and with tourists, and sometimes even gain control of the commodification process.[45] Thus, as in imperial times, local communities still manage to resist (or to bargain their way around) state directives, in order to preserve indigenous livelihood strategies. If these strategies do not work, Guizhou indigenous communities adopt new ones that suit their needs.

As I suggested earlier, Qing-era Guizhou was an arena for an ongoing argument between rulers and the ruled about power and legitimacy. In recent times, this argument has become a relatively civil conversation, but state hegemony in Guizhou still remains fragile and incomplete. During the Qing period, local resistance undermined imperial efforts to assert hegemony. Today, the quieter, but still persistent, voices of indigenous self-interest still prevent the central Chinese government from gaining full control over Guizhou's cultural and political space. The state is omnipresent but not omnipotent, and there are still myriad ways for the indigenes of Guizhou to resist and circumvent it.

NOTES

GZDJQ   *Gongzhong Dang Jiaqing chao zouzhe* 宮中檔嘉慶朝奏摺. (Secret palace memorials of the Jiaqing reign). Unpublished memorials compiled by and held at the National Palace Museum, Taipei.

GZDYZ   *Gongzhong Dang Yongzheng chao zouzhe* 宮中檔雍正朝奏摺 (Secret palace memorials of the Yongzheng reign). Compiled by the National Palace Museum. 32 volumes. Taipei: National Palace Museum Press, 1977–1980.

JBD   *Jiaobu Dang* 剿捕檔 (Record of pursuit and arrest). National Palace Museum, Taipei.

JCLZ mzl   *Junji chu lufu zouzhe, minzu shiwu lei* 軍機處祿復奏摺, 民族事務類 (Grand Council reference copies of palace memorials, minority affairs category). Number One Historical Archives, Beijing.

JQ   Jiaqing reign period (1796–1820), used in dates.

KX   Kangxi reign period (1662–1722), used in dates.

NQX   *Qingdai Jiaqing nianjian Guizhou Buyizu "Nanlong qiyi" ziliao xuanbian* 清代嘉慶年間貴州布依族 "南籠起義" 資料選編 (Collected materials on the "Nanlong Uprising" of the Buyi people during the Jiaqing Reign). Jointly compiled by the China Number One Historical Archives, the Southwest Guizhou People's Committee, and the Guizhou Buyi Studies Committee. Guiyang: Guizhou minzu chubanshe, 1989.

QL   Qianlong reign period (1736–1795), used in dates.

QSL-GZ   *Qing Shilu Guizhou ziliao jiyao* 清實錄貴州資料輯要 (A collection of materials on Guizhou from the Qing Veritable Records). Guiyang: Guizhou renmin chubanshe, 1962).

YZ   Yongzheng reign period (1723–1735), used in dates.

YZHZZ   *Yongzheng chao Hanwen zhupi zouzhe huibian* 雍正朝漢文硃批奏摺彙編 (Collection of Chinese-language palace memorials from the Yongzheng reign), ed. China Number One Historical Archives, 40 volumes. Nanjing: Jiangsu guji chubanshe, 1989.

YZZPYZ   *Yongzheng Zhupi Yuzhi* 雍正硃批諭旨 (The vermillion rescripts and edicts of the Yongzheng reign),10 volumes. Taipei: Wenyuan shuju, 1965 (reprint).

ZPZZ mzl *Zhupi zouzhe, minzu shiwu lei* 硃批奏摺, 民族事務類 (Palace memorials, minority affairs category). Number One Historical Archives, Beijing.

1 / GUIZHOU AND THE LIVELIHOODS APPROACH TO ZHONGJIA HISTORY

1   Aibida, *Qiannan shilue* (A handbook of Guizhou) (1750; reprint, Guiyang: Guizhou Renmin Chubanshe, 1992), 15.

2   In this book, the term *Zhongjia* will be used in reference to the late imperial period, and *Buyi* will be used when discussing the ethnic group in the People's Republic of China. The name *Buyi* and the Chinese characters used to represent it were approved by the Guizhou Nationalities Affairs Commission in August 1953, and "Bouyei" was the transcription adopted for foreign publications in 1991. See Wang Huiliang, "Lun Buyizu mingcheng ji jiancheng" (A discussion of the Buyi name and its short forms), *Buyi xue yanjiu* 1 (1989): 49–58.

3   Here, I use Jacob Whittaker's nuanced interpretation of the term *gaitu guiliu*. As he explains, the word *gui* implies "both a return to former conditions and the reestablishment of proper loyalty to the ruler." See his "Yi Identity and Confucian Empire: Indigenous Local Elites, Cultural Brokerage, and the Colonization of the Lu-ho Tribal Polity of Yunnan, 1174–1745" (PhD dissertation: University of California-Davis, 2008), 338.

4   Li Qingfu and Xu Xianlong, eds. *Buyi jianshi* (A concise history of the Buyi) (Beijing: Minzu chubanshe, 2008), 88–91.

5   Tim Forsyth and Jean Michaud, "Rethinking the Relationships between Livelihoods and Ethnicity in Highland China, Vietnam, and Laos," in *Moving Mountains: Ethnicity and Livelihoods in Highland China, Vietnam, and Laos*, eds. Jean Michaud and Tim Forsyth (Vancouver: University of British Columbia Press, 2011), 13. See also Terry McGee, "Foreword," in the same volume.

6   Forsyth and Michaud, "Rethinking the Relationships," 3.

7   Ibid.

8   James C. Scott, *The Art of Not Being Governed: An Anarchist History of Upland Southeast Asia.* (New Haven, CT: Yale University Press, 2009).

9   Forsyth and Jean Michaud, "Rethinking the Relationships," 13.

10 Christine Bonnin and Sarah Turner, "At what price rice? Food security, livelihoods, and state interventions in upland northern Vietnam," *Geoforum* 43 (2012): 95–105. See also Jean Michaud, "Hmong infrapolitics: A view from Vietnam." *Ethnic and Racial Studies*; Vol. 35, no. 11 (2012): 1853–73; and Sarah Turner, "Making a Living the Hmong Way: An Actor-Oriented Livelihoods Approach to Everyday Politics and Resistance in Upland Vietnam," *Annals of the Association of American Geographers* 102 (2012): 1–22.

11 The same can be said of the Khmu (of Laos), the Tai Lue and Hani (both of Yunnan), and the Tay and Tai (both of Vietnam), as well as of many other communities in the Massif. See, for example, Janet C. Sturgeon, "Rubber Transformations: Post-Socialist Livelihoods and Identities for Akha and Tai Lue Farmers in Xishuangbanna, China" in Michaud and Forsyth, *Moving Mountains*, 193–214. The Buyi—the direct descendants of the Zhongjia—have also developed strategies to preserve their identity in the face of challenges from China's increasingly market-oriented economy. As this volume was being written, Yu Luo, a PhD student in anthropology at Yale University, was conducting fieldwork that examines how the Buyi use ethnotourism, religion, and local festivals to negotiate state development programs.

12 See C. Patterson Giersch, *Asian Borderlands: The Transformation of Qing China's Yunnan Frontier* (Cambridge, MA: Harvard University Press, 2006); John E. Herman, *Amid the Clouds and Mist: China's Colonization of Guizhou, 1200–1700* (Cambridge, MA: Harvard University Press, 2007); and Whittaker, "Yi Identity and Confucian Empire."

13 When using these sources, I keep a wary eye out for the political agenda imposed by China's nationalistic ethnographers and historians, apparent in ideological flourishes and politically inspired turns of phrase. For example,

the editors of a folk narrative might put words like "oppression of the common people" into the mouth of an eighteenth-century Zhongjia teenager unlikely to have this Marxist terminology in her vocabulary. In other instances, modern-day editors might refer to the Nanlong Uprising as an example of "multinationality unity" when all historical evidence indicates that the overwhelming majority of participants were Zhongjia. The insurgents did include a handful of Han mercenaries and a few "Miao" (that is, neither Han nor Zhongjia) who were press-ganged into the rebel army.

14 Because these texts use Chinese characters to represent the sounds rather than the meanings of Zhongjia words, they are often incomprehensible to historians literate in Chinese (and even to those conversant in Buyi). The script was never standardized and often varies from locality to locality. See David Holm, *Killing a Buffalo for the Ancestors: A Zhuang Cosmological Text from Southwest China* (DeKalb, IL: Southeast Asia Publications, 2003), 45–48.

15 See, for example, Zhou Guomao, Wei Xingru, and Wu Wenyi, eds. *Buyizu Mojing wenxue* (Mojing religious literature of the Buyi) (Guiyang: Guizhou renmin chubanshe, 1996). David Holm's *Killing a Buffalo for the Ancestors* provides an annotated translation of two texts commonly used in sacrifices. Holm's companion book, *Recalling Lost Souls: The Baeu Rodo Tai Cosmogonic Texts from Guangxi in Southern China* (Bangkok: White Lotus, 2004), explores the myths and rituals surrounding Baeu Rodo and Mo Loekgyap, two personages often revered as the founding ancestors of the Zhuang and Buyi. Although Holm conducted his fieldwork in northern Guangxi communities officially identified as Zhuang, he discovered that the local dialect and religious practices closely resembled those of the Buyi in Guizhou. He thus refers to his research subjects as "Guangxi Bouyei." See Holm, *Killing a Buffalo*, 12–13.

16 On reading against the grain, see James Scott, *Domination and the Arts of Resistance: Hidden Transcripts* (New Haven, CT: Yale University Press 1990), 87. See also Peter C. Perdue, "Military Mobilization in Eighteenth-Century China, Russia, and Mongolia," *Modern Asian Studies* 30, no. 4 (1996): 783–87.

17 As Jean Michaud notes, economically and politically weak societies facing strong outside pressures are changed by those pressures, but also "actively and creatively use what power they have to interpret, adapt, and even subvert these pressures." See Michaud, "Hmong infrapolitics," 1856.

18 I would suggest that the Zhongjia possessed what Jean Michaud calls a "perceptive resilience . . . founded on an understanding that domination is a fact of life, that the stakes include cultural as much as physical survival, and that with each action come consequences." See Michaud, "Hmong infrapolitics," 1869.

19 Sherry Ortner, *Anthropology and Social Theory: Culture, Power, and the Acting Subject* (Durham, NC: Duke University Press, 2006), 143–44.

20 See Giersch, *Asian Borderlands*; Herman, *Amid the Clouds and Mist*; and Whittaker, "Yi Identity and Confucian Empire."

21 James C. Scott, *Seeing Like a State: How Certain Schemes to Improve the Human Condition Have Failed* (New Haven, CT: Yale University Press, 1998), 3.

22 James A. Millward, *Beyond the Pass: Economy, Ethnicity, and Empire in Qing Central Asia, 1759–1864* (Stanford: Stanford University Press, 1998), 239.

23 Emma Jinhua Teng, *Taiwan's Imagined Geography: Chinese Colonial Travel Writing and Pictures, 1683–1895* (Cambridge, MA: Harvard University Press, 2004), 239–43.

2 / NATURAL, HUMAN, AND HISTORICAL LANDSCAPES

1 Xu Xiake, "Qianri youji" (A diary of travels in Guizhou) in *Xu Xiake youji* (The travel diaries of Xu Xiake), 2 volumes (Shanghai: Shanghai Antiquities Publishing House, 1991 reprint) I: 621–77. For his exploration of the Beipan and Nanpan Rivers, see "Panjiang Kao" in *Xu Xiake youji* II: 1123–28. For a summary of Xu's travels in Yunnan, see Giersch, *Asian Borderlands*, 17–20. For more general information on Xu Xiake's career and writings, see Li Chi, *The Travel Diaries of Hsu Hsia-k'e* (Hong Kong: The Chinese University of Hong Kong, 1974); see also Julian Ward, *Xu Xiake (1587–1641): The Art of Travel Writing* (Richmond, Surrey: Curzon Press, 2001).

2 Xu died before he could edit the diaries, and they were published in their original form. See Richard Strassberg, *Inscribed Landscapes: Travel Writing from Imperial China* (Berkeley and Los Angeles: University of California Press, 1991), 319.

3 Like many of his contemporaries in late imperial China, Xu used the term "Miao" indiscriminately to describe the non-Han peoples he encountered in Guizhou. For some of Xu's more upbeat observations about the region's natural beauty, see his description of the mountain landscapes outside Guiyang in *Xu Xiake youji* II: 636–37, translated in Ward, 105. See also Xu's description of the Baishui waterfalls in *Xu Xiake youji* I: 651–52. The Baishui waterfalls are located at modern-day Huangguoshu, approximately 322 kilometers (200 miles) southwest of Guiyang, and today they are one of Guizhou's main tourist attractions.

4 During his investigation of the Pan Rivers, for instance, Xu discovered that he could not see the river source because a mountain always stood in his way. See *Xu Xiake youji* I: 660, cited in Ward, *Xu Xiake*, 109.

5 Based on modern ethnic patterns of the Dingfan region the people he encountered were probably ancestors of today's Buyi.

6 *Xu Xiake youji* I: 639–42.

7 *Xu Xiake youji* I: 642–45.

8 The Lolo were most likely the ancestors of the people today known as the Yi.

9 He Weifu, *Qingdai Guizhou shangpin jingjishi yanjiu* (Research on the economic history of commodities in Qing dynasty Guizhou) (Beijing: Zhongguo jingji chubanshe, 2007), 3. Guangdong receives 1500–2000 mm of rain per year, Fujian 800–1900 mm, Hunan 1250–1750 mm, and Guangxi 1000–2000 mm. See http://www.chinamaps.org/china/china-map-of-precipitation-annual .html.

10 http://www.allcountries.org/china_statistics/1_18_monthly_sunshine_hours _of_major.html. Both Wenjiang and Chongqing are located in Sichuan.

11 Modern precipitation and temperature statistics are taken from Chai Xingyi, et al. *Zhonghua renmin gongheguo diming cidian: Guizhou sheng* (A dictionary of place names in the People's Republic of China: Guizhou province) (Beijing: Shangwu yin shuguan, 1994), 2–4. See also Robert Jenks, *Insurgency and Social Disorder in Guizhou* (Honolulu: University of Hawaii Press, 1994), 11–12.

12 Aibida, *Qiannan shilue*, 200, 222.

13 George Babcock Cressey, *Land of the 500 Million: A Geography of China* (New York: McGraw Hill, 1955), 223–26. See also Caihua He, Kanging Xiong, Xiaoling Li, and Xing Cheng, "Karst Geomorphology and its Agricultural Implications in Guizhou, China," *Suppl. Geogr. Fis. Dinam. Quat.*III, T. 4 (1998), 121.

14 Although Yangshuo in Guangxi, and Yunnan's Stone Forest (Shilin) claim China's finest karst topography, southwestern Guizhou also has its share of striking landscapes. The rural areas outside the city of Xingyi (Nanlong) offer some of the most stunning vistas anywhere in China.

15 T. R. Tregear, *A Geography of China* (Chicago: Adline Publishing Company, 1965), 265. See also Jenks, *Insurgency and Social Disorder in Guizhou*, 13–14. For a detailed look at karst soils and their impact on Guizhou's agriculture, see He, et al., "Karst Geomorphology," 123–25.

16 Buckwheat and millet are still common foods in Guizhou. During my 2001 visit, I dined with a Xingyi family who enjoyed their rice mixed with steamed buckwheat and millet. Another interesting feature of Guizhou cuisine is that nearly every meal includes at least one boiled vegetable, typically squash or green beans. The vegetables are flavored with chili pepper mixed in to some of the vegetables' cooking liquid. One professor at Guizhou Normal Univer-

sity explained that this is a legacy of leaner times, when people boiled their vegetables because they could not afford cooking oil.

17 See Tregear, 266-67; *Guizhou tongzhi* (Gazetteer of Guizhou province), 1741, 15: 3b, 4a-4b; Aibida, *Qiannan shilue*, 49. See also Claudine Lombard-Salmon, *Un Exemple d'acculturation Chinoise, Guizhou au XVIIIeme siecle* (An example of Chinese acculturation: Guizhou in the eighteenth century) (Paris: Ecole Francais d'Extreme-Orient, 1972), 168.

18 This section is inspired by a similar discussion in Jenks' *Insurgency and Popular Disorder in Guzhou*, 18-20. Jenks uses population and cultivated acreage data to establish a quantitative basis for the subsistence crisis in nineteenth-century Guizhou. My aim here is to do the same for eighteenth-century Guizhou.

19 James Lee, "Food Supply and Population Growth in Southwest China, 1250-1850," *The Journal of Asian Studies* 41, no. 4 (August 1982): 723-24.

20 Ho Ping-ti, *Studies on the Population of China, 1368-1953* (Cambridge, MA: Harvard University Press, 1959), chapters 2 and 3.

21 Lee, "Food Supply and Population Growth," 723-29. It should be noted that in 1775, the Qianlong emperor declared a new commitment to maintaining an accurate registration, and he ordered provincial officials to make sure that everyone was counted. This initiative, rather than true demographic expansion, accounts for the increase of one million persons between 1765 and 1775. Lee notes that in spite of this effort, up to one-quarter of southwest China's population remained unregistered after 1775.

22 Yang Bin, "Differentiation and analysis of the population documents in the early Qing dynasty" *Chinese Journal of Population Science* 1997, 9 (I): 1-8. James Lee suggests that the mid-nineteenth century population was around 7 million. See his "Food Supply and Population Growth in Southwest China," 729.

23 Wang Yeh-chien, *Land Taxation in Imperial China* (Cambridge, MA: Harvard University Press, 1973), 29.

24 Ge Quansheng, Junhu Dai, Fanneng He, Jingyun Zheng, Zhimin Man, and Yun Zhao, "Spatiotemporal dynamics of reclamation and cultivation and its driving factors in parts of China during the last three centuries," *Progress in Natural Science* 14, no. 7 (July 2004): 608. These figures roughly square with Dwight Perkins' estimate of 17 million mu (1.1 ha) by the late eighteenth century. See Dwight Perkins, *Agricultural Development in China, 1368-1968* (Chicago: Aldine, 1969), 234. According to Robert Jenks' calculations, Perkins' estimate equaled about 6.5 percent of Guizhou's total land surface. Most likely, peasants learned to make better use of marginal lands and hillsides,

and terracing became more common. See Jenks, *Insurgency and Social Disorder in Guizhou*, 19.

25 Ge, et al., "Spatiotemporal dynamics," 608.

26 Lombard-Salmon estimates that more than 56 percent of Guizhou's eighteenth-century population was non-Han. See Lombard-Salmon, *Un Exemple d'acculturation Chinoise*, 170.

27 See David M. Deal and Laura Hostetler, trans., *The Art of Ethnography: A Chinese Miao Album* (Seattle: University of Washington Press, 2006). See also Hostetler, *Qing Colonial Enterprise: Ethnography and Cartography in Early Modern China* (Chicago: University of Chicago Press, 2001), 5–6.

28 Chapter 4 also includes a discussion of Zhongjia religion and its influence on local livelihood choices.

29 Both the Bo Y and the Giay reside in the northeastern provinces of Ha Giang and Lao Cai, and they are probably the descendants of Zhongjia refugees who fled Guizhou during the eighteenth and nineteenth centuries. Numbering only 1,450 persons, the Bo Y rank 46th in population among Vietnam's 54 officially recognized ethnic groups, while the Giay, rank 25th with 38,000 people. See http://www.vietnamembassy.org.uk/population.html for these 2007 population estimates. Although the Vietnamese government classifies these groups as two distinct nationalities, linguists generally agree that both are subgroups of the Buyi. See, for example, Holm, *Killing a Buffalo*, 9; William J. Gedney, "Yay, a Northern Tai Language in North Vietnam," *Lingua* 14 (1965): 180–93; and Jerold A. Edmondson, "Change and Variation in Zhuang," in *Papers from the Second Annual Meeting of the Southeast Asian Linguistics Society*, ed. Karen L. Adams and Thomas John Hudak (Arizona State University: Program for Southeast Asian Studies, 1994), 149.

30 One of the criminal cases examined in chapter 4 highlights the close ties between the Zhongjia and the Nong. Imperial officials usually wrote character *Nong* with the character component meaning "dog" (犭農). This study combines the "dog" radical (犭) with the homophonous character *nong* (農, meaning farmer or peasant). In a few Qing sources, *Nong* is written with the "human" character component (儂).

31 Northern Zhuang and Southern Zhuang are informal designations used by linguists and anthropologists. They are not official ethnic classifications. The Zhuang language encompasses two major dialect groups, Northern and Southern. David Holm suggests that these two dialects might be more accurately classified as separate languages, for there is greater linguistic difference between them than there is between Northern Zhuang and Buyi, or between Southern Zhuang and the Nung and Tay languages of northern Vietnam.

Furthermore, although the Nung and Tay are recognized as separate ethnic groups in Vietnam, in China, they are all classified as Zhuang. See Holm, *Killing a Buffalo*, 7–8. See also Snyder, "Bouyei Phonology," 378.

32 Wil C. Snyder and David Holm have suggested that the languages within the Northern and Central groups form a linguistic continuum extending from Guizhou into Vietnam. See Snyder, "Bouyei Phonology," 378; see also Holm, *Killing a Buffalo*, 7–8. For a more in-depth discussion of the taxonomy of Kadai languages, see Jerold A. Edmondson and David B. Solnit, eds., *Comparative Kadai: The Tai Branch* (Arlington TX: University of Texas at Arlington Summer Institute of Linguistics, 1997), 2. See also Anthony Diller, "Introduction," in *The Tai-Kadai Languages*, ed. Anthony V. N. Diller, Jerold A. Edmonson, and Luo Yingxian (London and New York: Routledge, 2008), 3–8.

33 For a historical overview of the Hundred Yue, see Zhou Guoyan, "An Introduction to the Kam-Tai (Zhuang-Dong) Group of Languages in China" in *Languages and Cultures of the Kam-Tai (Zhuang Dong) Group: A Word List (English-Thai version),* edited by Zhou Guoyan and Somsonge Burusphat (Bangkok: Sahadhammika Co. Ltd, 1996), 4–7. For a discussion of the DNA and linguistic evidence linking today's Kadai populations to the Baiyue, see Jerold A. Edmondson, "The power of language over the past: Tai settlement and Tai linguistics in southern China and northern Vietnam" in *Studies in Southeast Asian languages and linguistics,* ed. Jimmy G. Harris, Somsonge Burusphat and James E. Harris (Bangkok: Ek Phim Tai Co. Ltd., 2007), 39–64.

34 Edmondson, "The power of language over the past," 48. See also Zhou Guoyan, "Linguistic and Historical Explanations of the Names for the Buyi, a Group of Tai People in Southwestern China," *Proceedings of the Fourth International Symposium on Languages and Linguistics, Pan-Asiatic Linguistics* (January 8–10, 1996), 970.

35 Zhou Guoyan, "An Introduction to the Kam-Tai (Zhuang-Dong) Group of Languages in China,"4.

36 Zhou Guoyan, "Linguistic and Historical Explanations," 970.

37 Holm, *Killing a Buffalo*, 12.

38 As Patricia Ebrey writes, "We have to infer that . . . [non-Han in southern China] claimed descent from Chinese migrants either because they wanted to believe it (looking down on non-Han themselves), or because it was in their best interest to do so (for local politics, social prestige, or whatever)." See Patricia Ebrey, "Surnames and Han Chinese Identity," in *Negotiating Ethnicities in China and Taiwan*, edited by Melissa J. Brown (Berkeley: Institute for East Asian Studies, University of California, 1996), 23.

39 When I interviewed a Buyi family near Xingyi in 2001, they claimed to be

the descendants of settlers who had arrived in Guizhou from Jiangsu during the Ming period. Buyi scholar Yu Luo (see chapter 1) has also reported many claims of Jiangsu descent. Personal e-mail correspondences, June 8, 2010 and June 14, 2010. For further discussion of these avowed Jiangnan origins and the accompanying genealogies, see "Tantao Ceheng Buyizu yuan" (Investigating the origins of the Buyi nationality in Ceheng), *Ceheng wenshi ziliao* (Literary and historical materials from Ceheng) 3 (1985): 74–75. This anonymous article hereafter cited as "Tantao Ceheng."

40 Holm, *Killing a Buffalo*, 11. Katherine Kaup suggests that Zhuang genealogies showing Jiangnan or Huguang origins may also be falsified for similar reasons. See her *Creating the Zhuang: Ethnic Politics in China* (London: Lynne Rienner Publishers, Inc., 2000), 90. Jeffrey Barlow also notes that many Zhuang, "[who] lived sufficiently close to Han Chinese to learn their language and cultural practices . . . would later claim that their ancestors had been Han Chinese and that living in isolated districts, they had early received local influences which had rusticated them." See Barlow's online manuscript, "The Zhuang," http://mcel.pacificu.edu/as/resources/zhuang/zhuang9.htm #_edn15, Chapter 9.

41 Gu Yin, "Buyizu zuyuan yanjiu zongshu" (A summary of research on the origins of the Buyi nationality), *Buyi xue yanjiu* 6 (1998): 23. Chu was a powerful kingdom based in present-day Hunan. Its territory extended into northern Guangxi. Gu notes, however, that some Qing-era local gazetteers disputed the idea that the Zhongjia descended from Ma Yan's troops. A Miao album entry on the "Kayou Zhongjia" of southwestern Guizhou also hints at Yongguan origins. See Deal and Hostetler, *The Art of Ethnography*, 13

42 Samuel R. Clarke, *Among the Tribes in Southwest China* (London: Morgan and Scott, Ltd., 1911), 95.

43 Zhou Guoyan, "Linguistic and Historical Explanations," 980.

44 The final "x" in *Boux* indicates the fourth tone in both Buyi and Zhuang. It is not pronounced as a consonant. See Holm, *Killing a Buffalo for the Ancestors*, 8.

45 Holm, *Recalling Lost Souls*, 6.

46 For a discussion of the various characters used to write the name "Zhuang," see Huang Jiaxin, *Zhuangzu diqu tusi zhidu yu gaitu guiliu yanjiu* (Research on the tusi system and gaitu guilu in Zhuang nationality regions) (Hefei: Hefei gongye daxue chubanshe, 2007), 30.

47 Zhou Guoyan, "Linguistic and Historical Explanations," 980. See also his "An Introduction to the Kam-Tai Group of Languages in China," 6. In both pieces, Zhou offers and then rejects alternate hypotheses for the origins of

the term *Zhongjia*. One theory suggests that the word *Zhongjia* derived from homophonic words meaning "heavy armor," a reference to the armor worn during wars of the Song, Yuan, and Ming periods. Another explanation suggests that the name derives from the character meaning "to cultivate" (*zhong* 種), a reference to the Zhongjia's rice-farming livelihood.

48   According to Zhou Guoyan, the modern Buyi never refer to themselves as "Buzhong" or "Zhong." See his "An Introduction to the Kam-Tai Group of Languages in China," 6.

49   Wang Huiliang, "Lun Buyizu mingcheng ji jiancheng," 50–51. The final "k" in *bouxhek* and *bouxhak* indicates the seventh tone in Buyi and Zhuang. See Holm, *Killing a Buffalo*, 224.

50   In some respects, the nomenclature in Guizhou parallels the ecological and ethnic stratifications described in Leach's classic study of mainland Southeast Asia. See Edmund. R. Leach, "The Frontiers of 'Burma," *Comparative Studies in History and Society* Vol. 3, no. 1 October 1960): 49–68.

51   Wang Huiliang, "Lun Buyizu mingcheng ji jiancheng," 50–51 and Holm, *Killing a Buffalo*, 9. The final "z" in *bouxnongz* indicates the second tone in Buyi and Zhuang, and the final "h" in *bouxloeh* indicates the sixth tone.

52   Holm, *Killing a Buffalo*, 9.

53   Interestingly, many residents of northern Guangxi also identify themselves as *Bouyeix*. In southern Guangxi, by contrast, many local residents use the self-appellations *Bouxnungz* and *Bouxdoj*. See Zhou Guoyan, "An Introduction to the Kam-Tai Group of Languages in China," 2. See also "Tantao Ceheng," 75. (The final "z" in *Bouxnungz* indicates the fourth tone in Zhuang, and the final "j" in *Bouxdoj* indicates the third tone. See Holm, *Killing a Buffalo*, 8–9, 223).

54   This decision, which was made at a special meeting convened by the Guizhou Nationalities Affairs Commission, was not taken lightly. There were at least twenty other names in the running, including "Buyueyi," and "Buyue." Some delegates at the meeting argued that "Buyueyi" was the closest approximation of the group's autonym, but others objected to the idea of creating a three-character name because other ethnic groups employed one- or two-character names. Still others were uncomfortable about using the character *yue*, perhaps because of its connections to the Yue peoples of Chinese antiquity. See Thomas S. Mullaney, *Coming to Terms with the Nation: Ethnic Classification in Modern China* (Berkeley: University of California Press, 2011), 111–12.

55   The character used to write the name Zhuang was officially changed from 僮 to 壮 in 1965. See Huang Jiaxin, *Zhuangzu diqu tusi zhidu*, 30.

56 According to Katherine Palmer Kaup, Guizhou Nationality Affairs officials insisted that the Buyi in that province did not want to be labeled Zhuang. See *Creating the Zhuang*, 88.

57 Holm, *Killing a Buffalo*, 7–8.

58 Kaup, *Creating the Zhuang*, 89.

59 Mullaney, *Coming to Terms with the Nation*, 88. A similar issue arose along the Yunnan-Sichuan border. The Pumi ethnic group was divided into two separate categories, according to provincial boundaries; those in Yunnan were classified as Pumi, while those in Sichuan were classified as Zang. See Stevan Harrell, "The Nationalities Question and the Prmi Problem," in *Negotiating Ethnicities in China and Taiwan*, ed. Melissa J. Brown (Berkeley: Institute for East Asian Studies, University of California, 1996), 274–96.

60 Holm, *Killing a Buffalo*, 8–10.

61 During the 1950s, Chinese officials considered dividing Guangxi into Eastern (predominantly Han) and Western (predominantly Zhuang) administrative areas that would better reflect ethnic distribution throughout the province. The idea was abandoned in favor of unifying the province into the Guangxi Zhuang Autonomous Region, one of five provincial-level autonomous regions in China. See Kaup, *Creating the Zhuang*, 92–96. For problems arising from the classification of the Zhuang in Yunnan, see Kaup, "Regionalism Versus Ethnic Nationalism in the People's Republic of China," *The China Quarterly*, 172 (2002): 863–84.

62 Changing provincial boundaries is difficult, although not impossible. Another solution might be to maintain the Guangxi-Guizhou border but allow the Buyi category to cross it.

63 Holm, *Killing a Buffalo*, 11.

64 According to Yu Luo, however, there seems to be a growing recognition, particularly among members of the communities along the Guizhou-Guangxi border, that the Buyi and Zhuang share more similarities than differences. It seems unlikely that anyone from either side of the Buyi -Zhuang divide will mount a campaign to change the official nomenclature, but members of both ethnic groups will continue to explore their shared heritage in an informal way. E-mail correspondence and conversations, June-August 2011 and March 2012.

65 *Guizhou tongzhi* (Gazetteer of Guizhou province) 1697, 30: 21b; *Nanlong fuzhi* (Gazetteer of Nanlong prefecture) 1765, 2: 18.

66 Quoted in Hostetler, *Qing Colonial Enterprise*, 151.

67 *Xilong zhouzhi* (Gazetteer of Xilong department), 1673, 6: 2a.

68 The dog character component was also used to represent the ethnonyms of

other non-Han groups, including the Zhuang, the Miao, and the Yao. It could even be appended to the character for *Hui* (回), the name for Chinese Muslims. David Holm notes that the dog component originally referred to the classical Chinese myth of Panhu, the legendary canine revered as the ancestor of many non-Han peoples in southern China. Over time, this orthographic convention increasingly "reflected and contributed to a view, common in Chinese society at the time, that the southern non-Han peoples were sub-human." See Holm, *Recalling Lost Souls*, 5. On the application of the dog radical to Muslim populations, see Atwill, *The Chinese Sultanate: Islam, Ethnicity, and the Panthay Rebellion in Southwest China, 1856–1873* (Stanford: Stanford University Press, 2005), 25–26 and Jonathan N. Lipman, *Familiar Strangers: A History of Muslims in Northwest China* (Seattle: University of Washington Press, 1997), 41, note 54.

69 Here, as in Xu Xiake's account, "Miao" is a generic term for non-Han ethnic groups.

70 Aibida, *Qiannan shilue*, 223.

71 For more on this, see chapter 3.

72 As Donald Sutton observes in his study of the Miao in Hunan Province, "Acculturation does not mean assimilation, that is, a change of identification." See his "Ethnicity and the Miao Frontier," in *Empire at the Margins: Culture, Ethnicity, and Frontier in Early Modern China*, ed. Pamela Kyle Crossley, Helen F. Siu, and Donald S. Sutton (Berkeley: University of California Press, 2006), 220. For more on this, see chapter 4.

73 Clarke, *Among the Tribes*, 97.

74 Ibid., 98.

75 Ibid., 100. Clarke noted, however, that unlike their Han counterparts, Zhongjia women in rural areas generally did not bind their feet and often worked alongside men in the rice fields.

76 Ibid., 107–8.

77 Shi Jizhong "Qian Gui bianjiang Zhuangzu Buyizude tingmu zhidu" (The tingmu system of the Zhuang and Buyi nationalities in the Qian-Gui [Guizhou-Guangxi] borderlands) in *Xinan minzu shehui xingtai yu jingji wenhua leixing* (The social formations and cultural and economic types of the ethnic minorities in southwest China) (Kunming: Yunnan Educational Publishing House, 1997), 292.

78 For more on the *mogong* (called *bumo* in the Buyi dialects of northwestern Guangxi and southwestern Guizhou), see David Holm, *Killing a Buffalo*, 21–24 and chapter 4 of this book.

79 Shi Jizhong, "Qian Gui bianjiang," 298–99.

80 Ibid., 300.

81 *Nanlong fuzhi* 1765, 2: 20a–b. See also Li Qingfu and Xu Xianlong, *Buyizu jianshi*, 78–79.

82 Li Qingfu and Xu Xianlong, *Buyizu jianshi*, 88–89. See also He Weifu, *Qingdai Guizhou shangpin jingjishi yanjiu*, 117–19, 238–42.

83 Stevan Harrell, "The History of the History of the Yi," in *Cultural Encounters on China's Ethnic Frontiers*, ed. Stevan Harrell (Seattle: University of Washington Press, 1995), 85.

84 Both the Nanzhao and the Dali controlled territory in present-day Yunnan. See Herman, *Amid the Clouds and Mist*, chapter 1.

85 John Herman, "The Mu'ege Kingdom: a brief history of a frontier empire in Southwest China" in *Political Frontiers, Ethnic Boundaries, and Human Geographies in Chinese History*, ed. Nicola Di Cosmo and Don J. Wyatt (London: Routledge Curzon, 2003), 245–85.

86 John Herman, "The Cant of Conquest: Tusi Offices and China's Political Incorporation of the Southwest Frontier" in *Empire at the Margins: Culture, Ethnicity, and Frontier in Early Modern China*, ed. Pamela Kyle Crossley, Helen F. Siu, and Donald S. Sutton (Berkeley: University of California Press, 2006), 151.

87 Herman, "The Mu'ege Kingdom," 265.

88 Herman, *Amid the Clouds and Mist*, chapters 5–6.

89 The names San Miao, You-Miao, and Miao-Min appear in the Chinese classics and some early historical writings, but it is doubtful that these groups were Miao in the modern sense of the word. Jenks posits that in these earliest sources, "Miao" was simply used as a generic for the non-Han peoples of southern China. References to the Miao continue through the Qin and early Han but disappear from the historical record until the Song dynasty. Thereafter, and especially from the Ming dynasty onward, the name "Miao" appears in historical writing with increasing frequency, often in a compound such as "Miaoren" or "Miaoman." See Jenks, *Insurgency and Social Disorder in Guizhou*, 32.

90 Scott, *The Art of Not Being Governed*, 140–41.

91 During the 1970s and 1980s, many Hmong fled Laos for the temporary shelter of refugee camps in Thailand. Some were resettled in third countries such as the United States, Canada, Australia, France, and even Sweden. Some Hmong refugees made permanent homes in Thailand, and some were eventually repatriated to Laos. Today, the Miao of China number around 7.5 million. Their classification as a single nationality remains problematic. As Norma Diamond explains, it is difficult to see how the Stalinist criteria for nationali-

ties apply to the Miao, given that many subgroups speak mutually unintelligible dialects, and do not share a common territory, scattered as they are over several different provinces. See her "Defining the Miao: Ming, Qing, and Contemporary Views," in *Cultural Encounters on China's Ethnic Frontiers*, ed. Stevan Harrell (Seattle: University of Washington Press, 1995), 92.

92 Diamond, 99–100.

93 Jenks, *Insurgency and Social Disorder in Guizhou*, 31–32; Hostetler, *Qing Colonial Enterprise*, 106–7. For a complete list of these names, see Hostetler, "Chinese Ethnography in the Eighteenth Century: Miao Albums of Guizhou Province" (PhD dissertation, University of Pennsylvania, 1995), 159–204.

94 Diamond, "Defining the Miao," 95–96: Jenks, *Insurgency and Social Disorder in Guizhou*, 33.

95 Jenks, *Insurgency and Social Disorder in Guizhou*, 33–35.

96 Diamond, "Defining the Miao," 95.

97 To the extent that Ming population statistics can be trusted, it appears that the registered Han population of Guizhou at least doubled between 1502 and 1602. According to James Lee's estimates, there were around 265,000 registered Han in Guizhou in the former year and approximately 530,000 a century later. These figures include military populations as well as civilian households. See his "Food Supply and Population Growth in Southwest China, 1250–1850," 715.

98 The six "routes" were Yuanshun (modern-day Guiyang), Bozhou (modern-day Zunyi), Xintai (modern-day Guiding), Puding (modern-day Anshun), Puan, and Wusa (modern-day Weining).

99 Herman, *Amid the Clouds and Mist*, 101. The provincial administration commissioner was the early Ming version of a provincial governor. R. Kent Guy translates this term "commissioner for the promulgation and dissemination of government policies." See his *Qing Governors and their Provinces: The Evolution of Territorial Administration in China, 1644–1796* (Seattle: University of Washington Press, 2010), 34.

100 For more on the establishment of Guizhou province, see Herman, "The Mu'ege Kingdom," 6–21. See also his "The Cant of Conquest," 136–39 and *Amid the Clouds and Mist*, 94–102.

101 The Yuan and Ming also instituted the *tusi* system in Guangxi, Yunnan, Guangdong, and Sichuan, in the westernmost regions of Huguang (Hubei and Hunan), and in several other provinces with large non-Han populations.

102 For a list of the names for all the civil and military native offices in use during the Ming and Qing periods, see John Herman, "National Integration and Regional Hegemony: The Political and Cultural Dynamics of Qing State

Expansion, 1650–1750" (PhD dissertation, University of Washington, 1993), 24–27. For a succinct discussion of the *tusi* system, see also John Herman, "Empire in the Southwest: Early Qing Reforms to the Native Chieftain System," *Journal of Asian Studies* 56, no. 1 (February 1997): 50.

103 F. W. Mote, *Imperial China, 900–1800* (Cambridge, MA: Harvard University Press, 1999), 704–5.

104 James Lee, "Food Supply and Population Growth," 715.

105 Herman, "The Mu'ege Kingdom," 260.

106 For a detailed account of Yongli's peripatetic reign, see Lynn Struve, *The Southern Ming, 1644–1662* (New Haven: Yale University Press, 1984), chapter 5.

107 Jobtei (in Chinese Zhaobutai), the Manchu general in charge of southwestern Guizhou, received military assistance from the Cen native officials who controlled the Guangxi-Guizhou borderlands. See *Dading fuzhi (Gazetteer of Dading prefecture)* 1850, 48: 3a.

108 Jobtei received assistance from Cen Jilu, the native prefect of Sicheng in Guangxi. Until this point in his career, Wu Sangui was best known as the erstwhile Ming general who in 1644 allowed Qing forces to enter China at the Shanhai Pass, the easternmost gate of the Great Wall. As chapter 3 explains, Wu Sangui soon fell out of favor with Qing authorities, and so, in due course, did Cen Jilu's successors.

109 *Dading fuzhi,* 48: 3a.

110 See Struve, *The Southern Ming,* 169–78.

111 Kai-fu Tsao, "The Rebellion of the Three Feudatories Against the Manchu Throne in China, 1673–1681: Its Setting and Significance" (PhD diss., Columbia University), 1965, 52–53.

112 Ibid., 60.

3 / THE CONSOLIDATION OF QING RULE

1   The largest sub-provincial unit was the prefecture (*fu*). The department (*zhou*) was subordinate to the prefecture and usually had jurisdiction over at least one county (*xian*).

2   In a richly detailed chapter, Kent Smith describes the two-year campaign to pacify this small corner of Guizhou and its impact on subsequent policy in southwestern China. See Kent Clarke Smith, "Ch'ing Policy and the Development of Southwest China: Aspects of Ortai's Governor-Generalship, 1726–1731" (PhD diss., Yale University, 1971), 26–39. For brief accounts of the campaign in Dingfan-Guangshun, see also Lombard-Salmon, *Un exemple d'acculturation Chinoise,* 231–32, and Guy, *Qing Governors and Their Provinces,* 340–43.

3 Smith, "Ch'ing Policy and the Development of Southwest China," 26–39. See also Guy, *Qing Governors and their Provinces*, 334–48. Both Smith and Guy spell *Ortai* based on a romanization of the Manchu name. In the old Wade-Giles system it is spelled *O-erh-tai*. Other scholars spell it *Eertai*, using the *pinyin* romanization system.

4 Smith, "Ch'ing Policy and the Development of Southwest China," 97–100.

5 For detailed accounts of the violence in northeastern Yunnan and southeastern Guizhou, see Smith, "Ch'ing Policy and the Development of Southwest China," 157–71 and 256–89, respectively. For southeastern Guizhou, see also Herman, "National Integration and Regional Hegemony," chapters 4 and 6. For a discussion of the violence in southern Yunnan, see Giersch, *Asian Borderlands*, 43–63.

6 Hostetler, *Qing Colonial Enterprise*, 30, 119.

7 Copper was a key component of Qing coins. For more on the Yunnan copper industry, see Smith, "Ch'ing Policy and the Development of Southwest China," chapter 4.

8 Aibida, *Qiannan shilue*, 229.

9 *Yongzheng Zhupi Yuzhi* (The vermillion rescripts and edicts of the Yongzheng reign) (Taipei: Wenyuan shuju, 1965), 5: 2603. Ortai memorial YZ 4/9/19. Hereafter cited as YZZPYZ. Dates are rendered according to the Chinese lunar calendar, using the Chinese order: year/month/day.

10 Kent Smith asserts that Han colonization and settlement were unintended effects of Qing policy rather than an underlying motive. At one point, Ortai had suggested dispossessing the Zhongjia altogether and turning their land over to soldiers under the military colony (*tuntian*) system. Ortai proposed to settle Chinese farmers on any land not allocated to the military, with the express purpose of preventing Zhongjia from reoccupying the area. He abandoned this scheme, although he did insist that Zhongjia land ownership be regulated according to Chinese patterns, using deeds and official seals. As Smith writes, "The Zhongjia were efficient farmers upon whom officials now had the necessary leverage to exact payment of taxes. The introduction of Chinese officialdom . . . may have put Zhongjia at a disadvantage vis-à-vis land-hungry Chinese, but this was a by-product rather than a purpose of imperial policy for the region." See "Ch'ing Policy and the Development of Southwest China," 98.

11 Scott, *Seeing Like a State*, 3, 186–87, 190. Susan Mann has also noted that, like early modern European states, the Qing showed an "increasing capacity for seeing like a state." See her "Mann on Hostetler," in *Journal of Colonialism and Colonial History* vol. 2, no. 3 (Winter 2001).

12   These concepts were originally put forth by the anthropologist E. R. Leach in his work on pre-colonial Burma and later amplified by James Scott. See Leach, "The Frontiers of 'Burma,'" 185–87; see also Scott, *Seeing Like a State*, 186–87.

13   Leach, "The Frontiers of 'Burma,'"185–87. As James Scott notes, "Such spaces, it goes without saying, have served as refuges for fleeing peasants, bandits, rebels, bandits, and the pretenders who have often threatened kingdoms." See Scott, *Seeing Like a State*, 187. It could be argued that the Prince of Gui, the self-styled Southern Ming emperor, took advantage of the non-state spaces in southwestern China to mount his resistance against the Qing.

14   Daniel McMahon suggests that *gaitu guiliu* in the Miao regions of western Hunan illustrated the Qing state's desire to transform non-state spaces into state spaces. He suggests that "non-state spaces" are analogous to the remote mountainous regions known as *aoqu*. See his "Restoring the Garden: Yan Ruyi and the Civilizing of China's Internal Frontiers, 1795–1805" (PhD diss., University of California-Davis, 1998), 333–34. Although he does not use the precise terminology, John Herman makes a similar case for the Guzhou region of southeastern Guizhou. See his "National Integration and Regional Hegemony," chapter 4.

15   A fourth category could be used to describe indigenous polities that were largely independent of the imperial state, such as the Nasu Yi states of northwestern Guizhou and Yunnan. And a fifth category might describe the Tai polities of southern Yunnan that paid dual fealty to China's imperial state and the kingdoms of mainland Southeast Asia. See Herman, *Amid the Clouds and Mist*, Whittaker, "Yi Identity and Confucian Empire," and Giersch, *Asian Borderlands*.

16   During the spring and summer of 1659, Beijing renewed the investiture of more than forty *tusi* throughout Guizhou. See He Renzhong, et al., *Guizhou tongshi. Di san juan, Qingdai de Guizhou* (A comprehensive history of Guizhou, part 3, Qing dynasty Guizhou) (Beijing: Dangdai Zhongguo chubanshe, 2002), 223.

17   This measure was originally proposed by Guizhou Governor Zhao Tingchen. See Herman, "Empire in the Southwest," 48–49.

18   Herman, "National Integration and Regional Hegemony," 54–55.

19   Herman, "Empire in the Southwest," 60–66.

20   Giersch, *Asian Borderlands,* 44. See also Yingcong Dai, *The Sichuan Frontier and Tibet: Imperial Strategy in the Early Qing* (Seattle: University of Washington Press, 2009), 28–29.

21   After Wu captured and executed the last Ming pretender (the Prince of Gui,

whom Wu pursued into Burma) in 1662, he was named a Prince of the Blood and subsequently gained control over all the provincial officials in Yunnan and Guizhou. Wu claimed that tax revenues and profits from his monopolies would be used for public works. See Tsao, "The Rebellion of the Three Feudatories," 58–60, 68.

22 In particular, Wu Sangui targeted the Shuixi region, the traditional stronghold of the powerful An family. The Qing court authorized Wu to depose An Kun, the Nasu Yi native official, on grounds that An had collaborated with Ming loyalists who had straggled into Shuixi. To be sure, the native ruler had taken up arms, but only as a result of Wu's repeated provocations. The Shuixi region was subsequently divided into four prefectures, all of them under Wu's personal supervision. In 1683, the Kangxi Emperor restored the Shuixi ruling clan's official titles, and this clan remained in power until 1727. See Herman, *Amid the Clouds and Mist*, 201–15.

23 Kai-fu Tsao estimates that Wu commanded 64,000 troops by 1665, costing the Qing more than nine million taels annually. See his "The Rebellion of the Three Feudatories," 65–68. For more on Wu's self-aggrandizing schemes, see Yingcong Dai, "The Rise of the Southwestern Frontier under the Qing, 1640–1800" (PhD diss., University of Washington, 1996), 86–93.

24 This rebellion, the so-called War of the Three Feudatories, began when the Kangxi emperor ordered Wu Sangui and two other feudatories, Geng Jingzhong, and Shang Kexi, to resign their hereditary governorships. Wu then killed the regularly appointed governor of Yunnan and proclaimed a new dynasty, the Zhou. By 1674, he had occupied six provinces in southern and southwestern China, and had set up a new capital in Hunan. Later that year, the other two feudatories joined Wu's cause, bringing Fujian and Guangdong under the rebel banner. In 1678, Wu Sangui died in Hunan, leaving his throne to his grandson, who later retreated to Yunnan. The rebellion dragged on for another two years (until the younger Wu committed suicide in late 1681) and Qing armies quickly reestablished imperial control over the southwest. For a detailed account of the rebellion, see Tsao, "The Rebellion of the Three Feudatories," chapters 2 and 3. See also Herman, *Amid the Clouds and Mist*, 216–18.

25 One official who fell under the emperor's suspicion was Cai Yurong, governor-general of Yunnan and Guizhou from 1682 to 1686. At one time an imperial favorite for his role in suppressing Wu Sangui, Cai was eventually dismissed from office after he pushed for an aggressive policy against the native officials. See Dai, *The Sichuan Frontier and Tibet*, 28–29.

26 Smith, "Ch'ing Policy and the Development of Southwest China," 44.

27 For a comprehensive discussion of Yongzheng's reforms, see Pei Huang, *Autocracy at Work: A Study of the Yung-cheng Period, 1723-35* (Bloomington: Indiana University Press, 1975). See also see Mote, *Imperial China, 900-1800*, 887-911.

28 For example, Yongzheng legalized the tax surcharges that local officials traditionally assessed to augment their meager salaries and used the surcharges to subsidize merit increases for all officials. See Madeline Zelin, *The Magistrate's Tael: Rationalizing Fiscal Reform in Eighteenth-Century China* (Berkeley: University of California Press, 1984). The Yongzheng emperor also created an inner court haven where he could discuss policy with small, informal committees made up of his most trusted officials, and made expanded use of palace memorials (*zouzhe*), confidential reports submitted directly to the throne by a select group of officials. He adopted the use of palace memorials from the Kangxi Emperor, who had originally employed the secret communiqués to establish a private channel of communication with officials in the Imperial Household Department (*neiwu fu*). From there, the practice spread to other government organs in the capital and then to provincial officials. Whereas Kangxi had allowed only a few favored individuals to submit memorials, Yongzheng extended the privilege to a much larger number of men. This ensured a steady flow of information from all over the realm, and also enabled the emperor to cultivate close relationships with the memorialists by writing detailed responses in vermilion ink, known as vermilion rescripts (*zhupi*) on the original documents. As Smith explains, Ortai's relationship with Yongzheng flourished in large part as a result of their correspondence through memorials and rescripts. See his "Ch'ing Policy and the Development of Southwest China." For more detailed discussions on the inner court and palace memorial system, see Beatrice S. Bartlett, *Monarchs and Ministers: The Grand Council in Mid-Ch'ing China 1723-1830* (Berkeley: University of California Press, 1991). See also Mark C. Elliot, "The Manchu-language Archives of the Qing Dynasty and the Origins of the Palace Memorial System," *Late Imperial China* 22: 1 (June 2001): 48-55.

29 Edict of YZ 2/5/17, reprinted in *Qing Shilu Guizhou ziliao jiyao* (A collection of materials on Guizhou from the Qing Veritable Records) (Guiyang: Guizhou renmin chubanshe, 1962), 305. This collection hereafter cited as QSL-GZ. Also cited in Smith, "Ch'ing Policy and the Development of Southwest China," 45.

30 The transition from a conservative policy to a more aggressive one is summarized in Smith, 44-46. Ortai was a prime example of Yongzheng's "new men"—officials whose loyalty and talent compensated for a lack of family

connections and scholarly credentials. The Emperor preferred such officials to men of letters, whom he considered less likely to be his willing tools. "New men" owed their career success almost entirely to Yongzheng and thus became, in Smith's words, "eager instruments of [the emperor's] assault against the status quo in the empire." See Smith, "Ch'ing Policy and the Development of Southwest China," 14-16. For more on Yongzheng's "new men," see William T. Rowe, *Saving the World: Chen Hongmou and Elite Consciousness in Eighteenth-Century China* (Stanford: Stanford University Press, 2001), esp. 45-85.

31   The Guizhou governor expressed concern that the unlawful native officials in Dingfan-Guangshun would have a bad influence on the more quiescent ones. See YZZPYZ 1: 580-81, Mao Wenquan memorial YZ 2/10/24. Provincial officials dealing with the unrest in Nanlong also complained that the native rulers failed to hand criminals over to Qing authorities. See, for example, *Yongzheng chao Hanwen zhupi zouzhe huibian* (Collection of Chinese-language palace memorials from the Yongzheng reign), compiled by the Zhongguo di yi lishi dang'an guan. (Nanjing: Jiangsu guji chubanshe, 1989) 9: 8-10, YZ 5/2/2, Han Liangfu memorial. This collection hereafter cited as YZHZZ.

32   YZZPYZ 5: 2603, Ortai memorial, YZ 4/9/19.

33   Dai, *The Sichuan Frontier and Tibet*, 107-8. See also Giersch, *Asian Border-lands*, 44-45.

34   Aibida, *Qiannan shilue*, 43.

35   Most of the *tusi* in this region were Zhongjia, but a few were Miao. See Aibida, *Qiannan shilue*, 43, for a comprehensive list of the *fan*.

36   Smith, "Ch'ing Policy and the Development of Southwest China," 49.

37   *Guangshun zhouzhi* (Gazetteer of Guangshun department) 1846, 5: 14a and 17a-b, also cited in Smith, 54-55.

38   YZZPYZ 1: 574-75, Mao Wenquan memorial, YZ 2/5/14.

39   YZZPYZ 1: 575, imperial rescript on Mao Wenquan memorial, YZ 2/5/14.

40   YZZPYZ 1: 580-581, Mao Wenquan, 2/10/24. See also *Gongzhong Dang Yongzheng Chao* (Secret palace memorials of the Yongzheng reign) (Taipei: National Palace Museum, 1978), 4: 372-73, YZ 2/10/25, Gao Qizhuo memorial. This collection hereafter cited as GZDYZ. (Note: YZZPYZ is organized by memorialist, while GZDYZ is organized by date. References in this chapter are written to reflect the internal organization of each collection.) Mao Wenquan tried to hide Qing failures from the emperor for as long as possible. The true course of events came to light in Gao Qizhuo's memorials. See Smith, "Ch'ing Policy and the Development of Southwest China," 60-66.

41 GZDYZ 5: 773–76, YZ 3/1/26, Gao Qizhuo memorial.

42 Ibid.

43 YZZPYZ 1: 580, Mao Wenquan memorial, YZ 2/8/28. See also YZZPYZ 1: 581, Mao Wenquan memorial, YZ 2/10/24.

44 There was, however, one minor setback at the very beginning of the campaign. Before the Qing expeditionary force set out from Dingfan, five hundred Qing soldiers arrived in a village inhabited by members of the Qing Miao ethnic group, not Zhongjia. The inhabitants had already fled into a nearby grove, and the troops set up camp in the village. The troops burned down this and four other friendly Miao villages. The villagers, understandably enraged by the wanton destruction, surrounded and attacked the troops, wounding several. See YZZPYZ 1: 580–81, Mao Wenquan memorial, YZ 2/10/24, and GZDYZ 774, 3/1/26, Gao Qizhuo memorial.

45 Gong Yin, *Zhongguo tusi zhidu* [The *tusi* system in China] (Kunming: Yunnan minzu chubanshe, 1992), 840–41.

46 YZZPYZ 1: 582, Mao Wenquan memorial, YZ 2/11/17.

47 Ibid.

48 Smith, "Ch'ing Policy and the Development of Southwest China," 67.

49 Edict of YZ 3/4/13, reprinted in QSL-GZ, 497.

50 Shi Liha assumed this position in the spring of 1725, taking over from Mao Wenquan.

51 YZZPYZ 1: 322–23, Shi Liha memorial, YZ 3/10/13.

52 YZZPYZ 1: 327, Shi Liha memorial, YZ 4/3/20.

53 Gao Qizhuo's original plan called for the transfer of troops from Dading in northwestern Guizhou to Ding-Guang.

54 YZZPYZ 5: 2581, Ortai memorial, YZ 4/4/9.

55 YZZPYZ 5: 2581–82, Ortai memorial, YZ 4/4/9.

56 Ibid. Kent Smith notes that other provincial officials had lobbied for a nonviolent solution in Changzhai, but they did not have enough influence with the emperor to give their views force. See his "Ch'ing Policy and the Development of Southwest China," 77–80.

57 YZZPYZ 5: 2591, Ortai memorial, YZ 4/6/20.

58 YZZPYZ 5: 2593–94, Ortai memorial, YZ 4/7/9.

59 YZZPYZ 5: 2602, Ortai memorial YZ 4/8/19.

60 YZZPYZ 5: 2612–14, Ortai memorial, YZ 4/11/15.

61 Scott, *Seeing Like a State*, 65.

62 Sicheng was a native district (*tuzhou*) during the Ming dynasty, and was later elevated to a native prefecture during the early days of Qing rule.

63 By the late Ming period, the Cen clan controlled seven domains in central and northwestern Guangxi, making them the province's second-largest lineage group of native officials. The Huang lineage was the largest, with eleven domains. See Leo K, Shin, *The Making of the Chinese State: Ethnicity and Expansion on the Ming Borderlands* (New York: Cambridge University Press, 2006), 75, 82–90.

64 Claims to Han Chinese descent probably gave the Cens some leverage over the non-Han peoples they governed (many of whom made their own claims to Chinese ancestry, as noted in chapter 2), and enhanced their legitimacy in the eyes of Ming officialdom. See Ebrey, "Surnames and Han Chinese Identity," 23.

65 Shin, *The Making of the Chinese State*, 70; Huang Jiaxin, *Zhuangzu diqu tusi zhidu*, 228.

66 Shi Jizhong, "*Qian Gui bianjiang*," 292–93. The uprising was led by Nong Zhigao, who is still revered as a folk hero in many Zhuang regions. For a discussion of Zhuang relations with the Song state, see Jeffrey G. Barlow, "The Zhuang Minority of the Sino-Vietnamese Frontier in the Song Period," *Journal of Southeast Asian Studies*, 18, no. 2 (September 1987): 250–69. See also Barlow, "The Zhuang Minority in the Ming Era," *Ming Studies*, No. 28 (Fall 1989): 15–41.

67 Shi Jizhong, "*Qian Gui bianjiang*," 292–93. In recent years, scholars have questioned both the Cens' ancestral links to Cen Zhongshu and their purported Zhejiang roots. Although some historians still contend that the Cens moved to Guangxi from Zhejiang during the Song period, others have suggested that the family originated in Guangxi and belonged to the indigenous Zhuang elite. Still others argue for a middle ground in which the Cen family was originally Han Chinese but lived among the indigenous populations of Guangxi for so long that they internalized local culture and effectively became Zhuang. See Barlow, "The Zhuang," chapter 9, note 15. See also Huang Jiaxin, *Zhuangzu diqu tusi zhidu*, 228–31.

68 Huang Jiaxin, 230–31; Gong Yin, *Zhongguo tusi zhidu*, 1107. See also Shi Jizhong, "*Qian Gui bianjiang*," 292.

69 Shi Jizhong, "*Qian Gui bianjiang*," 292–93; Huang Yiren, *Buyizu shi* (A history of the Buyi nationality) (Guiyang: Guizhou renmin chubanshe, 1992), 147–49.

70 *Nanlong fuzhi* 2: 2a–2b.

71 It is not clear if the Cens had any dealings with the Southern Ming leaders based in southwestern China during the 1650s.

72 The first Cen native official to receive this title from the Qing was Cen Jilu.

73 YZZPYZ 5: 2627, Ortai memorial, YZ 5/1/25.

74 In 1667, Nanlong was made subordinate to Guiyang prefecture, even farther away. Twenty years later, it was placed under the jurisdiction of Anshun. See *Xingyi fuzhi*, 46: 9a. See also Aibida, *Qiannan shilue*, 219 and 227.

75 *Xingyi fuzhi* 46: 9a; see also edict of KX 50/8/13, reprinted in QSL-GZ, 496–97 and Aibida, *Qiannan shilue*, 222.

76 The Guangxi chieftain's name was Wang Shangyi. His adversary in Guizhou was A Jiu.

77 As noted earlier, the Huangcaoba garrison had only 1,500 troops, which may explain Cai's reluctance to use military force against the warring chieftains. Although Cai does not say as much in his memorial, it is possible that his colleagues' repeated humiliations in Dingfan-Guangshun two years earlier had taught him that Qing commanders could not afford to underestimate the Zhongjia.

78 *Yongzheng chao Hanwen zhupi zouzhe huibian* (Collection of Chinese-language palace memorials from the Yongzheng reign), ed. China Number One Historical Archives (Nanjing: Jiangsu guji chubanshe, 1989) 7: 896–97, YZ 4/8/16, Cai Chenggui memorial. This collection hereafter cited as YZHZZ.

79 YZZPYZ 5: 2627, Ortai memorial, YZ 5/1/25.

80 YZHZZ 9: 8–10, YZ 5/2/2, Han Liangfu memorial.

81 Edict of YZ 5/2/29, reprinted in *Qing shilu Guangxi ziliao huibian* (A collection of materials on Guangxi from the Qing shilu) (Nanning: Guangxi renmin chubanshe, 1982), Vol. 1: 245.

82 YZZPYZ 5: 2649, Ortai memorial, YZ YZ 5/i3/26.26.

83 YZHZZ 9: 601–2, YZ 5/4/8, Han Liangfu memorial.

84 As noted earlier, Zhejiang was supposed to be the Cen family's ancestral home, but much evidence suggests that the clan originated in Guangxi.

85 YZZPYZ 5:2663, Ortai memorial, 5/6/6. See also YZHZZ 10: 197–98, YZ 5/7/10, Cai Chenggui memorial.

86 YZHZZ 10: 81–84, Ortai memorial, YZ 5/6/27. See edict of YZ 5/8/20, reprinted in QSL-GZ, 258–59 and *Xingyi fuzhi* 46: 13a–15b. The former Guangxi territory of Luoke was originally placed under the jurisdiction of Yongfeng department, but in 1749, it was transferred to the jurisdiction of Dingfan department. Evidently, local officials determined that the transportation and communication routes between Luoke and Dingfan were better than those linking Luoke to Yongfeng.

87 *Xingyi fuzhi*, 9: 1a–10. See also Li Qingfu and Xu Xianlong, *Buyizu jianshi*, 76–77.

4 / LIVELIHOOD CHOICES IN THE MID-EIGHTEENTH CENTURY

1   See, for example, *Zhupi zouzhe, minzu shiwu lei* (Palace memorials, minority affairs category), 2074-15, QL 8/6/10, Guizhou surveillance commissioner Song Hou. These documents hereafter cited as ZPZZ mzl.

2   Michaud, "Hmong infrapolitics," 1862.

3   This chapter only includes cases on the Zhongjia found in the *minzu shiwu lei* category of the Palace Memorials (*zhupi zouzhe*) housed at the First Historical Archives in Beijing. I have also examined twenty-five murder cases from the collection of *Xingke tiben, tudizhaiwu lei* (Board of Punishments Office of Scrutiny, Routine Memorials, homicide cases related to disputes over land and debt). Interestingly, most of these cases involved Han-on-Han violence rather than violence within non-Han communities, or between Han and non-Han residents. Based on this small sampling, it appears that interethnic aggression was rare on a day-to-day basis. This is in keeping with William T. Rowe's observation about violence in southwestern China. As he notes, "Aggrieved parties resorted to arms to defend highly complex and specific local interests, and not necessarily along strict ethnic lines." See his *China's Last Empire: The Great Qing* (Cambridge, MA: Belknap Press, 2009), 79.

4   Michaud, "Hmong infrapolitics," 1857.

5   See, for example, ZPZZ mzl 2074-15. *Chipin wulai* is a set phrase often found in Qing criminal investigations. Mark McNicholas calls this a "documentary signpost." See Mark McNicholas, "Poverty Tales and Statutory Politics in Mid-Qing Fraud Cases," in *Writing and Law in Late Imperial China: Crime, Conflict, and Judgment*, eds. Robert E. Hegel and Katherine Carlitz (Seattle: University of Washington Press, 2007), 155-56.

6   Lombard-Salmon, *Un Exemple d'acculturation Chinose*, 182-97. See also He Weifu, *Qingdai Guizhou shangpin*, 166-71 and 174-77.

7   Lombard-Salmon, *Un Exempled'acculturation Chinose*, 199-203.

8   Ibid, 202. See also He Weifu, *Qingdai Guizhou shangpin*, 178-83 and 238-45.

9   Lombard-Salmon, *Un Exemple d'acculturation Chinose*, 205-6. See also He Weifu, *Qingdai Guizhou shangpin*, 224-33.

10 ZPZZ mzl 2074: 1-14 and 2075: 1-5.

11 ZPZZ mzl 1853: 1-7 and 1854: 1-2.

12 ZPZZ mzl 1963: 1-6.

13 The Qing sources cited throughout this chapter do not allow the participants in the criminal cases much room to speak. Qing officials either spoke for the

accused and the witnesses, or else the court reports heavily edited and fil-
tered the voices of the participants. In order to understand the perceptions
and motivations of the participants in each criminal case, the discussion
compares the official record of each case, wherever possible, with sources
relating to the indigenous Zhongjia religion known as Mo.

14 As we shall see, the ringleaders of the Ran Jing case of 1766 were captured in
Sichuan, but perpetrated most of their criminal activities in Guizhou.

15 ZPZZ mzl 2074–1, QL 8/3/21, Guizhou governor Zhang Guangsi. Huang San
hailed from a hamlet near Xilong, subordinate to Sicheng prefecture.

16 Ibid. The other men were named Wang Ali, Bu Xiujia, Wei Asan, Luo Long,
and Luo Awei.

17 Even if they encountered someone who could not speak Nong or Zhongjia,
they could always fall back on the local variant of Chinese.

18 ZPZZ mzl 2074–1. *Duangong* is a Daoist-influenced form of magic practiced
by several ethnic groups in southwestern China, notably the Qiang of western Sichuan. See Wang Mingke, *Qiangzai Han Zangzhijian* (The Qiang:
between Han and Tibetans) (Liaojing chubanshe, 2003), 253.

19 ZPZZ mzl 2074–1, QL 8/3/2, Guizhou governor Zhang Guangsi. See also
ZPZZ mzl 2074–2, QL 8/3/26, Anlong regional commander Song Ai; and
ZPZZ mzl 2074–15, QL 8/6/10, Guizhou surveillance commissioner (*ancha-
shi*) Song Hou.

20 ZPZZ mzl 2074–1. As noted in chapter 3, even after *gaitu guiliu* in this
region, many rural areas remained under the control of indigenous elites like
Wang Li.

21 It is not clear when the Zhuang and Buyi began using modified Chinese
characters to write their religious texts. Scholars in Guangxi cite a seventh-
century stone inscription as evidence that it could have been as early as the
Tang dynasty. Some Guizhou scholars, however, insist that the Zhongjia did
not begin using Chinese characters until after the *gaitu guiliu* reforms of the
Yongzheng reign, for it was only then that the Confucian education system
took root in southwestern Guizhou. This Sinocentric argument runs counter
to historical evidence. Confucian schools were established in Guizhou well
before the Yongzheng-era reforms. Moreover, these schools were not the only
vehicle for teaching Chinese literacy, for the Zhongjia had been interacting
with Han Chinese settlers and imperial officials for centuries before the Qing
period. See Holm, *Killing a Buffalo*, 46–51. The Mo texts bear striking parallels to the Vietnamese *chữ-nôm* script, which also used Chinese characters
to represent the local language. Whereas Mo script was used exclusively for
religious purposes, *chữ-nôm* was used to record vernacular literature. During

French colonial rule, *chữ-nôm* was replaced by *Quoc-ngu*, the Romanized script still used in Vietnam today.

22 As Holm explains, Mo authors sometimes used standard characters for phonetic and semantic readings; sometimes they created entirely new characters to represent words in their native tongue. The texts were incomprehensible to outsiders—and deliberately so. See Holm, *Killing a Buffalo*, 47–49.

23 ZPZZ mzl 2074-1.

24 ZPZZ mzl 2074-1 and ZPZZ mzl 2074-15. Wang Ali and Bu Xiujia were the two men who died resisting arrest. The Yongfeng department magistrate's name was Wang Yunhao, and the Nanlong prefectural magistrate was Yang Hui.

25 See chapter 2.

26 The sale of these positions provided the Qing government with an important source of revenue and also created a class of bureaucrats who helped link local communities to state entities. See Charles O. Hucker, *A Dictionary of Official Titles in Imperial China* (Reprint; Taipei: SMC Publishing Inc, 1995), 150, 303. See also Chung-li Chang, *The Chinese Gentry: Studies on their Role in Nineteenth-Century Chinese Society* (Seattle: University of Washington Press, 1955), 5, 7–8, 29–30; and Rowe, *China's Last Empire*, 50–54, 114.

27 See Donald Sutton, "Ethnicity and the Miao Frontier," 220.

28 Michaud, "Hmong infrapolitics," 1868–69.

29 ZPZZ mzl 2074-1 and ZPZZ mzl 2074-15. Wang Zuxian claimed that the mine was in Bengjia, a hamlet under the jurisdiction of Nanlong prefecture.

30 In the Buyi dialects of southwestern Guizhou, the term *bumo* (spelled *boumo* in some English publications) is written 布摩, while in the Zhuang dialects of northwestern Guangxi, it is written 布魔. In Qing sources, *bumo* is written *baomu* (報暮/抱暮) or sometimes *baomo* (抱莫). See Holm, *Killing a Buffalo*, 21–23.

31 ZPZZ mzl 2074-1. Unfortunately, the sources do not describe the magical acts or rituals that Baomu Bai performed, but the repertoire of *duangong* specialists typically included spells, chants, and dances to ward off evil and cure disease, and sometimes exorcisms.

32 Zhou Guomao, "*Mojing wenxue: yizhong qite de wenxue leixing*" (Mojing literature: a singular type of literature) in *Buyizu Mojing wenxue* (Mojing religious literature of the Buyi ethnic group) ed. Zhou Guomao, et al. (Guiyang: Guizhou renmin chubanshe, 1997), 1. For more on the role of the *bumo* in contemporary Zhuang and Buyi communities, see Holm, *Killing a Buffalo*, 21–22.

33 For more on Maoshan Daoism, see Isabelle Robinet, "*Shangqing*," in *The*

Encyclopedia of Taoism, Volume 2, ed. Fabrizio Pregadio (London: Rout-ledge, 2008), 858–66. See also Anna Seidel, "Taoist Messianism," *Numen*, 31, no. 2 (December 1984): 171–72. Meishan, another school of Daoism, is also widely practiced in Buyi and Zhuang communities. Meishan Daoism is espe-cially prevalent among the Yao of southwestern China, Vietnam, and Thai-land. The origins of this form of Daoism remain a subject of much debate, but some scholars postulate that it developed in Yao regions of western Hunan. When the Yao moved south into Guangxi and Guizhou, their reli-gious practices took root in Buyi and Zhuang communities. See Eli Alberts, *A History of Daoism and the Yao People of South China* (New York: Cambria Press, 2006).

34 Functional specification between the *bumo* and Daoist priests seems to vary across time and space. The distinction is clear in the old Buyi/Zhuang text, "Recitation on the Search for Water." When confronted with an epidemic, an ancient Zhuang king was advised to consult both *bumo* and Daoist priests: "In the middle of the night recite your prayer/Have a Taoist come and con-duct [the proceedings]/Invite a boumo to come and plead your case." The *bumo*, it seems, was entrusted with communications with the spiritual realm, while the Daoist priest was asked to carry out certain rituals. See Holm, *Recalling Lost Souls*, 106–8. In some communities, however, the same person might serve as either a *bumo* or a Daoist priest, as the occasion warranted. See Holm, *Killing a Buffalo*, 172. When I asked Buyi scholar Yu Luo about the distinction in Buyi communities today, she said that the *bumo* appear to be most actively involved in life cycle rituals such as births, funerals, and ances-tral worship. She added that many Buyi villagers are quick to say that the *bumo* is "not the same person" as the Daoist priest, but they cannot explain the different roles of these religious practitioners. E-mail correspondence, June 16, 2012 and July 2, 2012.

35 Cupellation is the process of applying extreme heat to ores or alloyed metals to separate noble metals like gold and silver from base metals like lead copper and zinc.

36 Huang San's testimony, at least as it is recorded in the Palace Memorials, evinces his unwavering faith in the existence of the "spirit silver." However, we should take this with a grain of salt. Qing officials, stymied as they were by this case, had a vested interest in portraying Huang San and other partici-pants as foolish rustics, mired in superstition and ignorance.

37 Wang Bujiang told officials that the hamlet was called Dongmajia, but this later proved to be a memory lapse or an outright lie. Subsequent testimony from other witnesses indicated that the hamlet's real name was Mumajia.

Huang Zuxian's real name was Huang Yilao, sometimes written Huang A Lao. In the Zhongjia dialects of eastern Yunnan, the diminutive "Yi" was sometimes used instead of the more commonplace "A." See ZPZZ mzl 2074–1 and ZPZZ mzl 2074–7.

38 ZPZZ mzl 2074–1.

39 Ibid.

40 Ibid. See also ZPZZ mzl 2074–7.

41 ZPZZ mzl 2074–7.

42 Ibid.

43 ZPZZ mzl 2074–1 and ZPZZ mzl 2074–7.

44 ZPZZ mzl 2074–1.

45 ZPZZ mzl 2074–1 and ZPZZ mzl 2074–15.

46 Ibid.

47 These two men, Huang San and Wang Zuxian, were accessories to a crime that officials had resolved to their satisfaction during the Yongzheng reign. See ZPZZ mzl 2075–1.

48 According to Brent Huffman, curator of www.ultimateungulate.com, "Guizhou province is just outside of the current range of the bharal, so the species—if present—would likely be quite rare." E-mail correspondence, March 7, 2012.

49 The wanderer was named Wang A'er, and his landlord was Wang Wenjia. See ZPZZ mzl 2074–5, QL 8/4/26, Guangxi governor Yang Xifu; and ZPZZ mzl 2074–6, QL 8/4/30, Guizhou governor Zhang Guangsi and Guizhou provincial military commissioner Han Dong. See also ZPZZ mzl 2074–15.

50 ZPZZ mzl 2075–3, QL 8/14/27, Zuojiang regional military commander Bi Ying.

51 ZPZZ mzl 2074–15.

52 ZPZZ mzl 2075–4, QL 8/8/6, Yunnan governor Zhang Yunsui.

53 The next six paragraphs are based on Zhupi zouzhe, minzu shiwu lei (Palace memorials, minority affairs category), 1853–1, QL 31/3/28, Fang Shijun.

54 Zhe Ruo, Li Bao, Luo Puti, and A Liu.

55 Zhu Bao and A Liu.

56 Dong Zhengyuan was probably not exaggerating his poverty. Daoists were marginalized in Qing China, for the Qing rulers practiced Tibetan Buddhism and promoted neo-Confucianism as the state doctrine. The government also tended to regard Daoism as a source of potential heterodoxy and social unrest, since its clergy tended to live in isolated monasteries, lacked a strong religious structure, and had inadequate financial support. The economic and social constraints must have been particularly acute for Daoists

living in one of China's poorest provinces. See Monica Esposito, "Daoism in the Qing," in *Daoism Handbook*, ed. Livia Kohn (Leiden: Brill, 2000), 623–24.

57 Again, Zhu Bao and A Liu.

58 Zhe Ruo , Li Bao , and Luo Puti.

59 The next four paragraphs are based on ZPZZ mzl 1853-2, QL 31/4/1, Aertai. Aertai should not be confused with the similarly named Ortai, who had served as Yunnan-Guizhou Governor-General forty years earlier.

60 *Qianlong chao shangyu dang* (Imperial edicts of the Qianlong reign), Compiled by the Number One Historical Archives, (Beijing: Dang'an chubanshe, 1991), 4: 870, item 2452, Court letter (*ziji*) to Fang Shijun, QL 31/4/21.

61 Ran Lang was also interrogated, but Ran Jing's confession provides the fullest account. Ran Hua had died of an illness en route. See ZPZZ mzl 1854-2, QL 31/5/12, Fang Shijun.

62 Ibid.

63 *Da Qingluli* (Great Qing code) (1740) (Reprint, Tianjin: Tianjin guji chubanshe, 1991), 22: 10–11. These crimes were regarded as much more serious than those committed in the homicide cases discussed earlier because they posed a potential threat to the dynasty. Plotting rebellion counted among the Ten Abominations (*Shi E*)—the most abhorrent offenses against persons or the state—enumerated in the preamble to the Qing Code. Plotting rebellion was one of the three capital crimes listed among the Ten Abominations, the other two being disloyalty *(moupan)* and treason *(mou dani)*. Sorcery involving prophecies was also a capital offense, punishable by immediate decapitation; and the same penalty applied to treason. See Philip A. Kuhn, *Soulstealers: The Chinese Sorcery Scare of 1768* (Cambridge: Harvard University Press, 1991), 87–88.

64 ZPZZ mzl 1854-2.

65 William T. Rowe, "Education and Empire in Southwest China: Ch'en Hungmou in Yunnan, 1733-1738," in *Education and Society in Late Imperial China*, ed. Benjamin A. Elman and Alexander Woodside (Berkeley: University of California Press, 1994), 417–57.

66 ZPZZ mzl 1963-1, QL 31/4/7, Fang Shijun. Wei Xuewen's friends were A Shou and Chen Ziyu.

67 Once again, "Miao" serves in these records as a generic term for the non-Chinese. Most likely, it refers to the Zhongjia and perhaps other smaller groups living in the Guiding region.

68 ZPZZ mzl 1963-3, QL 31/5/4, Fang Shijun.

69 Wei Xuewen's friend, Chen Ziyu, organized these activities.

70 ZPZZ mzl 1963–3.

71 ZPZZ mzl 1963–2.

72 ZPZZ mzl 1963–2 and 1963–3.

73 Edict of QL 31/5/13, reprinted in QSL-GZ, 1168–69.

74 ZPZZ mzl 1963–6, QL 31/6/6, Fang Shijun.

75 *Da Qing luli,* 23:254. As noted earlier, treason counted among the Ten Abominations.

76 The other conspirators included Yang Guochen, Chen Ziyu, A Shou, and three others.

77 ZPZZ mzl 1963–5, QL 31/6/6, Fang Shijun.

78 Today, it appears that some Hmong villagers in Vietnam have adopted a similar stance on state-mandated education. As Michaud writes, "I suspect many Hmong are not unhappy to limit . . . cultural dilution among their youth. They stick to what really matters: passing on ancestral knowledge through customary education, and limiting formal schooling to what is needed to learn some accountancy and become proficient enough in the national language to ensure good dealings." See "Hmong infrapolitics," 13.

79 Scott, *The Art of Not Being Governed,* 37.

5 / THE NANLONG UPRISING OF 1797

1 See, for example, *Gongzhong Dang Jiaqing chao zouzhe* (Secret palace memorials of the Jiaqing reign), compiled by and held at the National Palace Museum, Taipei, 3:2, 648, JQ 2/1/27, Feng Guangxiong memorial. This collection hereafter cited as GZDJQ.

2 Wei Qiluoxu's real name was Wei Chaoyuan. His nickname, "Seven-whisker Wei" was a reference to his wispy beard. Wang Niangxian's real name was Wang Acong. She is sometimes called "Immortal Maiden Wang" (Wang Xiangu). For consistency's sake, I will refer to them as Wei Qiluoxu and Wang Niangxian.

3 The Zhongjia had few guns during the early weeks of the rebellion; their arsenal consisted mainly of hunting knives. They acquired firearms later, after raiding Guizhou's towns and cities. This point will be considered later in the chapter. On the use of magic to neutralize an enemy's technological advantages, see Michael Adas, *Prophets of Rebellion: Millenarian Protest Movements against the European Colonial Order* (Chapel Hill: The University of North Carolina Press, 1979), 151.

4 *Qingdai Jiaqing nianjian Guizhou Buyizu "Nanlong qiyi" ziliao xuanbian* (Collected materials on the "Nanlong Uprising" of the Buyi people during the Jiaqing reign), comp. by China Number One Historical Archives, the

Southwest Guizhou People's Committee, and the Guizhou Buyi Studies Committee (Guiyang: Guizhou minzu chubanshe, 1989), 52–55. This collection hereafter cited as NQX.

5   The following collections of archival materials were used in this chapter: (1.) *Secret palace memorials of the Jiaqing Reign* (GZDJQ); (2.) *Jiaobu Dang* (Record of pursuit and arrest), hereafter cited as JBD; and (3.) Palace Memorial reference copies in the minority affairs category (*Junji chu lufu zouzhe minzu shiwu lei*) from the Number One Historical Archives in Beijing, reprinted in NQX. A comparison of the published NQX collection against the microfilmed versions at the archives revealed no discrepancies. The NQX references each *lufu* it reprints. In this chapter, the *lufu* citations will be provided in parentheses after each NQX entry; *Junji chu lufu zouzhe minzu shiwu lei* (Grand Council reference copies of palace memorials, minority affairs category) will hereafter be cited as JCLZ mzl.

6   These two Zhongjia narratives, "Wang Xiangu" and "Nanlong fanbing ge," are also included in NQX. Citations for these narratives will follow this format: NQX, page number, "Wang Xiangu" (or "Nanlong fanbing ge").

7   In Buyi oral tradition, narrative poems are epic tales that developed from folk songs. For descriptions of various forms of Buyi folk literature, see Zhou Guoyan et al., eds.,*Languages and Cultures of the Kam-Tai (Zhuang-Dong) Group: A Word List*, 24–32; and Huang Yiren, *Buyizu shi*, 187–88.

8   This indigenous account is a narrative poem in eighteen stanzas, recorded by Buyi ethnographers when they collected "Wang Xiangu." Sung verses alternate with spoken-word explanations, a typical pattern for this genre. See Zhou, *Languages and Cultures of the Kam-Tai*, 24–32.

9   For reasons that will be explored in the next section, PRC historians have mostly ignored the Buyi narratives.

10 James Scott, *Domination and the Arts of Resistance*, 87.

11 Claudine Lombard-Salmon's study of eighteenth-century Guizhou only mentions the rebellion in passing. See *Un exemple d'acculturation Chinoise*, passim. In his essay on the Liu military family of Xingyi (formerly Nanlong), Edward McCord makes a brief reference to the uprising. See Edward A. McCord, "Local Military Power and Elite Formation: The Liu Family of Xingyi County, Guizhou," in *Chinese Local Elites and Patterns of Dominance*, ed. Joseph W. Esherick and Mary B. Rankin (Berkeley: University of California Press, 1993), 162–90. Wang Niangxian also merits a short entry in a collection of eminent Chinese women. See "Wang Niangxian," in Lily Xiao Hong Lee, A. D. Stefanowska, and Clara Wing Chung-ho, eds. *Biographical dictionary of Chinese women: The Qing Dynasty* (Armonk: M. E. Sharpe, 1998).

12 As Stevan Harrell writes, "As representatives of their own *minzu*, and at the same time participants in this hegemonic state project, [scholars] participate in the two-way process of co-optation; their story gets told, and it is a glorious one, but it is told as a part of the larger story of the Chinese nation as a whole." Harrell also remarks that in recent years, the strictures on *minzu* scholarship have loosened somewhat. Although ethnography, ethnology, and linguistics are still devoted to the state projects of nation-building and development, these disciplines are no longer held to such a rigid, normalizing paradigm. See Harrell, *Ways of Being Ethnic in Southwest China* (Seattle: University of Washington Press, 2001), 45, 55.

13 The preface to NQX states that *Han ren* signifies Han landlords. See NQX, 4. The authors of *Guizhou tongshi* (A comprehensive history of Guizhou), however, allow the original phrase *tian jiang mie Han ren* to stand without qualification, leaving open the possibility that the rebels attacked Han residents without regard to their class background. It is worth noting that *Guizhou tongshi* is a more recent book (published 2002), and its authors are not Buyi. See He Renzhong, ed., *Guizhou tongshi. Di san juan, Qingdai de Guizhou* (A comprehensive history of Guizhou, part 3, Qing dynasty Guizhou). (Beijing: Dangdai Zhongguo chubanshe, 2002), 300.

14 The rebels typically attacked villages inhabited by ordinary Han peasants. Several rebel confessions indicate that the Zhongjia were enticed to join the insurrection with promises that they could get rich by plundering Han villages.

15 For many years, after Mao Zedong himself decreed that class struggle was the motive force of history, Chinese scholars had to treat "ethnic contradictions" as a sub-type of class contradictions. One scholar of the Nanlong Uprising allows that the rebellion arose from ethnic contradictions (*minzu maodun*) as well as class contradictions, but "ethnic contradictions" are never clearly defined. See, for example, Wu Changxing, "Qianxi Nanlong Buyizu qiyi baofa yuanyin" (A brief analysis of the reasons for the outbreak of the Nanlong Buyi Uprising), *Buyi xue yanjiu* 3 (1991): 71–78. See also Yan Yong and Fan Lixia, "Lun Nanlong qiyi shehui beijing, jingyan jiaoxun ji lishi yiyi" (Discussing the social background, experience, lessons, and historical significance of the "Nanlong Uprising"), *Buyi xue yanjiu* 3 (1991): 229–39.

16 See Chen Dingxiu, "Nanlong qiyi yuanyin" (A brief analysis of the origins of the Nanlong Uprising), *Buyi xue yanjiu* 3 (1991): 58–65, and Wu Changxing, 71–78. Several scholars refer to the Nanlong Uprising as a peasant rebellion (*nongmin qiyi*). See, for example, Huang Yiren, *Buyizu jianshi*. Interestingly, Huang Yiren simply calls it "the Buyi people's rebellion and struggle" (*Buyizu de qiyi douzheng*). See his *Buyizu shi*, 198.

17   Not even the Buyi scholars who collected and edited the indigenous narratives have much to say. They note that many events described in the narratives diverge from "historical facts" (that is, the events presented in the archival record and local gazetteers) but these scholars neglect to explain where and why these divergences occur.

18   Tian Yuan, "'Wang Xiangu,' 'Nanlong fanbing ge,' qianxi" (A brief analysis of "Wang Xiangu" and "Song of the Nanlong Resistance"), *Buyi xue yanjiu* 3 (1991): 286–90.

19   Huang, *Buyizu shi*, 188.

20   Jin may be on shaky historical ground here. The editors of NQX probably added these references to multi-ethnic participation to serve the same political aims expressed in Jin's article. There is no evidence to suggest that the Nanlong Uprising was a pan-ethnic rebellion. The Qing documents and the two indigenous narratives all indicate that the overwhelming majority of rebels were Zhongjia. As we shall see later in this chapter, the rebel leaders did enlist the help of a local Han outlaw, but he was one of just a few documented participants from outside the Zhongjia ethnic group.

21   Jin Anjiang, "Cong Nanlong qiyi kan jindai Buyizu diqu de minzu guanxi" (Looking at modern ethnic relations in Buyi regions since the Nanlong Uprising), *Buyi xue yanjiu* 3 (1991): 115–16, 119.

22   Perhaps these scholars were also reluctant to delve too deeply into the folk traditions of their own ethnic group, lest they betray support (real or perceived) for indigenous beliefs deemed inimical to socialism.

23   Leng Tianfang, "Zongjiao yu 'Nanlong qiyi'" (Religion in the 'Nanlong Uprising')," *Buyi xue yanjiu* 3 (1991): 130–38.

24   As David Atwill suggests in his work on nineteenth-century Yunnan, local resistance viewed over a long period of time reveals a sustained, logical response to external pressures. In the case of Yunnan, these pressures were "state and new-Han power groups that threatened Yunnanese cultural solidarity and economic livelihood." See Atwill, "Trading Places: Resistance, Ethnicity, and Governance in Nineteenth-Century Yunnan," in *Dragons, Tigers, and Dogs: Qing Crisis Management and the Boundaries of State Power in Late Imperial China*, Robert J. Antony and Jane Kate Leonard, eds. (Ithaca: Cornell University Press, 2002), 242.

25   Communities within Nanlong were divided into hamlets (*xiang*), each named after the four cardinal directions. These districts were further subdivided into hamlets. Dongsa was part of the "Northern District," or Beixiang. The headmen in charge of these districts were directly responsible to imperially appointed local officials.

26 Mo priestesses were renowned for their ability to predict the future and dispel evil spirits. According to one scholar, they did not always require the special training required of their male counterparts. Some of the priestesses acquired their powers after long illnesses. Also, they usually did not learn the scriptures used by the *bumo*. See Zhou Guomao, ed. *Yizhong teshu de wenhua dianji: Buyizu Mojing yanjiu* (A unique type of ancient texts: research on the Mojing religious literature of the Buyi ethnic group) (Guiyang: Guizhou renmin chubanshe, 2006), 3.

27 Some sources refer to "crossing the darkness" as *zouyin*. The terminology suggests Daoist influences in Zhongjia popular religion, as does the use of terms such as "immortal." See Li Rubiao, "'Nanlong qiyi' de zongjiao wenti" (The question of religion in the 'Nanlong Uprising'), *Buyi xue yanjiu* 3 (1991): 142. See also Wang Fangheng, "Nanlong qiyi zhong de wushu wenti" (The question of sorcery in the Nanlong Uprising), *Buyi xue yanjiu* 3 (1991): 147. The Northern Zhuang of Guangxi employ similar rituals called "crossing the passes" (*guoguan*) to cure children's illnesses. See Holm, *Recalling Lost Souls*, 14.

28 *Xingyi fuzhi*, 46: 19a–19b.

29 NQX, 143, Document #129 (JCLZ mzl JQ 2/8/24, Confession of Wang Niangxian).

30 *Xingyi fuzhi*, 46: 19b.

31 Based on David Holm's description, it seems that Wei Qiluoxu was a "ritual master" or *shigong* (師公), a broad descriptor for shamans, sorcerers, and exorcists who used a repertoire of magical and theatrical practices to drive away evil spirits. See *Killing a Buffalo*, 22–23.

32 NQX, 143, Document #129 (JCLZ mzl, JQ 2/8/24, Confession of Wei Qiluoxu). Here, the Zhongjia are referred to as "Miao," a generic term Qing officials often used for non-Han residents of southwestern China, without regard to their actual ethnicity.

33 Wei Qiluoxu was a social bandit in the most basic sense of the term; his aim was to steal from the relatively wealthy and redistribute among the very poor. For a discussion of social banditry in early twentieth-century Hunan, see Elizabeth Perry's essay, "Predatory Rebellion: Bai Lang and Social Banditry," in her *Challenging the Mandate of Heaven: Social Protest and State Power in China* (Armonk: M. E. Sharpe, 2002), 108–33.

34 NQX, 43–44, Document #58 (JCLZ mzl JQ 2/2/17), joint confession from Wang Asan, He Jima, Wei Aza, and Wang Jibao, four rebels captured during the early days of the suppression campaign. See also GZDJQ, 3:2, 713a–714, JQ 2/2/6, Feng Guangxiong memorial.

35 NQX, 143, Document #129 (JCLZ mzl, JQ 2/8/24, Confession of Wei Qiluoxu). See also *Xingyi fuzhi*, 46: 17b. I have translated "Yunnan cheng" as Kunming, the Yunnan provincial capital.

36 Wei Qiluoxu and Wang Niangxian never actually married; Wang Niangxian was already betrothed to a man in her village. According to Zhongjia custom, she and her husband lived separately for the first three years of their marriage. In any case, Wei Qiluoxu's allegiance was instrumental to his larger ambitions. As Elizabeth Perry notes, the scope of a bandit leader's control depended upon the kinds of outside coalitions he was able to forge. Such coalitions furnished protection for plundering purposes, and also served as "as stepping stones to a wider world of power and fame." See Perry's chapter, "Predators and Protectors: Strategies of Peasant Survival," in her *Challenging the Mandate of Heaven*, 21.

37 GZDJQ, 3:2, JQ 2/1/27, Feng Guangxiong memorial.

38 One account suggests that Zeng Tingkui committed suicide by stabbing himself in the abdomen. See *Xingyi fuzhi* 46: 19a–20a. According to Feng Guangxiong, however, Zeng fell ill during the Lunar New Year and was bedridden when the rebels attacked. When Zeng learned that Nanlong was under siege, he immediately ordered local military personnel to protect the city. Several days later, just before Zeng died, he again ordered civil officials, local gentry, and local militia to protect the city. Feng was quick to assure the court that Zeng had not been negligent or careless in any way. One wonders, however, if Feng was trying to cover for his subordinate's failure to take firmer action against Wang Niangxian's followers–or his own (Feng's) failure to report early activities to Beijing. See GZDJQ 3:2, 714b–717a, JQ 2/2/6, Feng Guangxiong memorial.

39 In this regard, the Nanlong Uprising might be considered a consequence of what William Rowe calls "governance on the cheap." At its peak, the Qing standing army, including both banner troops and the Chinese Green Standard Army, employed fewer than a million men to defend China's territory, and to protect and pacify a population of four to five hundred million. See Rowe, *China's Last Empire*, 32. The small size of the armed forces army kept military expenditures to a minimum, but it also created the potential for simultaneous rebellions in different parts of the empire.

40 More than thirty-one thousand troops from Yunnan and Guizhou had been transferred to the Hunan front, leaving only a few thousand to deal with the Zhongjia. See NQX, 59. For an analysis of the Hunan Miao Uprising, see Donald Sutton, "Ethnic Revolt in the Qing Empire: The 'Miao Uprising' of 1795–1796 Reexamined," *Asia Major* 3rd series, vol. 17, 1 (2003): 105–51. See

also Daniel McMahon, "Identity and Conflict on a Chinese Borderland: Yan Ruyi and the Recruitment of the Gelao During the 1795–97 Miao Revolt," *Late Imperial China* Vol. 23, No. 2 (December 2002): 53–86.

41 Le Bao's tenure in Yunnan and Guizhou was peripatetic, to say the least. Soon after his appointment to the governor-generalship in 1795, he was ordered to coordinate the Miao suppression on the Hunan-Guizhou border. He briefly returned to Yunnan in 1796, only to be ordered back to the Miao front when Hubei-Hunan governor-general Fukang'an died. After Le Bao secured a major victory in Hubei, the court ordered him to fight the Zhongjia in southwestern Guizhou. Shortly after the Zhongjia campaign ended in November 1797, Le Bao was appointed governor-general of Hubei and Hunan and continued to lead armies against the White Lotus rebels. See Arthur W. Hummel, ed., *Eminent Chinese of the Ch'ing Period* (Washington, D.C.: United States Government Printing Office, 1943), I: 444.

42 GZDJQ 3:2, 610, JQ 2/1/18, Feng Guangxiong memorial.

43 JBD, JQ 2/1/26.

44 GZDJQ 3:2, 648, JQ 2/1/27, Feng Guangxiong memorial.

45 As Donald Sutton rightly observes, " . . . acculturation does not mean assimilation, that is, a change of identification. See his "Ethnicity and the Miao Frontier," 220. David Atwill has also suggested that comments like "*yu qimin wuyi*" represented "the highest possible compliment" from Chinese intellectuals or Qing officials. See his *The Chinese Sultanate*, 32

46 Sang's motivations for joining the rebellion are not entirely clear. When Qing armies recaptured Nanlong in August 1797, he was too injured to make a confession. In any case, Le Bao labeled him a "treacherous Han" (Han *jian*) for aiding and abetting Wei Qiluoxu. GZDJQ 5:1, 269–72, JQ 2/8/23, Feng Guangxiong memorial.

47 NQX, 53 Document #63 (JCLZ mzl, JQ 2/3/2, Jiang Lan memorial).

48 GZDJQ 4:2, 832a–833b, JQ 2/7/2, Jiang Lan memorial.

49 GZDJQ 3:2, 714b–717a, JQ 2/2/6, Feng Guangxiong memorial.

50 During the Qing Dynasty, Anshun served as Guizhou's military nerve center; the provincial military commander was normally stationed there.

51 GZDJQ 3:2, 714b–717a, JQ 2/2/6, Feng Guangxiong memorial.

52 NQX, 49–51, Document #62 (JCLZ mzl, JQ 2/2/27, Feng Guangxiong).

53 Ibid. For the death of Cui Lin, see *Anshun fuzhi* (Gazetteer of Anshun prefecture) 1851, 44: 18a.

54 JBD JQ 2/2/27.

55 NQX, 52–55, Document #63 (JCLZ mzl, JQ 2/3/2, Jiang Lan memorial).

56 JBD, JQ 2/3/2.

57 The rebels had probably seized these guns from a Han village. Their weaponry varied from battle to battle, depending on what they had been able to steal in recent raids.

58 GZDJQ 3:2, 839–40, JQ 2/2/23, Feng Guangxiong and Zhulonga memorial.

59 GZDJQ 3:2, 838, JQ 2/2/23, Feng Guangxiong and Zhulonga memorial.

60 JBD, JQ 2/3/5.

61 NQX, 61–62, Document #70. Feng was especially concerned about Weiyuan (a key point on the eastward road to Hunan), and about Guzhou in southeastern Guizhou, which had been the locus of a major Miao uprising during the 1730s.

62 Ibid.

63 GZDJQ 4:2, 99–100, JQ 2/3/16, Le Bao and Feng Guangxiong memorial.

64 NQX 72–75, Document #75 (JCLZ mzl, JQ 2/4/8, Le Bao memorial).

65 NQX, 80–82, Document # 78 (JCLZ mzl, JQ 2/4/18, Le Bao memorial).

66 NQX, 86–88, Document # 81 (JCLZ mzl, JQ 2/5/1, Le Bao memorial).

67 The Mabie is a small tributary of the Hongshui River.

68 NQX, 99–100, Document # 89 (JCLZ mzl, JQ 2/5/11, Le Bao memorial). As discussed below, a highly exaggerated account of the rebels' victory at Mabie appears in the indigenous narrative "Wang Xiangu."

69 Wang Dengrong and Wang Tianlan.

70 The rebel commander at Yangchang was Wang Azhan.

71 NQX, 106–108, Document #94 (JCLZ mzl, JQ 2/5/23, Le Bao memorial). As noted earlier, Da Wang Gong was Wei Qiluoxu's second-in-command.

72 GZDJQ 4b: 642–645, JQ 2/6/18, Jiang Lan memorial and GZDJQ 4b: 688–90, JQ 2/6/29, Jiang Lan memorial.

73 NQX, 119–121, Document # 102 (JCLZ mzl, JQ 2/7/9, Le Bao memorial).

74 NQX, 141–144, Document #112 (JCLZ mzl, JQ 2/9/2, Le Bao memorial).

75 For Xingyi, see JBD, JQ 2/8/20. For Zhenfeng, see JBD, JQ 2/10/20.

76 JBD, JQ 2/10/6.

77 In Buyi oral tradition, narrative poems are epic tales that developed from folk songs. For descriptions of various forms of Buyi folk literature, see Zhou Guoyan, "An Introduction to the Kam-Tai (Zhuang-Dong) Group of Languages in China," 29.

78 NQX, 255–56, "Wang Xiangu."

79 Ibid., 257–58.

80 Ibid., 258–59. Here, the hands of PRC scholars may be at work. A discussion of social banditry, which reflects a lack of class consciousness, is omitted in favor of magic, thereby demonstrating that the Zhongjia needed the guiding hand of the Communists to lead them to scientific modernity.

81 Ibid., 260.

82 Ibid., 260–61. Here, Wang Niangxian speaks out against a longstanding grievance in Guizhou. The provincial treasury provided money for the requisition (*caimai*) of grain, firewood, and other raw materials from Zhongjia and Miao producers, but the local officials responsible for procuring these goods rarely paid for them. See Jenks, *Insurgency and Social Disorder in Guizhou*, 52.

83 NQX, 261–62, "Wang Xiangu."

84 Ibid., 264.

85 The term *kejia* here should not be confused with the Kejia ("Guest people" or Hakka) of southeastern China. The Zhongjia often referred to Han Chinese as "*kejia*" or guests. Indeed, migrants throughout China were often called "kejia." See NQX, 265, "Wang Xiangu."

86 NQX, 266, "Wang Xiangu."

87 Ibid., 267–68.

88 Ibid., 268.

89 Ibid., 269.

90 Ibid., 270.

91 Ibid., 270.

92 Ibid., 270–71.

93 Faith in this type of magic was common in other rebel movements. During the Saya San Rebellion of 1930–32, for example, Burman monks told recruits that they knew magical formulas that would turn twigs into war horses. See Adas, *Prophets of Rebellion*, 153.

94 NQX, 272, "Wang Xiangu."

95 Ibid., 272.

96 Ibid., 273.

97 Ibid., 273–74.

98 "Song of the Nanlong Resistance" appears to be an antiphonal song, or a song in which two performers (or groups of performers) sing alternately, one answering the other. Antiphonal singing is common among many Tai groups of southwestern China and Southeast Asia, often featured in festivals and courtship rituals. See Holm, *Recalling Lost Souls*, 14.

99 NQX, 294, "Nanlong fanbing ge."

100 The rhyme and symmetry of these Chinese verses suggests the hand of a post-1949 editor. NQX, 293, "Nanlong fanbing ge."

101 Ibid., 293–95.

102 Ibid., 296.

103 This general is identified in the narrative as Jia Jiangjun. The compilers of

NQX suggest that this was a local nickname for either Chang Shan or Zhulonga.

104 NQX, 296–97.

105 Ibid., 299, "Nanlong fanbing ge."

106 Before this point, the poem includes an episode describing the imperial rewards bestowed upon Le Bao and Jia Jiangjun, as well as the posthumous awards for the Qing officials killed in battle. This scene serves as an indirect way of boasting about the prowess of the Zhongjia rebels. That is, the Zhongjia rebels were worthy foes who exacted a heavy toll on the Qing troops.

107 NQX, 300, "Nanlong fanbing ge."

108 Ibid., 303.

109 Scott, *Domination and the Arts of Resistance*, 81.

110 For the reforms in western Hunan, see Daniel McMahon, "New Order in Hunan's Miao Frontier," *Journal of Colonialism and Colonial History*, 9:1 (Spring 2008).

111 NQX 195–99, Document #139 (JCLZ mzl, JQ 3/3/23, Feng Guangxiong and E'hui).

112 ZPZZ mzl 1916–1, JQ 5/6/27, Jueluo Langgan (覺羅琅玕).

6 / A LEGACY OF FRAGILE HEGEMONY

1 For a discussion of one such strategic marriage, see James Millward, "A Uyghur Muslim in Qianlong's Court: The Meanings of the Fragrant Concubine," *The Journal of Asian Studies* 53, no. 2 (May 1994): 427–58.

2 See Giersch, *Asian Borderlands*, 3–5, 91–96.

3 Millward, *Beyond the Pass*, 197. See also Hostetler, "Qing Connections to the Early Modern World: Ethnography and Cartography in Eighteenth-Century China." *Modern Asian Studies* 34, no. 3 (2000): 630–31; and Perdue, "Military Mobilization," 785, 788.

4 Millward, *Beyond the Pass*, 199. Evelyn S. Rawski has also demonstrated that Qing court culture incorporated many traditions from the Manchus, Mongols, Uighurs, and Tibetans. See her *The Last Emperors: A Social History of Qing Imperial Institutions* (Berkeley: University of California Press, 1998).

5 One product of the demand for information on Guizhou was Aibida's *Handbook of Guizhou* (*Qiannan shilue*). Aibida compiled this book for his own reference and for the benefit of future administrators while serving as Guizhou's governor in the early 1750s. He condensed information from local gazetteers and other contemporary geographic writings into a single, handy volume, organizing his material according to geographic region. Each of the thirty-two chapters is devoted to the political history, economy, climate, and

population of a single administrative unit. Aside from its practical function, the handbook carried considerable symbolic value. To refer to the concepts introduced in chapter 3, the volume functioned as a catalogue of the state spaces the Qing had delineated within Guizhou. The very act of committing geographic information to paper signaled that these sections of Guizhou had become part of the world known to—and under the jurisdiction of—the Qing state. In 1847, Guizhou Governor Luo Raodian revised the book and published it as *Qiannan zhifang shilue*. Interestingly, the handbook saw little use during the eighteenth century. The original copy was misplaced sometime after Aibida's tenure and only rediscovered in the 1820s.

6   Information in local gazetteers was organized topically, with each chapter subdivided according to geographic region. A chapter on local products, for example, would list all the crops grown in each geographic region. Likewise, a chapter on administrative history would list the information region by region. The disadvantage of this system was that one had to consult several chapters to find all the necessary information about a given place. Aibida simplified matters by organizing all the information on a given region into single chapters.

7   See Laura Hostetler, "Introduction: Early Modern Ethnography in Comparative Historical Perspective" in Deal and Hostetler, *The Art of Ethnography*, 159–60, 166–67.

8   Deal and Hostetler, *The Art of Ethnography*, 15.

9   Hostetler, *Qing Colonial Enterprise*, 159–60, 166–67.

10   Hostetler, "Introduction: Early Modern Ethnography," xli.

11   Hostetler, *Qing Colonial Enterprise*, 206.

12   As Laura Hostetler writes, "In essence, those who do the depicting define the peoples described. . . . [The] goal of the colonizer, or imperial authority, is precisely and unabashedly to learn about, or rather construct, the identity of those to be ruled. Such knowledge simplifies the task of governance." See Hostetler, "Qing Connections to the Early Modern World," 649–50.

13   Hostetler, "Chinese Ethnography in the Eighteenth Century: The Miao Albums of Guizhou Province" (PhD diss., University of Pennsylvania, 1995), 218, 222.

14   Perdue, "Military Mobilization," 788.

15   In other words, they had no "emancipatory visions," as Jean Michaud might call them. See Michaud, "Hmong infrapolitics," 1866.

16   This is in keeping with James Scott's comments on the hidden transcript: "By definition, the hidden transcript represents discourse—gesture, speech, practices—that is ordinarily excluded from the public transcript of subordi-

nates by the exercise of power. The practice of domination, then, creates the hidden transcript. If the domination is particularly severe, it is likely to produce a hidden transcript of corresponding richness. The hidden transcript of subordinate groups, in turn, reacts back on the public transcript by engendering a subculture and by opposing its own variant form of social domination against that of the dominant elite. Both are realms of power and interests." See *Domination and the Arts of Resistance*, 27.

17 As James Scott explains, "To continue the same routine means to go under in any case and it once again makes sense to take risks; such risks are in the interest of subsistence." See James C. Scott, *The Moral Economy of the Peasant: Rebellion and Subsistence in Southeast Asia* (New Haven, CT: Yale University Press, 1976, 26.

18 David A. Bello, *Opium and the Limits of Empire: Drug Prohibition in the Chinese Interior, 1729–1850* (Cambridge, MA: Harvard University Press, 2005), 240, 255, 257, 279.

19 Scott, *Seeing Like a State*, 3, 343.

20 Or, as Scott puts it, "The progenitors of such plans [for simplification] regarded themselves as far smarter and [more] farseeing than they really were, and at the same time, regarded their subjects as far more stupid and incompetent than they really were." *Seeing Like a State*, 343.

21 Clifton Crais calls this "a historical conversation between the rulers and the ruled." See Crais, "Chiefs and Bureaucrats in the Making of Empire: A Drama from the Transkei, South Africa, October 1880," *American Historical Review* vol. 108, no. 4 (October 2003): 1037.

22 Perdue, "Military Mobilization," 788.

23 Here, I understand a civilizing project in terms of Stevan Harrell's definition—an inherently unequal interaction in which one group, the civilizing center, claims a superior degree of civilization and undertakes to elevate the civilization of a peripheral group. See his "Civilizing Projects and the Reaction to Them," in *Cultural Encounters on China's Ethnic Frontiers*, ed. Stevan Harrell (Seattle: University of Washington Press, 1995), 3.

24 Harrell, "Civilizing Projects and the Reaction to Them," 36; see also McMahon, "Restoring the Garden," 335–36.

25 Scott, *Seeing Like a State*, 184.

26 Nicholas Thomas, *Colonialism's Culture: Anthropology, Travel, and Government* (Princeton: Princeton University Press, 1994), 105–6.

27 Millward, *Beyond the Pass*, 199–201; Teng, *Taiwan's Imagined Geography*, 239–40.

28 The distinction here is between nation and ethnic group. It carries very impor-

tant implications for politics in China today because Tibet and Xinjiang will likely never be pacified unless the CCP recognizes that the PRC is multinational and not just multicultural.

29 According to Pamela Kyle Crossley, the Manchus, Mongols, Han, Tibetans, and East Turkestanis earned their status by virtue of their contributions to the creation and development of the Qing state. See her *"Manzhou yuanliu kao* and the Formalization of the Manchu Heritage," *Journal of Asian Studies* vol. 46, no. 4 (November 1987): 780. See also Teng, *Taiwan's Imagined Geography*, 242.

30 Teng, *Taiwan's Imagined Geography*, 242–43.

31 Ibid., 245, figure 34.

32 Ibid., 246.

33 Beatrice S. Bartlett, Review of *The Last Emperors: A Social History of Qing Imperial Institutions,* in *Harvard Journal of Asiatic Studies,* Vol. 61, no. 1 (June 2001): 176–78.

34 Sutton, "Ethnicity and the Miao Frontier," 229.

35 Daniel B. Wright, *The Promise of the Revolution: Stories of Fulfillment and Struggle in China's Hinterland* (Lanham, MD: Rowman and Littlefield, 2003), 51–60.

36 BBC News Online, Monday 26 March 2001 (http://www.hartford-hwp.com/ archives/55/719.html).

37 *The New York Times,* June 30, 2008 (http://www.nytimes.com/2008/06/30/ world/asia/30iht-30riot.14086300.html?_r=1).

38 Caohai's winter wetland is a gathering ground for several species of endangered migratory birds, including the black crane.

39 Melinda Herrold, "The Cranes of Caohai and Other Incidents of Fieldwork in Southwest China," *Geographical Review,* Vol. 89, No. 3 (July 1999): 440–48.

40 Scott, *The Moral Economy of the Peasant,* 32–34.

41 As noted earlier, this is one of the central concerns in Yu Luo's PhD research at Yale University.

42 Timothy Oakes, "Selling Guizhou: Cultural Development in an era of Marketization," In *The Political Economy of China's Provinces,* eds. H. Hendrischke and C. Y. Feng, (London and New York: Routledge, 1999), 65.

43 Tim Oakes, "Cultural Strategies of Development: Implications for Village Governance in China," *The Pacific Review* 19, No. 1 (March 2006): 23–28.

44 Oakes, "Selling Guizhou," 65.

45 See Louisa Schein, *Minority Rules: The Miao and the Feminine in China's Cultural Politics.* (Durham NC: Duke University Press, 2000), 8.

CHINESE GLOSSARY

Aertai　阿爾泰
Aibida　愛必達
A Ji　阿幾
A Jin　阿近
A Jiu　阿九
A Liu　阿六
An　安
anchashi　按察使
Angu　安姑
Anlong　安龍
Annan　安南
Anshun　安順
aoqu　奧區
A Shou　阿受
Balongtun　巴隴屯
bashi　巴使
Baiyue　百越
bang gong du ri　幫工度日
Bangzha　棒鮓
Bao Changding　抱長定
baojia　保甲

Baomu Bai　報暮拜
Baomu Lun　報暮倫
Beipan River　北盤江
Beixiang　北鄉
Bengjia　崩戛
bingbu　兵部
bingwu mouni zhixin　並無謀逆
　之心
buzheng shi　布政使
Cai Chenggui　蔡成貴
Cai Yurong　蔡毓榮
caimai　採買
Ceheng *tongzhi*　冊亨同知
Cen　岑
Cen Jilu　岑繼祿
Cen Peng　岑彭
Cen Shumuhan　岑恕木罕
Cen Yingchen　岑映宸
Cen Zhongshu　岑仲淑
Chang Shan　常山
changshi　長詩

179

Changzhai　長寨

Chen Yuanxun　陳元勳

Chen Ziyu　陳資于

chipin wulai　赤貧無賴

Cui Lin　崔林

da huang yudi　大黃玉帝

Da Wang Gong　大王公

datong　大同

Dangzhan　當戰

dao dui dao lai qiang dui qiang,
　bing dui bing lai jiang dui jiang
　刀對刀來槍對槍, 兵對兵來將
　對將

Dayanjiao　大嚴腳

Di Qing　狄青

Dingfan-Guangshun　定番-廣順

Dong　侗

dong shen se　動甚色

Dongmajia　東馬甲

Dongsa　洞洒

Dong Zhengyuan　董正原

doubing　豆兵

duangong　端公

duzhihui shi　都指揮使

E'hui　鄂揮

fan　番

Fang Shijun　方世雋

Feng Guangxiong　馮光熊

fu　府

Fukang'an　福康安

fuyi　夫役

gaitu guiliu　改土歸流

Gao Qizhuo　高其桌

gongtian　公田

Guanling　關岭

Guangxi　廣西

guangxian　光仙

gui yin　鬼銀

Guiding　貴定

Guiyang　貴陽

Guizhou　貴州

guoguan　過關

guoyin　過隱

Guozijian　國子堅

Han *jian*　漢奸

Han Liangfu　韓良輔

Hanzu dizhu　漢族地主

He Zhanbie　賀占鱉

Hongshui River　紅水河

Huang A Lao　黃阿澇

Huang San　黃三

Huang Yilao　黃矣澇

Huang Zuxian　黃祖先

Huangcaoba　黃草壩

huangdi　皇帝

huangxian niangniang　皇仙
　娘娘

huogen　禍根

huxiang qikuang　互相欺誑

jia　甲

Jiaqing　嘉慶

jiansheng　堅生

jiangjun　將軍

jieji maodun　階級矛盾

Jobtei (Chinese: Zhaobutai)
　趙布泰

Kangxi　康熙

Kangzuo　康左

kejia　客家

Langdai　郎岱

Le Bao　勒保

Li Bao　李保

li Miao tongban　理苗通判
liangzhuang baixing　糧庄百姓
libu　吏部
Lolo　玀玀
lu　路
Lu Quan　盧全
Luo Puti　羅普替
Luo Shirong　羅士榮
Luoke　羅蚪
Luoping　羅平
Luoyue　駱越
Ma Huipo　馬會迫
Ma Yin　馬殷
Mabie River　馬別河
mapai　馬排
Mao Wenquan　毛文銓
Maoshan　茅山
Meishan　梅山
Miao　苗
Miao Wang　苗王
Miao tu　苗圖
minzu maodun　民族矛盾
minzu shi　民族史
minzu xue　民族學
Mo　摩
mogong　摩公
mou dani　謀大逆
moufan　謀反
moupan　謀叛
Mumajia　木馬甲
Nacha　哪喳
Nanlong　南籠
"Nanlong fanbing ge"　南籠反兵歌
Nanlong qiyi　南籠起義
Nanpan River　南盤江
nei shao　內哨

neidi　內地
neiwu fu　內務府
Nong　犭農/儂
Nong Zhigao　儂智高
nongmin qiyi　農民起義
nüpai　女仆
Ortai　鄂爾泰
Pan Youlin　潘有林
Pu'an　普安
Puping　埔平
Qi Ge　七格
Qianlong　乾隆
Ran Hua　然華
Ran Jing　然經
Ran Lang　然郎
sadou chengbing　洒豆成兵
Sang Hongsheng　桑鴻升
shanhou　善後
shao　哨
shaoshu minzu　少數民族
shen fan　神飯
sheng　生
shenxian di　神仙地
shenxian tian　神仙田
shexue　社學
Shi E　十惡
Shi Liha　石歷哈
shoubei　受備
shu　熟
shun Miao　順苗
Shunzhi　順治
Sicheng　泗城
Siniang　四娘
sitian　私田
sizhuang baixing　私庄百姓
Song Ai　宋愛

Song Hou 宋厚

Tian jiang mie Hanren, bing mie Miaomu bingyi 天將滅漢人，并滅苗目兵役

tianshen 天神

tianshuai 天帥

tianshuai xiangzhu 天帥相主

tianshun 天順

tianzi 天子

tidu 提督

ting 廳

tingmu 亭目

tongban 通判

toumu 頭目

tufu 土府

tuguan 土官

tumu 土目

tuntian 屯田

tusi 土司

tuxian 土縣

tuzhou 土州

wai shao 外哨

Wang A Jiang 王阿將

Wang Acong 王阿從

Wang A'er 王阿耳

Wang Azhan 王阿戰

Wang Bujiang 王卜將

Wang Dengrong 王登榮

Wang Huaming 王華明

Wang Li 王禮

Wang Ling 王令

Wang Niangxian 王孃仙

Wang Shangyi 土尚義

Wang Tianlan 王天爛

Wang Wenjia 王文甲

Wang Xiangu 王仙姑

Wang Yunhao 王允浩

Wang Zuxian 王祖先

Wangchengpo 望城破

Wei Chaoyuan 衛朝元

Wei Da Xiansheng 偉大先生

Wei Qiluoxu 衛七絡須

Wei Xuewen 衛學文

Wu Sangui 吳三貴

wufei piancai zhiyi 無非騙財之意

xian 縣

xianda 仙達

xianfa 仙法

xiangu 仙姑

xianghua 向化

xiangyong 鄉勇

Xincheng 新城

Xingyi 興義

Xi'ou 西甌

Xu Xiake 徐霞客

Xue Shiqian 薛世乾

xunfu 巡撫

Yangchang 洋場

Yang Hui 樣匯

yanluo 閻羅

yaoguai 妖怪

yaojing 妖精

yaoyan xitu shanhuo 妖言希圖煽惑

yaoyan yaoshu 妖言謠書

Yi 彝

Yi Bao 矣保

Yi Gen 矣根

ying 營

yixue 義學

Yongfeng 永豐

Yongning 永寧

Yongzheng 雍正

You River　右江

youji　遊擊

yu Hanren tong　與漢人同

yu qimin wu yi　與齊民無異

yu tianzi　玉天子

Yuan　元

Yun tengteng, shao Puping, Nanlong chi zaofan, sha shang Yunnan cheng　雲騰騰, 燒埔平, 南籠吃早飯, 殺上雲南城

Yunnan　雲南

Zeng Tingkui　曾庭奎

zhai　寨

Zhang Guangsi　張廣泗

Zhang Yulong　張玉隆

Zhang Yunsui　張允隨

zhangqi　瘴氣

Zhao Kun　趙坤

Zhao Tingchen　趙庭臣

Zhaotong　照通

Zhe Ruo　者若

Zhenfeng　貞豐

Zhenning　鎮寧

Zhongjia　仲家

zhou　州

Zhu Bao　主包

Zhulonga　珠龍阿

zhupi zouzhe　硃批奏摺

ziji　字寄

zongdu　總督

Zongjiao　宗角

zouyin　走隱

BIBLIOGRAPHY

ARCHIVAL SOURCES

N1HA: Number One Historical Archives, Beijing

PM: Palace Museum, Taipei, Taiwan

Gongzhong Dang Jiaqing Chao 嘉慶朝宮中檔. (Secret palace memorials of the Jiaqing reign). Taipei: National Palace Museum. Cited as GZDJQ (PM).

Jiaobu Dang 剿捕檔 (Record of pursuit and arrest). Cited as JBD (PM).

Junji chu lufu zouzhe, minzu shiwu lei 軍機處祿復奏摺, 民族事務類 (Grand Council reference copies of palace memorials, minority affairs category). Cited as JCLZ mzl (N1HA).

Xingke Tiben, tudi zhaiwu lei 刑科體本, 土地債務類 (Board of punishments office of scrutiny, routine memorials, homicide cases related to disputes over land and debt). (N1HA).

Zhupi zouzhe, minzu shiwu lei 硃批奏摺, 民族事務類 (Palace memorials, minority affairs category). Cited as ZPZZ mzl (N1HA).

PUBLISHED ARCHIVES

Gongzhong Dang Yongzheng chao 宮中檔雍正朝 (Secret palace memorials of the Yongzheng reign). Taipei: National Palace Museum, 1978. Cited as GZDYZ. [Note: YZZPYZ (see below) is organized by memorialist, while GZDYZ is organized by date. Citations are written to reflect the internal organization of each collection.]

Qianlong chao shangyu dang 乾隆朝上諭檔 (Imperial edicts of the Qianlong reign). Compiled by the Number One Historical Archives. Beijing: Dang'an chubanshe, 1991.

Qianlong chao zhengban tanwu dang'an xuanbian 乾隆朝懲辦貪污檔案選編 (A collection of archival materials on corruption cases from the Qianlong reign). Compiled by the Number One Historical Archives. Beijing: Zhonghua shuju, 1984.

Qingdai Jiaqing nianjian Guizhou Buyizu "Nanlong qiyi" ziliao xuanbian 清代嘉慶 間布依族 "南籠起義" 資料選編 (Collected materials on the "Nanlong Uprising" of the Buyi people during the Jiaqing Reign). Jointly compiled by the China Number One Historical Archives, the Southwest Guizhou People's Committee, and the Guizhou Buyi Studies Committee. Guiyang: Guizhou minzu chubanshe, 1989. Cited as NQX.

Qingdai qianqi Miaomin qiyi dang'an shiliao huibian 清代前期苗民起義檔案史料彙編 (Collected archival materials on the uprisings of the Miao people during the early Qing dynasty). 3 vols. Jointly compiled by the China Number One Historical Archives, the People's University Institute of Qing History, and the Guizhou Provincial Archives. Beijing: Guangming ribao chubanshe, 1987.

Yongzheng chao Hanwen zhupi zouzhe huibian 雍正朝漢文硃批奏折彙編 (Collection of Chinese-language palace memorials from the Yongzheng reign), edited by China Number One Historical Archives. Nanjing: Jiangsu guji chubanshe, 1989. Cited as YZHZZ.

Yongzheng Zhupi Yuzhi 雍正硃批諭旨 (The vermillion rescripts and edicts of the Yongzheng reign). Taipei: Wenyuan shuju, 1965. Cited as YZZPYZ. [Note: YZZPYZ is organized by memorialist, while GZDYZ (see above) is organized by date. Citations are written to reflect the internal organization of each collection.

PRIMARY AND SECONDARY SOURCES

Adas, Michael. *Prophets of Rebellion: Millenarian Protest Movements against the European Colonial Order.* Chapel Hill: University of North Carolina Press, 1979.

Aibida 愛必達. *Qiannan shilue* 黔南識略 (A handbook of Guizhou). 1750. Reprint, Guiyang: Guizhou renmin chubanshe, 1992.

Alberts, Eli. *A History of Daoism and the Yao People of South China.* New York: Cambria Press, 2006.

Anshun fuzhi 安順府志 (Gazetteer of Anshun prefecture), 1851.

Atwill, David G. *The Chinese Sultanate: Islam, Ethnicity, and the Panthay Rebellion in Southwest China, 1856–1873.* Stanford: Stanford University Press, 2005.

———. "Trading Places: Resistance, Ethnicity, and Governance in Nineteenth-

Century Yunnan." In *Dragons, Tigers, and Dogs: Qing Crisis Management and the Boundaries of State Power in Late Imperial China*. Edited byRobert J. Antony and Jane Kate Leonard, 245–72. Cornell East Asia Series, 114. Ithaca, NY: Cornell University Press, 2002.

Barlow, Jeffrey G. "The Zhuang." Electronic manuscript. http://mcel.pacificu.edu/as/resources/zhuang/zhuang9.htm#_edn15.

———."The Zhuang Minority in the Ming Era," *Ming Studies*, no. 28 (Fall 1989): 15–41.

———. "The Zhuang Minority of the Sino-Vietnamese Frontier in the Song Period," *Journal of Southeast Asian Studies* 18, no. 2 (September 1987): 250–69.

Bartlett, Beatrice S. "Imperial Notations on Ch'ing Official Documents in the Ch'ien-lung (1736–1795) and Chia-ch'ing (1796–1820) Reigns," *National Palace Museum Bulletin* 7, no. 2 (May-June 1972): 1–13 and no. 3 (July-August 1972): 1–13.

———. *Monarchs and Ministers: The Grand Council in Mid-Ch'ing China, 1723–1830*. Berkeley and Los Angeles: University of California Press, 1991.

———. "Review of *The Last Emperors: A Social History of Qing Imperial Institutions*." In *Harvard Journal of Asiatic Studies* 61, no. 1 (June 2001): 171–83.

———. "The Secret Memorials of the Yung-cheng Period (1723–1735): Archival and Published Versions." *National Palace Museum Bulletin* 9, no. 4 (September-October 1974): 1–12.

Bello, David A. *Opium and the Limits of Empire: Drug Prohibition in the Chinese Interior, 1729–1850*. Cambridge, MA: Harvard University Press, 2005.

Bonnin, Christine and Sarah Turner. "At what price rice? Food security, livelihoods, and state interventions in upland northern Vietnam." *Geoforum* 43 (2012): 95–105.

Buoye, Thomas. *Manslaughter, Markets, and Moral Economy: Violent Disputes over Property Rights in Eighteenth-century China*. Cambridge Studies in Chinese Literature, History and Institutions. Cambridge, UK: Cambridge University Press, 2000.

Burusuphat, Somsonge and Megan Sinnott, eds. *Kam-Tai Oral Literatures*. Bangkok: T& D Publishing, Ltd., 1998.

Cauquelin, Josiane. *Au Pays des Buyi: Une ethnie du berceau Thai, Province du Guizhou Chine*. Olizane: Les Cahiers de Peninsule, No. 4, 1998.

Chai Xingyi 柴興億, ed. *Zhonghua renmin gongheguo diming cidian: Guizhou sheng* 中華人民共和國地名詞典 : 貴州省 (A dictionary of place names in the People's Republic of China: Guizhou province). Beijing: Shangwu yin shuguan, 1994.

Chang, Chung-li. *The Chinese Gentry: Studies on their Role in Nineteenth-Century Chinese Society*. Seattle: University of Washington Press, 1955.

Chen Dingxiu 陳定秀. "Qianxi Nanlong qiyi yuanyin" 淺析南籠起義原因 (A brief analysis of the origins of the Nanlong Uprising). *Buyi i xue yanjiu* 3 (1991): 58–65.

Clarke, Samuel R. *Among the Tribes of Southwest China*. London: Morgan and Scott, Ltd.,1911.

Crais, Clifton. "Chiefs and Bureaucrats in the Making of Empire: A Drama from the Transkei, South Africa, October 1880." *American Historical Review* 108, no. 4 (October 2003): 1034–56.

Cressey, George Babcock. *Land of the 500 Million: A Geography of China*. New York: McGraw Hill, 1955.

Cronon, William, George Miles, and Jay Gitlin, "Becoming West: Toward a New Meaning for Western History."In *Under an Open Sky: Rethinking America's Western Past*. Edited by William Cronon, George Miles, and Jay Gitlin, 3–27. London and New York: W.W. Norton, 1992.

Crossley, Pamela K. "*Manzhou yuanliu kao* and the Formalization of the Manchu Heritage," *Journal of Asian Studies* 46, no. 4 (November 1987).

———, Helen F. Siu, and Donald S. Sutton, eds. *Empire at the Margins: Culture, Ethnicity and Frontier in Early Modern China*. Berkeley: University of California Press, 2006.

Dading fuzhi 大定府志 (Gazetteer of Dading prefecture), 1850.

Dai, Yingcong. "The Rise of the Southwestern Frontier under the Qing, 1640–1800." PhD dissertation, University of Washington, 1996.

———. *The Sichuan Frontier and Tibet: Imperial Strategy in the Early Qing*. Seattle: University of Washington Press, 2009.

Daqing luli 大清律例 (Great Qing code) 1740. Reprint. Tianjin: Tianjin guji chubanshe, 1991.

Deal, David M. and Laura Hostetler, trans., *The Art of Ethnography: A Chinese Miao Album*. Seattle: University of Washington Press, 2006.

Despeux, Catherine. "Talismans and Diagrams." Translated by Livia Kohn. In *Daoism Handbook*. Edited byLivia Kohn, 499–540. Leiden: Brill, 2000.

Diamond, Norma. "Defining the Miao: Ming, Qing, and Contemporary Views." In *Cultural Encounters on China's Ethnic Frontiers*. Edited by Stevan Harrell, 92–116. Seattle: University of Washington Press, 1995.

Diller, Anthony V. N., Jerold A. Edmonson, and Luo Yingxian, eds. *The Tai-Kadai Languages*. London and New York: Routledge, 2008.

Ebrey, Patricia. "Surnames and Han Chinese Identity." In *Negotiating Ethnicities in China and Taiwan*. Edited by Melissa J. Brown, 19–36. Berkeley: Institute of East Asian Studies Research Monograph 46 (University of California), 1996.

Edmondson, Jerold A. "Change and Variation in Zhuang." In *Papers from the Second Annual Meeting of the Southeast Asian Linguistics Society*. Edited by Karen L. Adams and Thomas John Hudak, 147–85. Arizona State University, Program for Southeast Asian Studies, 1994.

———. "The power of language over the past: Tai settlement and Tai linguistics in southern China and northern Vietnam." In *Studies in Southeast Asian languages and linguistics*. Edited by Harris et al., 39–64. Bangkok: Ek Phim Tai Co., Ltd., 2007.

——— and David B. Solnit, eds. *Comparative Kadai: The Tai Branch*. Arlington TX: University of Texas at Arlington Summer Institute of Linguistics, 1997.

Elliot, Mark C. "The Manchu-language Archives of the Qing Dynasty and the Origins of the Palace Memorial System." *Late Imperial China* 22, no. 1 (June 2001): 1–70.

Elvin, Mark. *The Retreat of the Elephants: An Environmental History of China*. New Haven and London: Yale University Press, 2004.

Esposito, Monica. "Daoism in the Qing." In *Daoism Handbook*. Edited by Livia Kohn, 623–59. Leiden: Brill, 2000.

Forsyth, Tim and Jean Michaud. "Rethinking the Relationships between Livelihoods and Ethnicity in Highland China, Vietnam, and Laos." In *Moving Mountains: Ethnicity and Livelihoods in Highland China, Vietnam, and Laos*. Edited by Jean Michaud and Tim Forsyth, 1–27. Vancouver: University of British Columbia Press, 2011.

Ge, Quansheng, Junhu Dai, Fanneng He, Jingyun Zheng, Zhimin Man, and Yun Zhao. "Spatiotemporal dynamics of reclamation and cultivation and its driving factors in parts of China during the last three centuries." *Progress in Natural Science* 14, no. 7 (July 2004): 605–13.

Gedney, William J. "Yay, a Northern Tai Language in North Vietnam," *Lingua* 14 (1965): 180–93.

Giersch, C. Patterson. *Asian Borderlands: The Transformation of Qing China's Yunnan Frontier*. Cambridge, MA: Harvard University Press, 2006.

———. "'A Motley Throng:' Social Change on Southwest China's Early Modern Frontier, 1700–1880." *The Journal of Asian Studies* 60, no. 1 (February 2001): 67–94.

Giersch, Charles Patterson Jr. "Qing China's Reluctant Subjects: Indigenous Communities and Empire Along the Yunnan Frontier." PhD dissertation, Yale University, 1998.

Gong Yin 龔蔭. *Zhongguo tusi zhidu* 中國土司制度 (The *tusi* system in China). Kunming: Yunnan minzu chubanshe, 1992.

Gu Yin 谷因. "Buyizu zuyuan yanjiu zongshu" (A summary of research on the origins of the Buyi nationality), *Buyi xue yanjiu* 6 (1998): 23–31.

Guangshun zhouzhi 廣順州志 (Gazetteer of Guangshun department), 1846.

Guizhou tongzhi 貴州通志 (Gazetteer of Guizhou province), 1697 and 1741.

Guy, R. Kent. *Qing Governors and their Provinces: The Evolution of Territorial Administration in China, 1644–1796.* Seattle: University of Washington Press, 2010.

Harrell, Stevan. "Civilizing Projects and the Reaction to Them." In *Cultural Encounters on China's Ethnic Frontiers.* Edited by Stevan Harrell, 3–36. Seattle: University of Washington Press, 1995.

———. "The History of the History of the Yi." In *Cultural Encounters on China's Ethnic Frontiers.* Edited by Stevan Harrell, 63–91. Seattle: University of Washington Press, 1995.

———. "The Nationalities Question and the Prmi Problem." In *Negotiating Ethnicities in China and Taiwan.* Edited by Melissa J. Brown, 274–96. Berkeley: Institute for East Asian Studies, University of California, 1996.

———. *Ways of Being Ethnic in Southwest China.* Seattle: University of Washington Press, 2001.

He, Caihua, Kanging Xiong, Xiaoling Li, and Xing Cheng, "Karst Geomorphology and its Agricultural Implications in Guizhou, China." *Suppl. Geogr. Fis. Dinam. Quat.*III, T. 4 (1998): 121–25.

He Renzhong 何仁種, ed. *Guizhou tongshi. Di san juan, Qingdai de Guizhou* 貴州通史: 第三卷: 清代的貴州 (A comprehensive history of Guizhou, part 3, Qing dynasty Guizhou). Beijing: Dangdai Zhongguo chubanshe, 2002.

He Weifu 何偉福. *Qingdai Guizhou shangpin jingjishi yanjiu* 清代貴州商品經濟史研究 (Research on the economic history of commodities in Qing dynasty Guizhou). Beijing: Zhongguo jingji chubanshe, 2007.

Herman, John E. *Amid the Clouds and Mist: China's Colonization of Guizhou, 1200–1700.* Cambridge, MA: Harvard University Press, 2007.

———. "The Cant of Conquest: Tusi Offices and China's Political Incorporation of the Southwest Frontier." In *Empire at the Margins: Culture, Ethnicity, and Frontier in Early Modern China,* Edited by Pamela Kyle Crossley, Helen F. Siu, and Donald Sutton, 135–70. Berkeley: University of California Press, 2006.

———. "Empire in the Southwest: Early Qing Reforms to the Native Chieftain System." *The Journal of Asian Studies* 56, no. 1 (February 1997): 47–74.

———. "The Mu'ege Kingdom: A brief history of a frontier empire in Southwest China." In *Political Frontiers, Ethnic Boundaries, and Human Geographies in Chinese History.* Edited by Nicola Di Cosmo and Don J. Wyatt, 245–85. London and New York: Routledge Curzon, 2003.

———. "National Integration and Regional Hegemony: The Political and Cultural

Dynamics of Qing State Expansion, 1650–1750." PhD dissertation, University of Washington, 1993.

Herrold, Melinda. "The Cranes of Caohai and Other Incidents of Fieldwork in Southwest China." *Geographical Review* 89, no. 3 (July 1999): 440–48.

Hind, Robert J. "The Internal Colonial Concept." *Comparative Studies in Society and History*, Vol. 26, no. 3 (July 1984): 543–68.

Ho, Ping-ti. *Studies on the Population of China, 1368–1953*. Cambridge, MA: Harvard University Press, 1959.

Holm, David. "The Exemplar of Filial Piety and the End of the Ape-Man: Dong Yong in Guangxi and Guizhou Ritual Performance." *T'oung Pao* 90 (June 2004): 32–64.

———. *Killing a Buffalo for the Ancestors: A Zhuang Cosmological Text from Southwest China*. DeKalb, IL: Southeast Asia Publications, Center for Southeast Asian Studies, Northern Illinois University, 2003.

———. *Recalling Lost Souls: The Baeu Rodo Tai Cosmogonic Texts from Guangxi in Southern China*. Bangkok: White Lotus, 2004.

Hostetler, Laura. "Chinese Ethnography in the Eighteenth Century: Miao Albums of Guizhou Province." PhD dissertation, University of Pennsylvania, 1995.

———."Introduction: Early Modern Ethnography in Comparative Historical Perspective." In David M. Deal and Laura Hostetler, trans., *The Art of Ethnography: A Chinese Miao Album*, xiv-lxvii. Seattle: University of Washington Press, 2006.

———. *Qing Colonial Enterprise: Ethnography and Cartography in Early Modern China*. Chicago: University of Chicago Press, 2001.

Hsiao Kung-chuan. *Rural China: Imperial Control in the Nineteenth Century*. Seattle: University of Washington Press, 1960.

Huang Jiaxin 黃家信. *Zhuangzu diqu tusi zhidu yu gaitu guiliu yanjiu* 壯族地區土司制度與改土歸流研究 (Research on the tusi system and gaitu guilu in Zhuang regions). Hefei: Hefei gongye daxue chubanshe, 2007.

Huang, Pei. *Autocracy at Work: A Study of the Yung-cheng Period, 1723–35*. Bloomington: Indiana University Press, 1975.

Huang Yiren 黃義仁. *Buyizu shi* 布依族史 (A history of the Buyi nationality). Guiyang: Guizhou minzu chubanshe, 1999.

———. *Buyizu zongjiao xinyang yu wenhua* 布依族宗教信仰與文話 (Religious beliefs and culture of the Buyi nationality). Beijing: Zhongyang minzu daxue chubanshe, 2002.

Hucker, Charles O. *A Dictionary of Official Titles in Imperial China*. Taipei: SMC Publishing, 1996.

Hummel, Arthur W., ed. *Eminent Chinese of the Ch'ing Period*. 2 volumes. Washington, D.C.: United States Government Printing Office, 1943.

Jenks, Robert D. *Insurgency and Social Disorder in Guizhou: The "Miao" Rebellion, 1854–1873*. Honolulu: University of Hawaii Press, 1994.

Jin Anjiang 金安江. "Cong Nanlong qiyi kan jindai Buyizu diqu de minzu guanxi" 從南籠起義看近代布依族地區民族關係 (Looking at modern ethnic relations in Buyi regions since the Nanlong Uprising). *Buyi i xue yanjiu* 布依學研究 3 (1991): 115–29.

Kaup, Katherine Palmer. *Creating the Zhuang: Ethnic Politics in China*. London: Lynne Rienner Publishers, Inc., 2000.

———. "Regionalism Versus Ethnic Nationalism in the People's Republic of China." *The China Quarterly* No. 172 (December 2002), 863–84.

Khanittanan, Wilaiwan. "Taoist Influence in Tai Languages and Cultures." In *SEALS XIV: Papers from the 14th annual meeting of the Southeast Asian Linguistics Society*, Volume I. Edited by Wilaiwan Khanittanan and Paul Sidwell, 185–92. Canberra: Australian National University, 2008.

Kleeman, Terry F. "Ethnic Identity and Daoist Identity in Traditional China." In *Daoist Identity: History, Lineage and Ritual*. Edited by Livia Kohn and Harold David Roth, 1–18. Honolulu: University of Hawaii Press, 2002.

Kuhn, Philip A. *Soulstealers: The Chinese Sorcery Scare of 1768*. Cambridge: Harvard University Press, 1990.

Langlois, John. D. "The Hongwu Reign." In *The Cambridge History of China*. Volume 9, *The Ming Dynasty Part 1*. Edited by Frederick W. Mote and Dennis Twitchett. Cambridge: Cambridge University Press, 1988.

Leach, Edmund R. "The Frontiers of 'Burma.'" *Comparative Studies in Society and History* Vol. 3, no.1 (October 1960): 49–68.

Lee, James. "Food Supply and Population Growth in Southwest China, 1250–1850." *Journal of Asian Studies*, 41, no. 4 (August 1982): 711–46.

Lee, Lilly Xiao Hong, A. D. Stefanowska, and Clara Wing Chung-ho, eds. *Biographical dictionary of Chinese women: The Qing Dynasty*. Armonk: M. E. Sharpe, 1998.

Leng Tianfang 冷天放. "Zongjiao yu 'Nanlong qiyi'" 宗教與'南籠起義' (Religion in the 'Nanlong Uprising'), *Buyi xue yanjiu* 3 (1991): 130–38.

Li Chi. *The Travel Diaries of Hsu Hsia-k'e*. Hong Kong: The Chinese University of Hong Kong, 1974.

Li, Huaiyin. *Village Governance in North China, 1875–1936*. Stanford: Stanford University Press, 2005.

Li Qingfu 李慶福 and Xu Xianlong 許憲隆, eds. *Buyizu jianshi* 布依族簡史 (A concise history of the Buyi nationality). Beijing: Minzu chubanshe, 2008.

Li Rubiao 黎汝標. "'Nanlong qiyi' de zongjiao wenti'" 南籠起義" 的宗教問題

(The question of religion in the "Nanlong Uprising"). *Buyi xue yanjiu* 3 (1991): 139–45.

Lin Jianzeng 林建增. "Guizhou de jingji fazhan he renkou zengjia" 貴州省的經濟發展和人口增加 (Guizhou's economic development and population growth). *Guizhou ribao*, September 9, 2003.

Lipman, Jonathan N. *Familiar Strangers: A History of Muslims in Northwest China*. Seattle: University of Washington Press, 1997.

Lombard-Salmon, Claudine. *Un exemple d'acculturation Chinoise: Guizhou au XVIIIeme siecle* (An example of Chinese acculturation: Guizhou in the eighteenth century). Paris: Ecole Francais d'Extreme-Orient, 1972.

Ma Ruxing 馬汝邢 and Cheng Chongde 程崇德. *Qingdai bianjiang kaifa* 清代邊疆開發 (The opening of frontiers during the Qing dynasty). 2 vols. Taiyuan: Shanxi People's Publishing House, 1998.

Mann, Susan. "Mann on Hostetler." In *Journal of Colonialism and Colonial History* vol. 2, no. 3 (Winter 2001).

McCord, Edward A. "Local Military Power and Elite Formation: The Liu Family of Xingyi County, Guizhou."In *Chinese Local Elites and Patterns of Dominance*. Edited by Joseph W. Esherick and Mary B. Rankin, 162–90. Berkeley: University of California Press, 1993.

McGee, Terry, "Forward." In *Moving Mountains: Ethnicity and Livelihoods in Highland China, Vietnam, and Laos*. Edited by Jean Michaud and Tim Forsyth, ix-xvi. Vancouver: University of British Columbia Press, 2011.

McMahon, Daniel. "Identity and Conflict on a Chinese Borderland: Yan Ruyi and the Recruitment of the Gelao during the 1795–97 Miao Revolt."*Late Imperial China* Vol. 23, no. 2 (December 2002): 53–86.

———. "New Order in Hunan's Miao Frontier," *Journal of Colonialism and Colonial History* 9, no.1 (Spring 2008).

———."Restoring the Garden: Yan Ruyi and the Civilizing of China's Internal Frontiers, 1795–1805." PhD dissertation, University of California-Davis, 1998.

McNicholas, Mark. "Poverty Tales and Statutory Politics in Mid-Qing Fraud Cases." In *Writing and Law in Late Imperial China: Crime, Conflict, and Judgment*. Edited by Robert E. Hegel and Katherine Carlitz, 143–60. Seattle: University of Washington Press, 2007.

Michaud, Jean. *Historical Dictionary of the Peoples of the Southeast Asian Massif*. Lanham, MD: The Scarecrow Press, 2006.

———. "Hmong infrapolitics: A view from Vietnam." *Ethnic and Racial Studies* Vol. 35, no. 11 (2012): 1853–73.

——— and Tim Forsyth, eds. *Moving Mountains: Ethnicity and Livelihoods in*

Highland China, Vietnam, and Laos. Vancouver: University of British Columbia Press, 2011.

Millward, James A. *Beyond the Pass: Economy, Ethnicity, and Empire in Qing Central Asia, 1759–1864.* Stanford: Stanford University Press, 1998.

———. "New Perspectives on the Qing Frontier." In *Remapping China: Fissures in Historical Terrain.* Edited by Gail Hershatter, Emily Honig, Jonathan N. Lipman, and Randall Stross, 113–29. Stanford: Stanford University Press, 1996.

———. "A Uyghur Muslim in Qianlong's Court: The Meanings of the Fragrant Concubine," *The Journal of Asian Studies* 53, no. 2 (May 1994): 427–58.

Mote, F. W. *Imperial China, 900–1800.* Cambridge, MA: Harvard University Press, 1999.

Mullaney, Thomas S. *Coming to Terms with the Nation: Ethnic Classification in Modern China.* Berkeley: University of California Press, 2011.

Nanlong fuzhi 南籠府志 (Gazetteer of Nanlong prefecture), 1765.

Oakes, Tim. "Cultural Strategies of Development: Implications for Village Governance in China." *The Pacific Review* 19, no. 1 (March 2006): 13–37.

Oakes, Timothy. "Selling Guizhou: Cultural Development in an Era of Marketization." In *The Political Economy of China's Provinces.* Edited by H. Hendrischke and C. Y. Feng, 27–67. London and New York: Routledge, 1999.

Ortner, Sherry. *Anthropology and Social Theory: Culture, Power, and the Acting Subject.* Durham, NC: Duke University Press, 2006.

Park, Nancy, and Robert Antony. "Archival Research in Qing Legal History." *Late Imperial China* 14, no. 1 (June 1993), 93–137.

Park, Nancy E. "Corruption in Eighteenth-century China," *Journal of Asian Studies* 56: no. 4 (November 1997): 976–1006.

Perdue, Peter C. *China Marches West: The Qing Conquest of Central Eurasia.* Cambridge, MA: Belknap Press of Harvard University Press, 2005.

———. "Comparing Empires: Manchu Colonialism." *International History Review* 20, no. 2 (June 1998): 238–62.

———. "Military Mobilization in Seventeenth and Eighteenth-Century China, Russia, and Mongolia." *Modern Asian Studies* 30, no. 4 (1996): 757–93.

Perkins, Dwight. *Agricultural Development in China, 1368–1968.* Chicago: Aldine, 1969.

Perry, Elizabeth J. *Challenging the Mandate of Heaven: Social Protest and State Power in China.* Armonk: M. E. Sharpe, 2002.

———. *Rebels and Revolutionaries in North China.* Stanford: Stanford University Press, 1980.

Pregadio, Fabrizio, ed. *The Encyclopedia of Taoism.* Volumes I and II. London: Routledge, 2008.

Prescott, John Robert Victor. *Boundaries and Frontiers*. Totowa, NJ: Bowman and Littlefield, 1978.

Qingdai de kuangye 清代的礦業 (Mining industries during the Qing dynasty). Compiled by the Institute of History, People's University. Beijing: Renmin daxue chubanshe, 1983.

Qing Shilu Guangxi ziliao huibian 清實錄廣西資料彙編, Volume 1 (A collection of materials on Guangxi from the Qing shilu). Jointly compiled by the Guangxi Zhuang Autonomous Region Bureau of Local Gazetteers and the Guangxi Zhuang Autonomous Region Library. Nanning: Guangxi renmin chubanshe, 1982.

Qing Shilu Guizhou ziliao jiyao 清實錄貴州資料輯要 (A collection of materials on Guizhou from the Qing Veritable Records). Guiyang: Guizhou renmin chubanshe. Cited as QSL-GZ.

Rawski, Evelyn S. *The Last Emperors: A Social History of Qing Imperial Institutions*. Berkeley: University of California Press, 1998.

Robinet, Isabelle. "*Shangqing*." In *The Encyclopedia of Taoism*, Volume 2. Edited by Fabrizio Pregadio, 858–66. London: Routledge, 2008.

———. *Taoism: Growth of a Religion*. Translated by Phyllis Brooks. Stanford: Stanford University Press, 1997.

Rowe, William T. *China's Last Empire: The Great Qing*. Cambridge, MA: Belknap Press, 2009.

———. "Education and Empire in Southwest China: Ch'en Hung-mou in Yunnan, 1733–1738." In *Education and Society in Late Imperial China*. Edited by Benjamin A. Elman and Alexander Woodside, 417–57. Berkeley: University of California Press, 1994.

———. *Saving the World: Chen Hongmou and Elite Consciousness in Eighteenth-century China*. Stanford: Stanford University Press, 2001.

Sahlins, Marshall. "What is Anthropological Enlightenment? Some Lessons of the Twentieth Century." *Annual Review of Anthropology* (1999): i–xxiii.

Schein, Louisa. *Minority Rules: The Miao and the Feminine in China's Cultural Politics*. Durham, NC: Duke University Press, 2000.

Scott, James C. *The Art of Not Being Governed: An Anarchist History of Upland Southeast Asia*. New Haven, CT: Yale University Press, 2010.

———. *Domination and the Arts of Resistance: Hidden Transcripts*. New Haven, CT: Yale University Press, 1990.

———. *The Moral Economy of the Peasant: Rebellion and Subsistence in Southeast Asia*. New Haven, CT: Yale University Press, 1976.

———. *Seeing Like a State: How Certain Schemes to Improve the Human Condition Have Failed*. New Haven, CT: Yale University Press, 1998.

————. *Weapons of the Weak: Everyday Forms of Peasant Resistance.* New Haven, CT: Yale University Press, 1985.

Seidel, Anna. "Taoist Messianism," *Numen* 31, no. 2 (December 1984):164–71.

Shi Jizhong 史繼忠. "Qian Gui bianjiang Zhuangzu Buyizude tingmu zhidu" 黔桂邊疆壯族布依族的亭目制度 (The tingmu system of the Zhuang and Buyi nationalities in the Qian-Gui [Guizhou-Guangxi] borderlands). In *Xinan minzu shehui xingtai yu jingji wenhua leixing* 西南民族社會形態與經濟文化類型 (The social formations and cultural and economic types of the ethnic minorities in southwest China). Edited by Shi Jizhong, 288–307. Southwest China Study Series. Kunming: Yunnan Educational Publishing House, 1997.

Shin, Leo K. *The Making of the Chinese State: Ethnicity and Expansion on the Ming Borderlands.* New York: Cambridge University Press, 2006.

Smith, Kent Clarke. "Ch'ing Policy and the Development of Southwest China: Aspects of Ortai's Governor-Generalship, 1726–1731." PhD dissertation, Yale University, 1971.

Snyder, Will C. "Bouyei Phonology." In *The Tai-Kadai Languages.* Edited by Anthony V. N. Diller, Jerold A. Edmonson, and Luo Yingxian, 378–88. London and New York: Routledge, 2008.

Spence, Jonathan D. *Ts'ao Yin and the K'ang-hsi Emperor: Bondservant and Master.* New Haven: Yale University Press, 1966.

Spencer, J. E. "Kueichou: An Internal Chinese Colony." *Pacific Affairs* 13, no. 2 (June 1940): 162–72.

Strassberg, Richard. *Inscribed Landscapes: Travel Writing from Imperial China.* Berkeley and Los Angeles: University of California Press, 1991.

Strickmann, Michel. *Chinese Magical Medicine.* Edited by Bernard Faure. Stanford: Stanford University Press, 2002.

Struve, Lynn A. *The Southern Ming, 1644–1662.* New Haven, CT: Yale University Press, 1984.

Sturgeon, Janet C. "Rubber Transformations: Post-Socialist Livelihoods and Identities for Akha and Tai Lue Farmers in Xishuangbanna, China." In *Moving Mountains: Ethnicity and Livelihoods in Highland China, Vietnam, and Laos,* edited by Jean Michaud and Tim Forsyth, 193–214. Vancouver: University of British Columbia Press, 2011.

Sun, E-tu Zen. "Ch'ing Government and the Mineral Industries Before 1800," *The Journal of Asian Studies* 27, no. 4 (August, 1968): 835–45.

————. "Mining Labor in the Ch'ing Period." In *Approaches to Modern Chinese History.* Edited by Albert Feuerwerker, Rhoads Murphey, and Mary C. Wright, 45–68. Berkeley and Los Angeles: University of California Press, 1967.

Sutton, Donald S. "Ethnicity and the Miao Frontier in the Eighteenth Century." In

    Empire at the Margins: Culture, Ethnicity, and Frontier in Early Modern China. Edited by Pamela Kyle Crossley, Helen F. Siu, and Donald S. Sutton, 190–228. Berkeley: University of California Press, 2006.

———. "Ethnic Revolt in the Qing Empire: The 'Miao Uprising' of 1795–1796 Reexamined." *Asia Major,* 3rd series, 17, no. 1 (2003): 105–51.

"Tantao Ceheng Buyizu yuan" 探討冊亨布依族源 (Investigating the origins of the Buyi nationality in Ceheng). *Ceheng wenshi ziliao* 冊亨文史資料 (Literary and historical materials from Ceheng) 3 (1985): 69–79.

Teng, Emma Jinhua. *Taiwan's Imagined Geography: Chinese Colonial Travel Writing and Pictures, 1683–1895.* Cambridge, MA: Harvard University Press, 2004.

ter Haar, Barend. "A New Interpretation of the Yao Charters." In *New Developments in Asian Studies: An Introduction.* Edited by Paul van der Velde and Alex McKay, 3–19. London and New York: Keegan Paul International, 1998.

Thomas, Nicholas. *Colonialism's Culture: Anthropology, Travel, and Government.* Princeton, NJ: Princeton University Press, 1994.

Tian Yuan 田原. "'Wang Xiangu,' 'Nanlong fanbing ge' qianxi" 王仙姑," "南籠反兵歌"淺析 (A brief analysis of "Wang Xiangu" and "Song of the Nanlong Resistance"). *Buyi xue yanjiu* 3 (1991): 286–90.

Took, Jennifer. *A Native Chieftaincy in Southwest China: Franchising a Tai Chieftaincy under the Tusi System of Late Imperial China.* Leiden: Brill, 2005.

Tregear, T. R. *A Geography of China.* Chicago: Aldine Publishing Company, 1965.

Tsao, Kai-fu. "The Rebellion of the Three Feudatories Against the Manchu Throne in China, 1673–1681: Its Setting and Significance." PhD dissertation, Columbia University, 1965.

Turner, Sarah. "Making a Living the Hmong Way: An Actor-Oriented Livelihoods Approach to Everyday Politics and Resistance in Upland Vietnam." *Annals of the Association of American Geographers* 102 (2012): 1–22.

Vansina, Jan. *Oral Tradition as History.* Madison: University of Wisconsin Press, 1984.

Wang Fangheng, 王芳恒. "Nanlong qiyi zhong de wushu wenti 南籠起義中的巫術問題 (The question of sorcery in the Nanlong Uprising)," *Buyi xue yanjiu* 布依学研究 3 (1991): 145–52.

Wang Huiliang 王惠良. "Lun Buyizu mingcheng ji jiancheng" 论布依族名称及简称 (A discussion of the Buyi name and its short forms). *Buyi xue yanjiu* 布依学研究 1 (1989): 49–58.

Wang Mingke 王明珂. *Qiangzai Han Zangzhijian* 羌在漢藏之間 (The Qiang: between Han and Tibetans). Liaojing chubanshe, 2003.

Wang Yeh-chien. *Land Taxation in Imperial China.* Cambridge, MA: Harvard University Press, 1973.

Ward, Julian. *Xu Xiake (1587–1641): The Art of Travel Writing*. Richmond, Surrey: Curzon Press, 2001.

Whittaker, Jacob Tyler. "Yi identity and Confucian empire: Indigenous Local Elites, Cultural Brokerage, and the Colonization of the Lu-ho Tribal Polity of Yunnan, 1174–1745." PhD dissertation, University of California-Davis, 2008.

Wright, Daniel B. *The Promise of the Revolution: Stories of Fulfillment and Struggle in China's Hinterland*. Lanham, MD: Rowman and Littlefield Publishers, Inc., 2003.

Wu Changxing 伍長胜. "Qianxi Nanlong Buyizu qiyi baofa yuanyin" 淺析南籠布依族起義爆發原因 (A brief analysis of the reasons for the outbreak of the Nanlong Buyi Uprising). *Buyi xue yanjiu* 3 (1991): 71–78.

Xilong zhouzhi 西隆州志 (Gazetteer of Xilong department), 1673.

Xingyi fuzhi 興義府志 (Gazetteer of Xingyi prefecture), 1851.

Xu Xiake 徐霞客. *Xu Xiake youji* 徐霞客游記 (The travel diaries of Xu Xiake). Original date unknown. 2 volumes. Shanghai: Shanghai Antiquities Publishing House, 1991.

Yan Yong 顔勇 and Fan Lixia 范麗霞. "Lun Nanlong qiyi shehui beijing, jingyan jiaoxun ji lishi yiyi" '南籠起義'社會背景,經驗教訓及歷史意義 (Discussing the social background, experience, lessons, and historical significance of the "Nanlong Uprising"). *Buyii xue yanjiu* 3 (1991): 229–39.

Yang Bin. "Differentiation and analysis of the population documents in the early Qing Dynasty." *Chinese Journal of Population Science* 9, no. 1 (1997): 1–8.

Zelin, Madeline. *The Magistrate's Tael: Rationalizing Fiscal Reform in Eighteenth-Century China*. Berkeley: University of California Press, 1984.

Zhou Guomao 周國茂, ed. "*Mojing wenxue: yizhong qite de wenxue leixing*" 摩經文學: 一種特奇特的文學類型 (Mojing literature: a singular type of literature). In *Buyizu Mojing wenxue* 布依族摩經文學 (Buyi Mojing religious literature of the Buyi ethnic group). Edited by Zhou Guomao, Wei Xingru 韋興儒, and Wu Wenyi 伍文義, 1–11. Guiyang: Guizhou renmin chubanshe, 1997.

———. *Yizhong teshu de wenhua dianji: Buyizu Mojing yanjiu* 一種特殊的文化典籍: 布依族摩經研究 (A unique type of ancient texts: Research on the Mojing religious literature of the Buyi ethnic group). Guiyang: Guizhou renmin chubanshe, 2006.

———, Wei Xingru 韋興儒, and Wu Wenyi 伍文義, eds. *Buyizu Mojing wenxue* 布依族摩經文學 (Mojing religious literature of the Buyi ethnic group). Guiyang: Guizhou renmin chubanshe, 1997.

Zhou Guoyan, "An Introduction to the Kam-Tai (Zhuang-Dong) Group of Languages in China." In *Languages and Cultures of the Kam-Tai (Zhuang Dong)*

Group: A Word List (English–Thai version). Edited by Zhou Guoyan and Somsonge Burusphat, 1–65. Bangkok: Sahadhammika Co. Ltd, 1996.

———. "Linguistic and Historical Explanations of the Names for the Buyi, a Group of Tai People in Southwestern China," *Proceedings of the Fourth International Symposium on Languages and Linguistics, Pan-Asiatic Linguistics* (January 8–10, 1996), 970. Accessed at sealang.net/sala/archives/pdf8/guoyan 1996linguistic.pdf.

——— and Somsonge Burusphat, eds. *Languages and Cultures of the Kam-Tai (Zhuang-Dong) Group A word list (English-Thai version).* Bangkok: Sahadhammika Co., Ltd., 1996.

INDEX

acculturation, versus assimilation, 147n72, 171n45

Aertai (governor of Sichuan), 164n59; investigation of crime, 74, 75

agency, indigenous, 8, 134; of marginalized peoples, 5; under Qing, 124–25

agriculture: Han, 30, 32; slash-and-burn, 30, 40; Zhongjia, 28–29, 30, 51, 58, 151n10

Aibida (governor of Guizhou), 17; *Handbook of Guizhou*, 121, 174n5, 175n6

A Ji, talisman of, 80

A Jin (Zhongjia strongman), 46–47

A Jiu, 158n76

alchemy: ceremonies of, 70; in Huang San case, 66, 67, 68, 70

A Liu, 163n54

An clan, 29–30; trade network of, 30; and Wu Sangui, 36

Angu, in Nanlong Uprising, 96

An Kun (Nasi Yi official), 153n22

Anlong (Guizhou province), 35, 85

Annan, in Nanlong Uprising, 96

Anshun prefecture (Guizhou), 4, 53; climate of, 14; military presence in, 72, 74; in Nanlong Uprising, 96, 100; provincial military command at, 171n50; Tunpu villages near, 133; Zhongjia raid on, 74, 75

A Shou (swindler), 165n76

Atwill, David, 168n24

Baeu Rodo (Zhuang ancestor), 138n15

Baishui waterfalls (Guizhou), 139n3

Balongtun, in Nanlong Uprising, 101

banditry: in Guizhou province, 12, 13, 38, 44, 45–47; social, 91, 107, 169n33

Bangzha, Qing attack on, 105

Bao Changding (Huang San case), 67, 68, 69

Baomu Bai (*bumo*), 67, 68, 69; practice of *duangong* magic, 66, 161n31

Baomu Lun (*bumo*), 68

Beixiang (Nanlong hamlet), 168n25

strength of, 100, 101; women, 97.
See also Nanlong Uprising
Zhou Guoyan, 21, 22, 144n47
"Zhuang," characters used for,
144n46, 145n55
Zhuang people: ancestors of, 138n15;
bumo of, 161n32; Chinese genealogies of, 20–21, 144n40; dialect
of, 138n15; ethnonyms of, 23, 24,
147n68; of Guangxi, 23; language
of, 142n31, 144n44; Meishan Daoism of, 162n33; Northern, 19, 24,

142n31, 169n27; relationships with
Buyi, 21, 23, 24, 63, 146n64; reli-
gious texts of, 160n21; rituals of,
169n27; Southern, 19, 20, 24, 142n31;
written language of, 160n21; of
Yongguan, 21
Zhu Bao, 164n57
Zhulonga (Guizhou provincial mili-
tary commander), 94, 96; engage-
ment with Zhongjia rebels, 102
Zhu Youlang. *See* Yongli
Zongjiao, Qing military presence in, 51

CPSIA information can be obtained at www.ICGtesting.com
Printed in the USA
BVOW08s2009190716

456161BV00003B/22/P